Aircraft of the National Air and Space Museum

Smithsonian Institution
Fourth Edition

Compiled by Claudia M. Oakes and
Kathleen L. Brooks-Pazmany and
edited by F. Robert van der Linden

Published for the National Air and Space Museum
by the Smithsonian Institution Press
Washington, D.C., and London

Copyright © 1991 Smithsonian Institution
All rights reserved
First edition, 1976; revised 1981, 1985, and 1991

Library of Congress Cataloging-in-Publication Data
National Air and Space Museum.
    Aircraft of the National Air and Space Museum /
Smithsonian Institution. — 4th ed.
        p.   cm.
    ISBN 1-56098-153-9 (alk. paper)
    1. Airplanes — Catalogs.   2. National Air and
Space Museum — Catologs.   I. Smithsonian Institution.
II. Title. TL506.U6W376 1991
629.133'074'753 — dc20   91–27296

British Library Cataloging-in-Publication Data available

On the title page: The Wright Flyer rises off the ground
    on December 17, 1903. Orville Wright pilots the
    aircraft, as Wilbur Wright looks on. (Photo: SI A26767B)

For permission to reproduce individual illustrations
    appearing in this book, please correspond directly
    with the owners of the works as listed in the picture
    captions. The Smithsonian Institution Press does
    not retain reproduction rights for these illustrations
    individually or maintain a file of addresses for photo
    sources. Photos for which a Smithsonian Institution
    (SI) negative number are given may be obtained
    through the National Air and Space Museum.

The paper used in this publication meets the minimum
    requirements of the American National Standard
    for Permanence of Paper for Printed Library Materials
    Z39.48-1984.

Printed in the United States of America

5 4 3 2 1
95 94 93 92 91

Contents

Introduction

In the six years since the last edition of *Aircraft of the National Air and Space Museum* the National Aeronautical Collection has continued to improve through a careful process of rational selection and reinterpretation. This continuing program will enhance the collection and provide an invaluable record of humankind's most notable achievements, as well as failings, from which all of us may gather important lessons for the future. In the pages that follow, you will see a selection of brief aircraft histories that will help to document a part of this important story

Today, the National Air and Space Museum preserves over 350 aircraft. While only a small number of these artifacts are displayed in the museum at any one time, aircraft are regularly rotated through our changing exhibits to allow you the opportunity to view the greatest number possible. At any given time, the majority are either on display at our Paul E. Garber Preservation, Restoration, and Storage Facility, which may be visited by appointment, or are on loan to other museums around the world. The remaining aircraft are stored behind the scenes at the Garber Facility or at Washington Dulles International Airport.

All of the aircraft presented in this catalog are either currently on display in the museum or have been on exhibit in the past. All of them belong to the museum and all of them are real. None of the aircraft described are replicas or mock-ups.

Since the last edition of this book was published in 1985, we have added a considerable number of aircraft to the collection. This catalog describes eight of these additions, including the Ecker Flying Boat in the Early Flight gallery, the Grumman G-21 Goose in the Hall of Air Transportation, the Lockheed U-2C in Looking at Earth, the Rutan Voyager in the south lobby, and the Pfalz D.XII, Voisin VIII, and SPAD XIII in our newest gallery, Legend, Memory, and the Great War in the Air. In the intervening years, the famed Grumman F6F Hellcat was also prominently exhibited. A complete list of our accessions is located in the Appendices.

I hope that you will find this latest version of our catalog an interesting and informative reminder of your visit to the National Air and Space Museum.

Tom D. Crouch
Chairman
Aeronautics Department

Aeronca C-2

Wingspan:	10.98 m (36 ft.)
Length:	6.10 m (20 ft.)
Height:	2.18 m (7 ft. 6 in.)
Weight:	Gross 318 kg (700 lb.)
	Empty 184 kg (406 lb.)
Engine:	Aeronca E-107A, 26 hp

The Aeronca C-2 of 1929 was the first successful light plane produced in the United States. Safe, economical, easy to fly, and built in number, this delightful but unassuming airplane changed the face of aviation by opening a market never before successfully tapped—that of private aircraft ownership. "Airknockers" or "Flying Bathtubs," as they were affectionately known, made it possible for the average person to fly.

Before the Aeronca C-2, civil aircraft were working machines. There was almost no private ownership, for the large and expensive airplanes of the decade following World War I had to work to earn their keep. Even the barnstormer's Jenny— despite romantic images—was strictly a commercial venture that bore little resemblance to the luxury of owning an automobile. The 1920s were the heyday of the sportsman pilot, when aircraft manufacturers catered to the lucrative but limited market of the very wealthy. Their large, elegant, and expensive biplanes were touted as the ideal way to attend yacht regattas and polo matches.

Charles Lindbergh's 1927 flight from New York to Paris in the *Spirit of St. Louis* heightened public awareness and acceptance of the airplane. Ironically, the Great Depression two years later further promoted the emergence of light airplanes by making the machines of the 1920s too

expensive to operate. These factors, and advances in airframe and engine technology, set the stage for one of the most significant trends in aviation between the wars. It became possible at last in the 1930s for a significant segment of American society to own and fly an airplane.

Squat and bug-eyed, the diminutive Aeronca C-2 was a simple airplane with modest performance and delightful characteristics. Its steel-tube fuselage and wooden wings were covered with fabric and braced with wires. The pilot, seated before a stick and rudder bar, had just four instruments: oil temperature, oil pressure, nonsensitive altimeter, and tachometer.

The single-seat C-2 was powered by a two-cylinder Aeronca E-107 engine rated at 26–30 hp. The Aeronca C-3, its bigger brother introduced in 1931, had the Aeronca E-113 engine, which was rated at 36–40 hp. With seating for two side by side, the C-3 offered greater utility than the C-2 and quickly became popular as a trainer.

In 1929 the Aeronca C-2 sold for $1,495. By mid-1930, the price had dropped to $1,245 as a result of the Depression. C-2s were economical at 1 cent a mile for oil and gas, and could often be rented for just $4.00 an hour. Furthermore, they were simple to fly, easy to maintain, and had no bad characteristics to spring on a novice pilot. As the first light airplane to be produced in number in

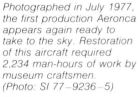

Photographed in July 1977, the first production Aeronca appears again ready to take to the sky. Restoration of this aircraft required 2,234 man-hours of work by museum craftsmen. (Photo: SI 77–9236–5)

Aeronca NX626N, serial #2, on its maiden flight in the fall of 1929. With its very long wing and low horsepower, the C-2 was almost a powered glider. (Photo: SI 74–10592)

Much was done to publicize the C-2 by noted pilot "Iron Hat" Johnston, shown here retrieving a can of gas in an Alameda, California, air show in November 1930. (Photo: SI A31980-L)

The design of the C-2 was based on that of Jean A. Roché's light plane. Standing with Roché, center, are John Dohse, who helped in the construction, and Harold Morehouse, who designed the engine. (Photo: SI A935-B)

the United States, the Aeronca C-2 was the Model T Ford of general aviation.

The Aeronautical Corporation of America, a small company whose name was shortened to Aeronca, was formed in 1928 at Lunken Airport near Cincinnati, Ohio. It bought production rights to a light airplane designed solely for recreational flying by French-born Jean A. Roché, Senior Aeronautical Engineer for the U.S. Army Air Service. The plane, reengineered for production by Roger E. Schlemmer of the University of Cincinnati's Aeronautical School, was designated the C-2. Work began on the prototype in 1929.

The first Aeronca flew on October 20, 1929. Painted bright yellow and orange, this plane was given serial number 2 (Roché's hand-built plane being considered the first of the type) and was assigned the registration NX626N. This airplane is

now in the collection of the National Air and Space Museum.

The first C-2s that Aeronca demonstrated at aviation expositions around the country won enthusiastic acceptance during the latter half of 1930. Despite the flood of competing light planes appearing on the scene by 1931, Aeronca maintained its dominance of the marketplace by introducing the two-seat C-3.

NX626N, the first Aeronca, flew for ten years with a variety of owners. In 1940, it was reacquired by the Aeronca Company for display at its new factory in Middletown, Ohio. Eight years later, Aeronca answered a call by the Smithsonian Institution for historic aircraft to add to its collection. NX626N was donated to the National Aeronautical Collection, where it remained in storage until its turn for restoration in 1976.

Jay P. Spenser

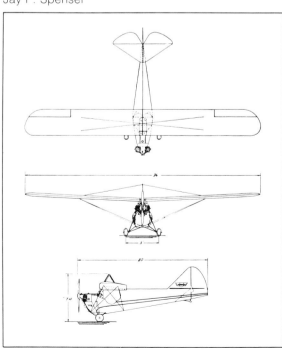

Albatros D.Va

Wingspan:	9 m (29 ft. 7 in.)
Length:	7.33 m (24 ft. 5/8 in.)
Height:	2.84 m (9 ft. 4 in.)
Weight:	Gross, 915 kg (2,017 lb.)
	Empty, 680 kg (1,499 lb.)
Engine:	Mercedes D IIIa 6-cylinder, in-line water cooled, 180 hp

The German Albatros D.Va fighter was widely used and well known in its time, though not considered one of the best World War I fighters. Although it failed to overcome the ascendancy gained by the Allied S.E.5s, Sopwiths, and SPADs, it fought on all fronts and was flown by nearly all of the principal German aces.

The series of famous Albatros fighters that concluded with the D.Va began in the summer of 1916 with the Albatros D.I Scout. Powered by an 160-hp Mercedes engine, it was soon followed by the D.II model, with only slight structural modifications. By early January 1917, the advanced D.IIIs were in production and joining frontline units. This model was basically a modified D.II with a narrow-chord lower wing similar to the French Nieuport. It met with immediate acceptance as the finest fighter the Germans had seen and consequently much was expected of it.

The D.V. was the next in the line of Albatros fighters. To improve performance, the prototype, completed in early 1917, was designed as a lighter airplane than the D.III. It was described as having the same wings as the D.III and a redesigned, more oval fuselage. Its initial weight margin of 70 pounds was soon lost because of modifications to correct structural weaknesses. Since both were powered by the 160-hp Mercedes six-cylinder water-cooled in-line engine, the performances of the two were quite similar.

Albatros D.Vs began reaching frontline units in May 1917, and one or both types served in nearly every German fighter unit. For even the average pilot the Albatros was easy to fly, without bad traits, and, above all, effective in combat.

An improved model, the Albatros D.Va was only slightly different from the D.V in that it incorporated a few structural improvements. Later models were equipped with the higher powered 180-hp Mercedes engine that improved the airplane's performance.

Many notable airmen flew D.Vs and D.Vas.

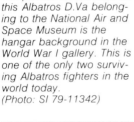

The perfect exhibit area for this Albatros D.Va belonging to the National Air and Space Museum is the hangar background in the World War I gallery. This is one of the only two surviving Albatros fighters in the world today.
(Photo: SI 79-11342)

Restoring this Albatros was one of the most challenging projects undertaken by the National Air and Space Museum. The airplane is original except for newly printed wing fabric, and fuselage plywood covering. (Photo: SI 79-4630)

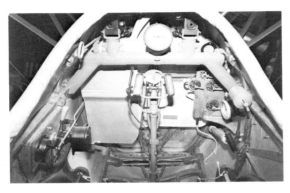

Compared to modern airplanes, the cockpit of the Albatros contains few controls. On the left handgrip of the control column is the throttle, and on the left side of the cockpit is the spark-advance handle. The large instrument in the center is the tachometer. (Photo: Smithsonian Institution)

Among these were Lt. Hermann Goering (twenty-two victories), who later was to head Hitler's Luftwaffe in World War II. Albatrosses of Jasta 21, led by the Bavarian ace Eduard von Schleich

(thirty-five victories), shot down forty-one French aircraft in the month of September 1917 alone. Other notable aces were Erich Loewenhardt (fifty-three victories), Ernst Udet (sixty-two victories), and Werner Voss (forty-eight victories). Manfred von Richthofen scored most of his eighty victories in the Albatros and not in the Fokker Triplane as legend implies. During an air duel in a D.V, von Richthofen, the "Red Baron," was seriously wounded, yet was able to nurse his crippled airplane to a safe landing before collapsing. Undaunted, he later flew another Albatros to lead his unit during the Battle of Cambrai.

The Albatros belonging to the National Air and Space Museum is painted with the original markings that it carried while in combat. The origin of the word "Stropp" remains unknown, but is typical of individualized markings created by the German pilots. The yellow and green tail stripes indentify this aircraft as having belonged to Jasta 46. This unit was formed on December 17, 1917, as part of Germany's Amerika Program to build German strength for a decisive blow before American equipment and manpower became an overwhelming factor against Germany.

The Stropp Albatros entered service sometime around February 1918, and several factors lead to the conclusion that its operational life ended before April 15, 1918, primarily based on the unchanged Patee-style cross insignias that were to be changed to the straight-sided cross by that date. This operational period for this Albatros is significant because it coincides with the German Spring Offensive of 1918, which included some of the heaviest air fighting of the war. Jasta 46 was stationed at the exact center of the German thrust that attempted to throw a wedge between the British and French armies. Losses during this campaign were unusually high. Battle damage to the museum's Albatros caused by a single bullet penetrating the fuel tank and engine was left unrepaired during its 1979 restoration.

Manufacture of the Albatros was discontinued around April 1918 after approximately 4,800 Albatros fighters of all types had been produced. Of the D.V and D.Va series, there is evidence that 2,505 or more were ordered, yet only one other example of this significant fighter survives, and that one is in the Australian War Memorial Museum in Canberra. There are no earlier models in existence anywhere.

Robert C. Mikesh

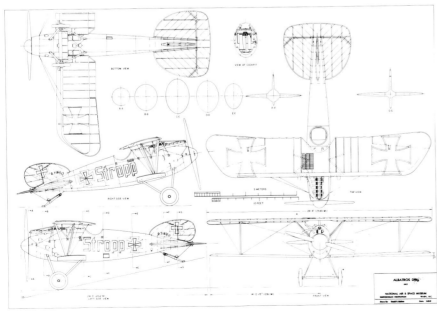

Beechcraft Bonanza "Waikiki Beech"

Wingspan:	10 m (32 ft. 9⅞ in.)
Length:	7.67 m (25 ft. 2 in.)
Height:	1.95 m (6 ft. 6½ in.)
Weight:	Gross, 1,750 kg (3,858 lb.)
	Empty, 738 kg (1,625 lb.)
Engine:	Continental E-165,165 hp

The Beechcraft Bonanza is one of general aviation's great success stories. This classic airplane first flew in 1947 and is still in continuous production with a conventional tail rather than the distinctive V-tail with which it first flew.

In addition to a generous acceptance within the aviation world, where it is regarded as the "Cadillac" of the single-engined light-plane field, the Bonanza also rates high marks in the industrial-design field. In a survey of 100 leading designers, design teachers, and architects, published in *Fortune* magazine, April 1959, the Bonanza was rated as one of the 100 best designs of mass-produced products.

Its fine performance encouraged a number of people to select the Bonanza for record-breaking flights. Probably the best known of these is the *Waikiki Beech*, in which Capt. William P. "Bill" Odom set two distance records. Both of these flights were sponsored by Beech Aircraft Corporation to demonstrate the efficiency and dependability of their plane.

In the log book of the *Waikiki Beech*, under the dates of March 6, 7, and 8, 1949, is the following entry: "X-country record-breaking flight: 36 hours 01 minutes, Honolulu to Teterboro, New Jersey.

Bill Odom, who piloted the Waikiki Beech *on two record-breaking flights, stands beside his colorful aircraft.*
(Photo: SI 75-11348)

Signed Wm. P. Odom, 97580." This brief entry summed up the flight, which covered 4,957.24 officially accredited great circle miles (5,273 actual miles). Of this distance, 2,474 miles were over the waters of the Pacific Ocean and 2,799 were over the North American Continent. The flight was completed at a total cost of less than $75 for fuel and oil. The average fuel consumption was 19.37 miles per gallon and average speed was 146.3 miles per hour.

A smooth takeoff from Hickam Field, Honolulu, began this epoch-making flight. It was uneventful, proceeding as planned except for two detours to avoid bad weather enroute. As he passed over Ohio, Odom changed his shirt and used his electric razor. When he stepped out of the Bonanza at Teterboro, he was clean-shaven and neatly dressed, as any young executive might be on arrival for a business conference.

In an earlier flight, on January 12, 1949, Odom had established a record for light-plane flights from Hawaii to the continental United States. The Bonanza was the first light plane to make this flight, a great circle distance of 2,406.9 miles, though Odom actually flew 2,900 miles. Severe weather over Nevada forced Odom to abandon his

The Waikiki Beech *makes a trial flight over Wichita before its famous Honolulu-to-New York flight.*
(Photo: SI 75-11351)

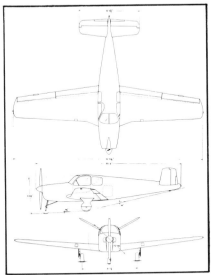

Warming up at the Honolulu airport, the Waikiki Beech *prepares to take off for New York.*
(Photo: SI 75-11349)

goal and return to Oakland 22 hours and 6 minutes after takeoff.

Following the Honolulu-to-Teterboro flight, Odom made a national tour with the Bonanza, after which it was turned over to the National Air Museum. In 1951 the plane was returned to Beech Aircraft to be refurbished, and was loaned to Congressman Peter F. Mack, Jr., for a worldwide goodwill flight. Leaving Springfield, Illinois, on October 7, 1951, the plane, rechristened *Friendship Flame*, visited forty-five major cities in thirty-five countries. One hundred thirteen days and 33,000 miles later, the plane returned to Wichita, Kansas, on April 19, 1952.

The *Waikiki Beech* was the fourth Bonanza built; the only modifications made to the otherwise standard Model 35 were the fixtures and tubing required to install the extra fuel tanks, 126 gallons in the cabin and a 62-gallon streamlined tank on each wing tip. The Bonanza is regarded as a classic aircraft design of the post-World War II era and is easily identified by its distinctive V-tail. Though a number of other design refinements contributed to the efficiency of this airplane, the "butterfly tail" is its most distinguishing outward characteristic. This unique feature was tested during the waning years of World War II and found promising. The most important advantages of this design were the reduction in the number of parts and in weight. Control response with the V-tail is equivalent to conventional tail surfaces of 40 percent greater area.

Early in 1975 the *Waikiki Beech* was once again refurbished by Beech for exhibit in the new National Air and Space Museum. In recognition of its two significant record flights, the plane carries its "Waikiki Beech" markings on the left side of the fuselage and the "Friendship Flame" markings on the right.

Louis S. Casey

Beechcraft C17L

Wingspan:	9.75 m (32 ft.)
Length:	7.44 m (24 ft. 5 in.)
Height:	2.59 m (8 ft. 6 in.)
Weight:	Gross 1,435.6 kg (3,165 lb.)
	Empty 827.8 kg (1,825 lb.)
Engine:	Jacobs L-4MB, 225 hp

The Model 17, the first aircraft produced by the Beech Aircraft Corporation of Wichita, Kansas, was a gamble for Walter Beech, president of the company, and Ted Wells, vice-president and chief designer of the aircraft. Produced during the depths of the Great Depression, this expensive aircraft was designed as a high-speed, comfortable business airplane. The gamble was successful, and 781 Beech 17s were produced in eight different series.

The first series of Beech Staggerwings, in which only two were built, was known as the Model 17R. The aircraft had fixed landing gear that was well faired with wheel pants and it was powered with a 420-hp Wright R-760 engine. It had a steel-tube fuselage and wing spar structure. The upper wing was inversely staggered behind the lower wing, and this design gave the Model 17 its unique shape and name. The fuselage was faired with wood formers and stringers and was covered with fabric. Top speed of the aircraft was over 200 mph and yet the landing speed was only 60–65 mph. Such performance was remarkable for the time. Despite its promise, the aircraft was difficult to sell, largely because of its cost. Clearly, some compromises in performance had to be made if it was to be more competitive.

By 1934, a new series retaining the overall design of the earlier airplanes and known as the Model B17L was being produced. The major modifications were the installation of retractable landing gear, wings of a different airfoil, the use of wood wing spars instead of steel ones, and a 225-hp Jacobs L-4 power plant. The use of retractable gear, which was not common at the time, as well as parallel improvements in streamlining and weight reduction, gave the aircraft a maximum speed of 175 mph and a landing speed of 45 mph. The Beech Company advertised the performance and economy of the new series and emphasized the pilot's visibility from the aircraft and the plane's gentle stall characteristics, both due to the staggered wing arrangement. The redesigned aircraft had hit the target, and sales improved significantly.

The company also built two Model A17s with fixed landing gear and Wright R-1820 Cyclone engines. The engine on the second of these two powerful planes developed 710 hp. The aircraft had a maximum speed of 250 mph, making it the fastest commercial aircraft of its time and the fastest Model 17 ever built.

Although the airborne performance of the early Model 17s was impressive, the aircraft did not have desirable landing characteristics. The tall landing gear made ground loops a problem and the nose-heavy condition made three-point landings difficult. The Model C17 introduced in 1936 corrected these problems. It had shorter landing gear, and the angle of incidence of the horizontal stabilizer was changed to get the tail down while landing.

The Beech Corporation not only had a successful corporate aircraft, but a winner in

The National Air and Space Museum's Beechcraft Staggerwing in its original configuration about 1936. (Photo: SI 84–9345)

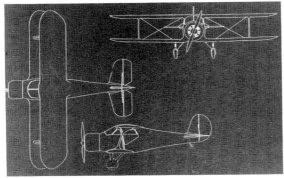

Beechcraft Model C17L in the Golden Age of Flight gallery in the National Air and Space Musuem. (Photo: SI 84–8281–10)

racing circles. NC15835, a Model C17R, piloted by Louise Thaden and Blanche Noyes, won the 1936 Bendix Trophy Race. Other stock Beechcraft won two major air races in Miami in 1936. In 1937, Jacqueline Cochran set a 1,000-kilometer speed record averaging over 320 kph (200 mph). Staggerwings also did well in the 1937 and 1938 Bendix Races.

The Model D17 Staggerwing was the first major design change since the Model B17. The fuselage was lengthened. This change improved the landing characteristics by giving more leverage to the elevator. The ailerons were moved to the upper wings to prevent interference with the air flow over the flaps. The hand-operated brake, which was coordinated with the rudder pedals, was replaced with foot-operated brakes, which simplified braking considerably. These and other airframe modifications improved the basic design of the Staggerwing.

The Model D17S Staggerwing, equipped with a 450-hp Pratt and Whitney R-985 engine, was produced in larger numbers than any other model During World War II, the U.S. Army Air Forces and the U.S. Navy purchased all the Model D17S aircraft for transporting personnel.

The Beechcraft Staggerwing in the National Air and Space Museum, serial number 93, was manufactured on July 3, 1936, and registered as NC15840. It was a Model C17B powered with a 285-hp Jacobs L-5M engine. The original owner of the aircraft was Mr. E. E. Aldrin (father of astronaut Edwin "Buzz" Aldrin), who was with the Standard Oil Development Company in New York City. The list price of the aircraft was $10,260.00. The aircraft was equipped with numerous extras, including expensive instrumentation, electrical bonding, rear seat parachutes, a magneto-equipped engine, and a custom paint scheme using the colors and logo of Standard Oil. The company installed a radio transmitter and receiver for communication and a radio compass for navigation, equipment essential for a corporate aircraft.

NC15840 was damaged and repaired many times throughout its flying career. A number of repairs to the wings of the aircraft reflect the problem of ground looping. The aircraft eventually had its hand-operated brake removed and replaced with toe-operated brakes.

Shortly after World War II, the aircraft was changed to a Model C17L with the installation of a 225-hp Jacobs L4-MB engine. The new engine

Beechcraft Model A17F with Wright Cyclone engine. (Photo: SI 84–9347)

allowed the use of a controllable pitch prop, the efficency of which offset the lower horsepower of the new engine.

From 1936 to 1980, NC15840 had nineteen different owners. It was operated by several oil companies as well as charter and sight-seeing businesses. During World War II, it flew coastal patrol with the Civil Air Patrol. Between 1961 and 1980 the aircraft was inactive. In 1981, it was donated to the National Air and Space Museum by Desert Air Parts of Tucson, Arizona.

The fact that NC15840 survived so long is a testimony to the masterful design of Walter Beech, Ted Wells, and their associates. The aircraft was technologically advanced for its time, and its beauty will always remain a classic in aircraft design.

Rick Leyes and Dorothy Cochrane

Beechcraft Model G17S. (Photo: SI 84–9346)

Beechcraft D.18

Wingspan:	14.5 m (47 ft. 7 in.)
Length:	10.4 m (33 ft. 11 ½ in.)
Height:	2.8 m (9 ft. 2 ½ in.)
Weight:	Gross, 3,967 kg (8,750 lb.)
	Empty, 2,584 kg (5,697 lb.)
Engines:	Two Pratt and Whitney Wasp, Jr., 450 hp

On January 15, 1937, the Beechcraft Model 18 made its first demonstration flight at the factory in Wichita, Kansas, and it continued in production for thirty-two years. This low-wing, all-metal, twin-engine monoplane was originally intended as a six-to-eight-passenger executive or feeder airline transport. As the years passed, however, the Model 18 was adapted to many uses; in all, thirty-two different versions were produced.

When production began on the Model 18 in 1937, there was virtually no market for this airplane in the United States. At the time, air transportation in the United States was a trunkline operation, and few feeder lines existed. Acceptance of the Model 18 by foreign and charter lines was immediate, however. The Model 18A, which operated on interchangeable ski- or float-landing gear, was an ideal adaptation for snowbound areas and for lake and interisland service. Prairie Airlines of Alberta, Canada, for example, ordered several of these airplanes for use in delivering airmail over a route that extended from Prince Albert to North Battleford, south to Saskatoon and Moose Jaw, finally joining up with the main route of Trans-Canada Airlines at Regina. Also, businessmen

were favorably impressed with the performance of the Model 18 as an executive transport, with orders coming from Alaska, Canada, and Puerto Rico.

On January 13, 1939, Beech began negotiations with the U.S. Government on a contract for a photoreconnaissance version of the 18. Fourteen of these aircraft, designated Type F-2, were ordered as part of the Emergency Procurement Program. This order was followed by a contract for eleven C-45 personnel transports. Later that year, Beech began negotiations with the Chinese Government for a bomber trainer. This version had a clear plastic nose, a single gun turret on the upper fuselage, and a machine gun in a tunnel in the rear floor. It also had internal bomb racks, which carried up to twenty 25-pound bombs.

That year also saw a standard Beech 18S set a new flight record while on a demonstration tour, flying from Bogotá to Barranquilla, Colombia, a distance of 450 miles, in 1 hour, 54 minutes. Later the same plane made a 1,350-mile flight from Maracay, Venezuela, to Miami, Florida, in 6 hours, the first known nonstop flight between those two cities. To further demonstrate the capable performance of the Beech Model 18, Walter Beech

The National Air and Space Museum's Model D18S, N522B, served as an air ambulance for fifteen years. (Photo: SI 77-7744)

entered a D-18S in the 1940 Macfadden Race from St. Louis to Miami. With "Ding" Rankin as his pilot, Beech crossed the finish line in Miami in 4 hours, 37 minutes, to win first place. Their average speed for the flight was 234.097 mph.

The advent of World War II brought more orders for Beech military versions, both from the United States and foreign governments. The AT-7 was used for training student navigators; the AT-11 was an advanced trainer for specialized training of bombardiers. In fact, about 90 percent of the U.S. Air Force's navigators and bombardiers received their training on AT-7s and AT-11s. The U.S. Navy SNB-1 was similar to the AT-11, the SNB-2 to the AT-7. The JRB-1 was a radio-control airplane for target or drone aircraft. The Navy's personnel transports similar to the C-45 were known as JRB-2, JRB-3, and JRB-4.

With the end of the war came the end of military production, although many of these aircraft remained in service for years. By October 1945 Beech was back into full commercial aircraft production. The first aircraft off the line was the newest model, the D18S, which incorporated a number of improvements. Structural modifications allowed for an increase in maximum weight. New landing gear, brakes, and tires were installed. The D18S was powered by two 450-hp Pratt and Whitney Wasp, Jr., engines with Hamilton Standard constant speed propellers. It was the premier executive transport among businessmen.

On December 10, 1953, the prototype of the Super 18, the last version of the Beech 18, made its first flight. The last three production aircraft were delivered in November 1969. More than 9,000 Model 18s had been produced since 1937, and in 1970 more than 2,000 were still being flown in the United States alone.

In 1958 Mike Mitchell bought what is now the National Air and Space Museum's aircraft from the F.H. Hogue Produce Company. It was already ten years old, but still in good condition. For fifteen years, he flew N522B as an air ambulance, operating out of Sky Harbor Air Service in Phoenix, Arizona. The aircraft was modified to accommodate up to ten ambulatory patients. Stretcher patients could be placed on a lounge running fore and aft. During the fifteen years that Mitchell used this plane, he flew a total of a million and a quarter miles, transporting nearly fifteen thousand patients. He donated it to the Smithsonian in 1976.

Kathleen L. Brooks-Pazmany

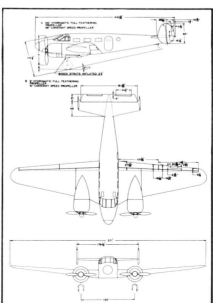

Bell 206L-1 LongRanger II "Spirit of Texas"

Rotor diameter:	11.27 m (37 ft.)
Length:	10.13 m (33 ft. 3 in.)
Width:	1.32 m (4 ft. 4 in.)
Height:	3.6 m (11 ft. 8 in.)
Weight:	Gross 1,800 kg (4,000 lb.)
	Empty 936.5 kg (2,081 lb.)
Engine:	Allison 250-C28B
	500 hp

Conventional layout, low-cost maintenance, and good flying qualities make the Bell LongRanger a popular choice for company transport. (Photo: SI 84-9612)

On September 25, 1973, Bell Helicopter announced an improved version of the venerable JetRanger. Named the Model 206L-1 LongRanger II, it introduced Bell's revolutionary new Noda-Matic suspension system for the transmission and a stretched fuselage 26 inches longer than that on the JetRanger. The additional space left room for a third side window, the most recognizable visual feature of the LongRanger. Bell Helicopter Textron's Model 206L-1 LongRanger II, and its older brother JetRanger, may be the most familiar helicopters in the western world. To date, over 5,000 JetRangers and 900 LongRangers have been produced, and it seems that the type will stay in production for years to come.

Development of the Model 206 started in the late 1950s, the intended goal being to compete for the U.S. Army's light observation helicopter (LOH) program, carried out in 1961. But the Hughes Helicopters entry, designated OH-6 by the Army and now known as the Hughes 500, won the contest. However, Bell introduced the aircraft, commercially named the JetRanger, to the civilian market with excellent results. Military work came for the JetRanger in 1968 when the U.S. Navy bought forty aircraft, called TH-57A SeaRangers, for use as trainers. The Model 206 has since filled several

military contracts, the most recent order for more SeaRangers coming from the Navy.

Simplicity, reliability, and utility characterize the Jet and LongRanger aircraft. Bell's trademark, the two-blade teetering main rotor combined with small, high-output turbine engines, made the Model 206 easy and inexpensive to fly and maintain by both the corporate owner and troops in the field.

The Noda-Matic system in the LongRanger greatly reduced a shortcoming that was almost traditional in helicopters—vibration. By suspending the transmission at certain points from a metal beam, vibration levels were reduced so that the LongRanger's ride compared with that of a fixed-wing turboprop aircraft.

Besides civilian and military users in the United States, thirty-six other countries have bought this helicopter. The Model 206 is also built under license in Italy by Agusta.

Using easy-to-maintain engines, uncomplicated flight control systems, and cabin interiors that can be modified in minutes from passenger to cargo configuration, Bell has made these helicopters almost as efficient to operate as fixed-wing airplanes.

These attributes were demonstrated when a

A difficult landing in the Pacific Ocean was made halfway between Kushiro, Japan, and Shemya Island, Alaska, aboard the container ship S.S. President McKinley by the Spirit of Texas. (Photo: SI 84-9613)

206L-1 LongRanger II named the Spirit of Texas and flown by H. Ross Perot Jr. and Jay Coburn completed the first circumnavigation of the world by helicopter on September 30, 1982. Their journey began 29 days, 3 hours, and 8 minutes earlier on September 1.

For their trip around the world, which began and ended in Fort Worth, Texas, Perot and Coburn flew a LongRanger with full navigation equipment, survival gear, and emergency items. Also added were pop-out floats, and a 151-gallon auxiliary fuel tank in place of the rear seat. An additional five hours' endurance was added to enable the Spirit of Texas to fly eight hours without refueling.

An Allison 250-C28B turbine engine performed flawlessly for 246.5 hours of flight, flying more than 10 hours a day, over open ocean, barren desert, and tropical rain forest. Average ground speed for the trip around the world was 117 mph. The LongRanger is capable of a maximum speed of 150 mph.

The Spirit of Texas made its last landing at Andrews Air Force Base on November 15, 1982. From there, it was transferred to the National Air and Space Museum for display, and later it was donated by H. Ross Perot to become a permanent part of the National Aeronautical Collection. Russell E. Lee

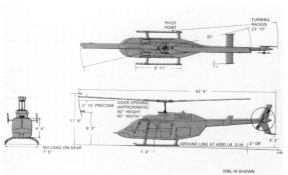

Flying across thousands of acres of ranchland, today's cattleman inspects the same amount of acreage in a day from his LongRanger that yesterday's cowboy covered in a month by horse. (Photo: SI 84-9611)

Perot and Coburn fly the Spirit of Texas past Reunion Tower in Ft. Worth on final approach for landing, completing the round-the-world flight on September 30, 1982. The aircraft consumed 57,756 pounds of turbine fuel flying a distance of 24,699 miles. (Photo: SI 84-9610)

Bell UH-13J

Rotor diameter:	11.3 m (37 ft. 1 ½ in.)
Fuselage length:	9.87 m (32 ft. 4 ¾ in.)
Weight:	Gross, 1,293 kg (2,850 lb.)
	Empty, 744 kg (1,640 lb.)
Engine:	Lycoming VO-540-B1B, 260 hp

The Bell UH-13J Ranger was the first helicopter to carry a President of the United States. This is now the most practical method of transporting the President and his staff over short distances. (Photo: Bell Helicopter Company)

The White House announced in early 1957 that two Bell helicopters, UH-13Js, with special interiors had been purchased for use by President Dwight D. Eisenhower for his short trips—primarily between the White House and Washington National Airport.

This decision marked the coming of age of helicopters, as officials entrusted with the safety of the President approved one for his use. The helicopter eliminated many security problems, and could deliver the President directly to his waiting aircraft or to the White House lawn.

President Eisenhower made the first presidential helicopter trip on July 13, 1957, at 2:10 p.m. aboard one of these UH-13Js, from the White House south lawn to a military command post at a remote location. Acting in his capacity as commander-in-chief of the armed forces, Eisenhower made this trip as part of a military exercise. Piloting him was Air Force Maj. Joseph E. Barrett. James Rowley, chief of the White House

Secret Service detachment, accompanied the President.

In a second Air Force helicopter, piloted by Capt. Lawrence R. Cummings, was Eisenhower's personal physician and a Secret Service agent.

In early 1958, after less than one year of operation, the presidential helicopter mission was assigned jointly to the Army and Marines, utilizing a larger type of craft, able to carry more members of the President's staff. The two Bell helicopters were transferred to the 1,001st Helicopter Squadron at Bolling Air Force Base, Washington, D.C., for continued service. Although they never again carried a President after this one flight, they did carry many high-ranking Department of Defense personnel—both civilian and military. Numerous foreign dignitaries also were flown in the aircraft.

By 1967, after ten years of service, the two Bell helicopters were retired. The aircraft that actually carried the President, 57-2729, was presented to

The south lawn of the White House proved to be a suitable landing site for the Bell UH-13J. This helicopter could carry three passengers at nearly 100 mph. (Photo: Bell Helicopter Company)

The first and only time that President Eisenhower used the UH-13J during its one year of service was on July 13, 1957, when he flew to a military command post not far from Washington, D.C. The Army and Marine Corps now provide this service in much larger helicopters. (Photo: Bell Helicopter Company)

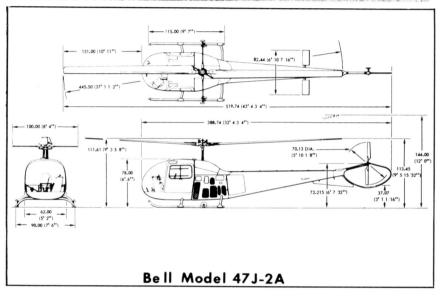

Bell Model 47J-2A

the National Air and Space Museum. The sister ship, 57-2728, went to the Air Force Museum at Dayton, Ohio.

These first presidential helicopters were equivalent to the commerical model of the Bell 47J. They were advanced models of the type that was first certificated in 1946 for carrying passengers. Wider, with more sophisticated equipment and greater power than its predecessors, the UH-13J seated three across with plenty of leg room for the passengers. The pilot sat alone up front, with the instrument console to the left for maximum visibility. The nose was a plastic bubble with about 120 degrees of vision in all directions, tinted to cut down glare. Normal cruising speed was between 90 and 100 mph.

The Bell Model 47 and its many variants were produced in large quantitites to serve both military and civilian needs, not only in the United States but in many foreign countries as well.
Robert C. Mikesh

Bell X-1 "Glamorous Glennis"

Wingspan:	8.54 m (28 ft.)
Length:	9.41 m (30.9 ft.)
Height:	3.31 m (10.85 ft.)
Weight:	Launch configuration, 5,557 kg (12,250 lb.) Landing configuration, 3,175 kg (7,000 lb.)
Engine:	Reaction Motors, Inc., XLR-11-RM-3 (Model A6000C4), 6,000-lb. static thrust

On October 14, 1947, flying the Bell XS-1 #1, Capt. Charles E. "Chuck" Yeager, USAF, became the first pilot to fly faster than sound. The XS-1, later designated X-1, reached Mach 1.06, 700 mph, at an altitude of 43,000 feet, over the Mojave Desert near Muroc Dry Lake, California. The flight demonstrated that aircraft could be designed to fly faster than sound, and the concept of a "sound barrier" crumbled into myth.

The XS-1 was developed as part of a cooperative program initiated in 1944 by the National Advisory Committee for Aeronautics (NACA) and the U.S. Army Air Forces (later the U.S. Air Force) to develop special manned transonic and supersonic research aircraft. On March 16, 1945, the Army Air Technical Service Command awarded the Bell Aircraft Corporation of Buffalo, New York, a contract to develop three transonic and supersonic research aircraft under project designation MX-653. The Army assigned

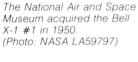

The National Air and Space Museum acquired the Bell X-1 #1 in 1950. (Photo: NASA LA59797)

the designation XS-1 for Experimental Sonic-1.

Bell Aircraft built three rocket-powered XS-1 aircraft. The National Air and Space Museum now owns the XS-1 #1, serial 46-062, named *Glamorous Glennis* by Captain Yeager in honor of his wife. The XS-1 #2 (46-063) was flight-tested by NACA and later was modified as the X-1E Mach 2+ research airplane. (The X-1E is currently on exhibit outside the NASA Flight Research Center, Edwards, California.) The X-1 #3 (46-064) had a turbopump-driven, low-pressure fuel feed system. This aircraft, known popularly as the X-1-3 *Queenie*, was lost in a 1951 explosion on the ground that injured its pilot. Three additional X-1 aircraft, the X-1A, X-1B, and X-1D, were constructed and test-flown. Two of these, the X-1A and X-1D, were also lost, as a result of propulsion-system explosions.

The two XS-1 aircraft were constructed from high-strength aluminum, with propellant tanks

In the fall of 1946 the Bell X-1 #2 was taken to Muroc Dry Lake, California, for its initial powered flight. This photo of the aircraft being carried to launch altitude by a B-29 was taken December 9, 1946. (Photo: Bell Aerospace Co.)

This is the instrument panel of the museum's specimen X-1 #1. (Photo: SI A47619)

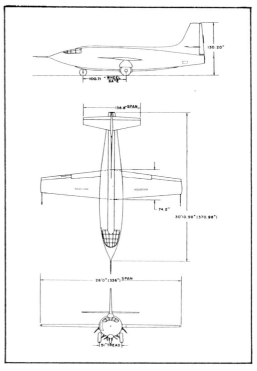

The Reaction Motors, Inc., XLR-11-RM-3 Model A6000C4 engine in the X-1 used liquid oxygen and diluted ethyl alcohol for propellants. (Photo: USAF 8814A.C.)

fabricated from steel. The first two XS-1 aircraft did not utilize turbopumps for fuel feed to the rocket engine, relying instead on direct nitrogen pressurization of the fuel-feed system. The smooth contours of the XS-1, patterned on the lines of a .50-caliber machine gun bullet, masked an extremely crowded fuselage containing two propellant tanks, twelve nitrogen spheres for fuel and cabin pressurization, the pilot's pressurized cockpit, three pressure regulators, a retractable landing gear, the wing carry-through structure, a Reaction Motors, Inc., 6,000-pound-thrust rocket engine, and more than five hundred pounds of special flight-test instrumentation.

Though originally designed for conventional ground takeoffs, all X-1 aircraft were air-launched from Boeing B-29 or B-50 Superfortress aircraft. The performance penalties and safety hazards associated with operating rocket-propelled aircraft from the ground caused mission planners to resort to air-launching instead. Nevertheless, on January 5, 1949, the X-1 #1 *Glamorous Glennis* successfully completed a ground takeoff from Muroc Dry Lake, piloted by Chuck Yeager. The maximum speed attained by the X-1 #1 was Mach 1.45 at 40,130 feet, approximately 957 mph, during a flight by Yeager on March 26, 1948. On August 8, 1949, Maj. Frank K. Everest, Jr., USAF, reached an altitude of 71,902 feet, the highest flight made by the little rocket airplane. It continued flight test operations until mid-1950, by which time it had completed a total of nineteen contractor demonstration flights and fifty-nine Air Force test flights.

On August 26, 1950, Air Force Chief of Staff Gen. Hoyt Vandenberg presented the X-1 #1 to Alexander Wetmore, then Secretary of the Smithsonian Institution. The X-1, General Vandenberg stated, "marked the end of the first great period of the air age, and the beginning of the second. In a few moments the subsonic period became history and the supersonic period was born." Earlier, Bell Aircraft President Lawrence D. Bell, NACA scientist John Stack, and Air Force test pilot Chuck Yeager had received the 1947 Robert J. Collier Trophy for their roles in first exceeding the speed of sound and opening the pathway to practical supersonic flight.

Richard P. Hallion

Bell XP-59A Airacomet

Wingspan:	14.93 m (49 ft.)
Length:	11.83 m (38 ft. 10 in.)
Height:	3.76 m (12 ft. 3¾ in.)
Weight:	Gross, 5,443 kg (12,562 lb.)
	Empty, 3,320 kg (7,320 lb.)
Engines:	Two General Electric I-A, 1,250-lb. thrust

The Bell XP-59A Airacomet was the first American turbojet airplane to fly. Three XP-59A Airacomets were completed, and the National Air and Space Museum has the XP-59A #1 aircraft, U.S. Army Air Forces serial number 42-108784. Development of the XP-59A began in October 1941, with a contract from the government to the Bell Aircraft Corporation of Buffalo, New York. Design and construction of the aircraft took place in greatest secrecy, and the designation XP-59A was specially chosen as a cloak for the Airacomet, for the XP-59A designation had originally referred to an abortive piston-engine fighter project that Bell had abandoned.

The XP-59A owed its existence to a visit made to Great Britain by the Army Air Forces chief, Maj. Gen. Henry H. "Hap" Arnold, in April 1941. While there, General Arnold had learned of the development of Britain's first jet aircraft, the Gloster E.28/39, powered by a jet engine designed by British jet pioneer Frank Whittle. Immediately upon

The historic Bell XP-59 #1, America's first turbojet aircraft to fly, is shown at Muroc Dry Lake, California. (Photo: Bell Aerospace Co.)

his return to the United States Arnold arranged for Whittle engines to be made available to this country. General Electric was selected as the engine contractor, and Bell received a go-ahead to develop a testbed airframe. The XP-59A was the result.

The first XP-59A Airacomet arrived at Muroc Dry Lake, California, for its initial flight trials in mid-September 1942. On October 1, 1942, Bell test pilot Robert M. Stanley completed the aircraft's first flight. During this initial trial flight, Stanley kept the landing gear fully extended and did not exceed an altitude of 25 feet. Later in the day, three more flights were made, to an altitude of 100 feet. Then, on October 2, 1942, the XP-59A completed an additional four flights, attaining an altitude of 10,000 feet.

After these trial flights, the XP-59A was modified to carry a flight test observer in an open cockpit in the nose of the airplane ahead of the pilot. Because of an occasional tendency of early jet

This P-59B-1 is one of only fifty production aircraft completed.
(Photo: Bell Aerospace Co.)

engines to start only after much coaxing, this XP-59A received the unofficial nickname "Miss Fire."

The XP-59A was powered by two General Electric-manufactured Type I-A centrifugal-flow jet engines. The I-A engine was based on the design of the British Whittle W2B. Each I-A engine produced 1,250 pounds of static thrust, giving the XP-59A a maximum speed of 390 mph. In March 1942 the Bell Company had received a follow-on contract for thirteen YP-59A test and evaluation aircraft to examine the plane's military suitability. The first YP-59A arrived for flight testing at Muroc in June 1943. In mid-1943 Bell proposed that the Army Air Forces acquire 300 P-59 production fighter aircraft, but the AAF decided to order only 100, as the P-59 was clearly outclassed by contemporary piston-engine fighters such as the North American P-51, Republic P-47, and Lockheed P-38. In fact, only fifty Airacomet production aircraft were ever completed, these consisting of twenty P-59As and thirty P-59Bs. The YP-59A, P-59A, and P-59B Airacomets were all powered by the more powerful General Electric I-16 (J-31) turbojet engine. The P-59B was assigned to the 412th Fighter Group, which used the aircraft for pilot familiarization with the handling and performance characteristics of jet aircraft. The production P-59A and B aircraft had an armament of one 37-mm M-4 cannon with 44 rounds and three .50-caliber machine guns with 200 rounds per gun. Maximum performance of the production P-59 aircraft was 409 mph at 35,000 feet. While good, this performance was exceeded by many Allied and Axis piston-engine fighters.

Even after the XP-59A began flight operations, the plane's existence was a closely guarded secret. Officials at one point disguised the XP-59A with a dummy four-bladed propeller to fool onlookers into thinking that the Airacomet was a conventional plane. Mechanics removed the "propeller" before flight and reinstalled it after the plane landed.

Because of America's delayed entry into the jet propulsion field, no American jet aircraft saw combat service in World War II. The Gloster Meteor, a British jet fighter, did serve briefly at the war's end against the V-1 "buzz bomb," but it was Nazi Germany that made the most of jet propulsion. Before the end of the war, Germany had the Messerschmitt Me.262 jet fighter and the Arado Ar 234 jet bomber in operational service.

The historic XP-59A #1 aircraft is the direct ancestor of all American jet-propelled airplanes.

Richard P. Hallion

The Army ordered thirteen YP-59As in 1942 for test and evaluation at Muroc Dry Lake, California.
(Photo: Bell Aerospace Co.)

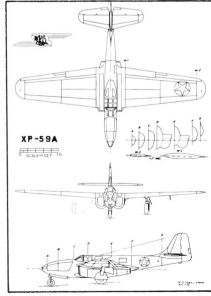

The production aircraft, including the P-59A, were powered by the GE 1-16 (J-31) engine.
(Photo: Bell Aerospace Co.)

(Diagram: Courtesy Ronald D. Neal)

XP-59A

SCALE·FEET

Bensen Gyro-Glider and Gyro-Copter

Gyro-Glider	Length:	3.45 m (11 ft. 4 in.)
	Width:	1.22 m (4 ft.)
	Height:	1.91 m (6 ft. 3 in.)
	Weight:	Gross, 136 kg (300 lb.)
		Empty, 58 kg (128 lb.)
Gyro-Copter	Length:	3.45 m (11 ft. 4 in.)
	Height:	1.91 m (6 ft. 3 in.)
	Weight:	Gross, 227 kg (500 lb.)
		Empty, 110 kg (247 lb.)
	Engine:	McCulloch 4318E, 90 hp

In 1953 Igor Bensen, a Russian immigrant to the United States, realized a twenty-five-year-old dream—the establishment of his own aircraft company. Since fleeing to the West during the Russian Revolution, Bensen had patented thirty-six inventions, had participated in early helicopter research for the General Electric Company, had organized and directed the Research Department at Kaman Aircraft Corporation, and had been a test pilot for both the Air Force and the Navy. His new company was formed to develop light, safe rotary-wing aircraft for use by private individuals.

His original Gyro-Glider, built in 1954, took two men two weeks to complete. Designed to be towed behind a small automobile, the Gyro-Glider took off when the car reached 25 mph. If there were winds above 25 mph, the aircraft could lift off by itself, like a kite.

No pilot's license was required to operate the Gyro-Glider, nor did the aircraft itself need to be licensed. It was equipped with a single-stick control for forward flight, turning and banking, and going up and down. Stalling was impossible, because the rotor continued to turn even when the airspeed was zero.

The Gyro-Glider was basically a lightweight tubular aluminum T-shaped structure. The forward arm supported the seat, towing arm, rudder bar, and landing-gear nose wheel. The rear bar carried the stabilizing fin and rudder. The two rotor blades, mounted at the top of the T-frame, had a diameter of 20 feet, 6 inches.

There were several options available for building the Gyro-Glider. The complete aircraft could be purchased, a kit with parts was available, or a set of plans with building and flying instructions could be purchased. Materials were readily available anywhere, since plywood, aluminum, or steel could be used. No welding was involved in the construction.

Because the aircraft measured only 5 × 6 × 11 feet and could be taken apart with a pair of wrenches, it could be transported inside a car and stored in a garage, basement, or attic.

On July 22, 1965, the first Gyro-Glider made was donated to the Smithsonian Institution. This colorful little aircraft was yellow with blue trim and a red seat. One rotor tip was painted red and one blue. "Bensen Gyro-Glider" was printed on both vertical stabilizers.

The Bensen Gyro-Glider is being towed into the air. (Photo: SI 74-2692)

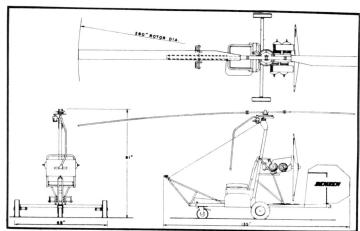

Igor Bensen presents his Gyro-Copter to Louis S. Casey and Paul E. Garber of the Smithsonian Institution on May 14, 1969. (Photo: SI 74-2693)

The Gyro-Copter duplicates the route of the Wright brothers' historic first flight and is seen flying over the monument at Kitty Hawk, North Carolina. (Photo: SI 74-2691)

The Gyro-Copter, first flown on December 6, 1955, was a powered version of the Gyro-Glider. It, too, was designed to be constructed from a set of plans, costing about $30, or from a prefabricated kit, costing $995. Engines were available ranging in price from $495 to $1,195. As few as forty man-hours were required for kit assembly.

The airframe was a square tubular aluminum structure with a single, two-blade rotor of laminated plywood. The controls consisted of a single stick with a twist-grip throttle and foot pedals for the rudder, steering bar, and brakes. As with the Gyro-Glider, spinning and stalling could not occur, for autorotation would allow the aircraft to settle gently into a normal landing with no power.

Also like the Gyro-Glider, the Gyro-Copter could be stored in any garage, since it required a space only 5½ × 6 × 20 feet. For added convenience, the Gyro-Copter Model B-8M, put into production in 1957, was roadable. No equipment had to be changed or removed for the conversion from aircraft to automobile: the blades were simply locked in the fore-and-aft position. On the road it could reach speeds up to 35 mph. Several were successfully driven on highways and through heavy city traffic during public demonstrations.

Besides their use as a pleasure craft, Gyro-Copters could be used for terrain and pipeline aerial surveillance and sport and forestry patrol. In England one was modified for crop spraying. All three branches of the military had several in their inventories, and they carried Air Force designation X-25.

The best known of the Gyro-Copters was the Spirit of Kitty Hawk, so named because on the sixtieth anniversary of the Wright brothers' historic flight, this aircraft became the first to duplicate exactly the first powered flight. It took off from the same spot, flew at the same speed, and covered the same distance as the Wright aircraft.

Not only did the Spirit of Kitty Hawk make that interesting flight, but in May 1967 and June 1968 it set twelve world and national autogiro speed, distance, and altitude records. Among these were speed over a 100-kilometer closed course (82.5 km/hr.), cross-country distance over a straight line (84 miles in 1 hour, 25 minutes), and maximum altitude (7,200 feet). The aircraft held more records than any other nonmilitary rotary aircraft in the world.

On May 14, 1969, at a ceremony before the American Helicopter Society, the Spirit of Kitty Hawk was presented to the Smithsonian for the National Aeronautical Collection.
Claudia M. Oakes

Blériot Type XI

Wingspan:	8.52 m (28.5 ft.)
Length:	7.63 m (25.5 ft.)
Weight:	Gross, 450 kg (990 lb.)
	Empty, 326 kg (720 lb.)
Engine:	Gnome, 50 hp

The Blériot Type XI was the most famous and successful of several classic airplanes that emerged during the miraculous summer of 1909, when all of Europe seemed to be taking to the sky.

Louis Blériot, a French engineer and manufacturer of automobile head lamps, had first become interested in aeronautics in 1901–2, when he constructed an experimental ornithopter. During the next eight years he moved through a series of ten distinct aircraft designs, only one of which was capable of making a flight of more than ten minutes.

His next effort, the Type XI, primarily designed by engineer Raymond Saulnier, was first flown at Issy-les-Moulineaux on January 23, 1909. Blériot achieved immortality in this craft on July 25, 1909, when he made the first airplane crossing of the English Channel, covering the 40 kilometers between Calais and Dover in 36 minutes, 30 seconds.

In the wake of the Channel flight, Blériot received the first of many orders for the Type XI monoplane. Variants of the original 1909 machine, produced by the Blériot firm, foreign licensees, and enthusiastic amateur builders in Europe and America, were a dominant force in aeronautics before World War I.

The National Air and Space Museum's specimen was manufactured by Blériot Aéronautique at Levallois, Perret, France, in 1914. Powered by a 50-hp Gnome rotary engine, it is a standard Type XI of the immediate prewar period, featuring wing-warping for lateral control and the castering undercarriage that eased the problem of crosswind landings.

The craft was purchased by the Swiss aviator John Domenjoz, a Blériot company flight instructor, on July 31, 1914. Domenjoz, who planned an extensive exhibition tour, ordered the machine specially strengthened and added a heavy harness to support the pilot during inverted flight.

With the outbreak of war in Europe, Domenjoz took his new machine to South America, where he developed a reputation for daring aerobatics. Flying at Buenos Aires in April 1915, he performed 40 consecutive loops in 28 minutes, a feat that earned him the soubriquet "upside-down Domenjoz."

He arrived in New York the following September and almost immediately made headlines with a series of loops over the Statue of Liberty.

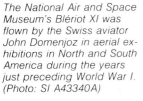

The National Air and Space Museum's Blériot XI was flown by the Swiss aviator John Domenjoz in aerial exhibitions in North and South America during the years just preceding World War I. (Photo: SI A43340A)

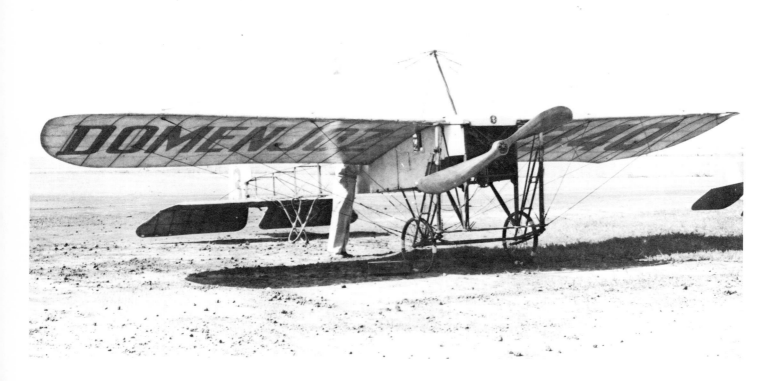

Domenjoz and his Blériot continued their tour
through the South and Midwest in 1915 and 1916.
 During World War I Domenjoz served as a test
pilot and flight instructor in France and the United
States. When he returned to France in 1920, the
Blériot was stored in a Long Island barn, where it
was eventually discovered and refurbished for
display in a Long Island Museum. The Smithsonian
obtained the machine in 1950. It was restored
once again by the National Air and Space Museum
in 1979 for exhibit in the Early Flight gallery.
Tom D. Crouch

John Domenjoz earned the
name "upside-down Do-
menjoz" after performing
forty consecutive loops in
28 minutes.
(Photo: SI 78-14970)

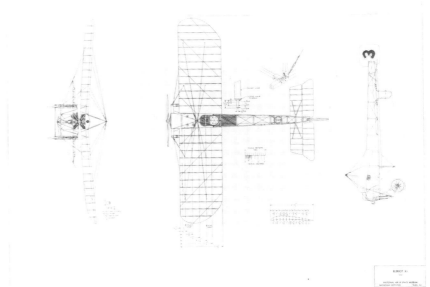

Boeing 247D

Wingspan:	22.55 m (74 ft.)
Length:	15.72 m (51 ft. 7 in.)
Height:	3.70 m (12 ft. 1¾ in.)
Weight:	Gross, 7,623 kg (16,805 lb.)
Engines:	Pratt and Whitney S1H1-G, 550 hp.

The National Air and Space Museum's Boeing 247D is important both as an aircraft type and as a famous plane in its own right. It was flown in the 1934 MacRobertson England-Australia Race by famed racing pilot Roscoe Turner and Clyde Pangborn, finishing in third place; it then went on to three other productive careers before being given to the museum.

The first Boeing 247 made its initial flight on February 8, 1933, and the plane's performance confirmed the wisdom of what had been to that date a daring gamble on the part of Boeing's management. Three key men—President Phillip G. Johnson, Vice President Claire Egtvedt, and Chief Engineer C. N. Monteith—chose to develop the transport potential of their successful Boeing B-9 twin-engine bomber rather than stick to the orthodox trimotor and biplane design of the day.

The group of United Airlines predecessors (Boeing Air Transport, Pacific Air Transport, National Air Transport, and Varney Air Lines) determined to replace its entire fleet by ordering sixty of the 247s, thereby gaining a tremendous advantage over competitors, for the new airplane had made all other transports obsolete overnight.

The all-metal, low-wing 247 combined a retractable landing gear, two supercharged air-cooled engines, and, in later models, controllable pitch propellers, with totally new standards in passenger comfort. The ten passengers and three crew members enjoyed excellent soundproofing, a low vibration level, plush seats, and, for the first time, cabin air conditioning.

On May 22, 1933, the new 247 entered cross-country service, making the journey from San Francisco to New York in 19½ hours, compared to the previous 27-hour air travel time.

Curiously, the inability of other airlines to obtain the 247 worked to Boeing and United's net disadvantage, for Trans World Airlines went to Douglas for a competitive aircraft, and the result was the famous DC series, which made the 247, in turn, obsolete.

The original 247 had a top speed of 182 mph and cruised at 170 mph compared to the 115 mph of the Ford Tri-motor then in general use. Boeing attempted to match the Douglas aircraft by creating the 247D, an improved version with a 200-mph top speed and 189-mph cruise. Earlier 247s were modified to 247D standards, but the airplane

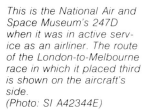

This is the National Air and Space Museum's 247D when it was in active service as an airliner. The route of the London-to-Melbourne race in which it placed third is shown on the aircraft's side.
(Photo: SI A42344E)

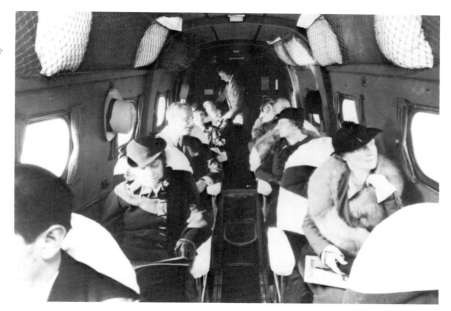

Ten passengers could be carried in comfort in the 247. Note the obstacle—the main wing spar—in the middle of the aisle. The inconvenience it caused was accepted as part of the price of the great structural strength of the plane.
(Photo: SI 75-12099)

did not have the necessary growth potential to compete and was soon relegated to shorter route segments and smaller airlines.

The museum's aircraft made its first flight on September 5, 1934. It was leased from United by Turner and modified with extra fuel tanks to provide a range of more than 2,500 miles for the 1934 MacRobertson Race. Turner, Pangborn, and Reeder Nichols took off from Mildenhall, England on October 20, 1934, and landed 92 hours, 55 minutes, and 30 seconds later at Melbourne, Australia, finishing in third place. The race was won by an English de Havilland DH 88 Comet; second place went to a KLM-operated Douglas DC-2.

The 247 had an actual flying time of a little over eighty-five hours for the 11,300-mile distance and might have finished second were it not for some engine problems and a three-hour navigational error.

The airplane was returned to United where it served in regular airline service until 1937, when it was sold to the Union Electric Company of St. Louis for use as an executive transport. In 1939 it was purchased by the Department of Commerce Air Safety Board (CAS), which used it for fourteen years before presenting it to the museum in 1953. The aircraft served so well in so many experiments with the CAS that it received the affectionate nickname "Adaptable Annie."

To highlight the most interesting aspects of the 247's career, the airplane is displayed with two sets of markings. The left side is marked as it was when flown by Colonel Turner in 1934, carrying the NR-257Y registration; the right side is marked as the aircraft was flown by United, with the NC 13369 registration.

The original gray anodized aluminum finish of the 247 was badly weatherworn, and it was necessary to repaint it in a color as near to the original as possible. Fortunately, the two engine cowlings and the vertical tail surface were in relatively good condition, and they were left in their original unpainted anodized finish.

In 1974 United Air Lines made a grant that permitted the National Air and Space Museum to have the aircraft restored to its present status by CNC Industries, Camp Springs, Maryland.
Walter J. Boyne

Clyde Pangborn and Col. Roscoe Turner are shown at Heston Airport, England, prior to the historic London-to-Melbourne race.
(Photo: SI 72-8422)

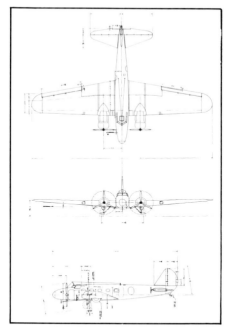

Boeing F4B-4

Wingspan:	9.15 m (30 ft.)
Length:	6.10 m (20 ft. 1 in.)
Height:	2.84 m (9 ft. 4 in.)
Weight:	Gross, 1,639 kg (3,611 lb.)
	Empty, 1,069 kg (2,354 lb.)
Engine:	Pratt and Whitney R-1340-16, 550 hp

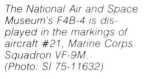

The National Air and Space Museum's F4B-4 is displayed in the markings of aircraft #21, Marine Corps Squadron VF-9M. (Photo: SI 75-11632)

Developed as a private venture, the Boeing F4B/P-12 series served as the primary fighter of the U.S. Navy and U.S. Army Air Corps in the early years of the Great Depression. The F4B/P-12 continued to serve the nation in numerous roles until the early 1940s. It was Boeing's and the Army's last biplane and wooden-wing fighter design. The large quantity produced was a significant factor in establishing Boeing as an important aircraft manufacturer and in maintaining the firm through the economic hardships of the thirties.

First flown on June 25, 1928, Models 83 and 89 were designated XF4B-1 and delivered to the Navy for evaluation. Convinced of the merits of the craft after extensive trials, the Navy purchased twenty-seven production examples, the first being delivered in the summer of 1929 to the Red Rippers of VB-1B on the U.S.S. *Lexington*. The new fighter was capable of reaching speeds of more than 176 mph, and could carry five 24-pound bombs under each wing, with either one 500-

pound bomb or one 41 IMP-gallon fuel tank beneath the fuselage. As a fighter, the F4B-1 mounted two .30-caliber machine guns synchronized to fire through the propeller arc.

Following the success of the first series, the Navy contracted for forty-six improved versions in June 1930 with deliveries beginning in January of the next year. The F4B-2 differed in having a redesigned ring cowling, improved split-axle undercarriage, and Friese ailerons. Maximum speed was increased to 186 mph, and the plane could carry four 116-pound bombs.

Encouraged by the Navy's results with the XF4B-1, the Army placed an order for ten similar machines with the carrier-hook deleted. The first P-12 was flown to Central America on a goodwill mission by then Capt. Ira C. Eaker in February 1929. The next model, the P-12B, was an upgraded version with Friese ailerons and a shorter undercarriage, of which ninety were produced. In June 1930 the Army Air Corps

When F4B-4 BuAer #9241 came out of the factory in 1933, it was assigned as aircraft #2, Marine Corps Squadron VF-10M, North Island, San Diego. (Photo: SI A48452)

The Boeing P-12 series was the Army's adaptation of the Navy's F4B carrier fighter.

The aircraft was received by the Smithsonian in these U.S. Navy markings of VF-1 (Navy fighting squadron) "Top Hat," even though the aircraft never served with that squadron. (Photo: SI A47357)

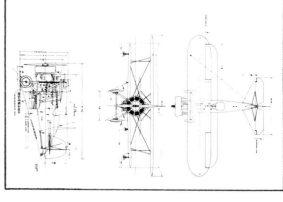

contracted for 131 P-12C models, which incorporated the P-12B airframe with a ring cowl and a cross-axle undercarriage. Although the last thirty-five of the order were labeled D models, they were identical to the P-12C. The naval equivalent was the F4B-2.

While production of the F4B-2 was in progress, Boeing began development of a new version. Instead of the bolted alloy tube fuselage of the earlier plane, the F4B-3 had an all-metal semimonocoque fuselage. The two-spar, fabric-covered wings with corrugated metal control surfaces were retained. The engine was the Pratt and Whitney R-1340-10, which was fitted with a drag ring. The Navy contracted for seventy-five examples of the F4B-3; the first plane was delivered on Christmas Eve, 1931. Built for the Army as the P-12E, the new version represented Boeing's largest Army contract since the MB-3A of 1921. Of the 135 ordered, 110 were delivered as P-12Es. The remaining twenty-five were delivered as P-12Fs, employing SR-1340G powerplants for increased high-altitude performance.

The fourth and final version of the F4B series was the F4B-4. Essentially an F4B-3 with a broader chord fin and a larger headrest for an inflatable life raft, the F4B-4 was first ordered in April 1931, and the last of the ninety-two aircraft were delivered on February 28, 1933. Twenty-one of these planes were assigned to the Marine Corps. The F4B-4 maintained the good flight characteristics of the earlier versions despite greater weight and increased power. Only when overloaded and at maximum speed did the F4B-4 exhibit any instability.

Total production of the F4B/P-12 reached 586; almost 350 were ordered by the Army. Two were sent to Thailand where one remains today on display in the Royal Thai Air Force Museum, and twenty-five were built for Brazil. Of these, only one ever saw combat. Model 281, from which the F4B-3 and P-12E developed, was sold to China where it was downed by the Japanese after accounting for two of its three attackers.

The machine that is on display in the National Air and Space Museum is one of the twenty-one F4B-4s built for the Marine Corps, the only difference being the absence of an arrester hook. Number 9241 was shipped from the Boeing factory in Seattle on December 20, 1932, arriving nine days later at the North Island Air Station in San Diego, California. This F4B-4 was assigned as the number two aircraft in Marine Fighting Squadron 10 and served there until July 1933. All of the F4B-4s of the squadron were transferred to VF-9M at Quantico, Virginia, where number 9241 flew until replaced by more modern Grumman F3F-2s. After this, the aircraft served as a trainer until purchased by the Bureau of Air Commerce and stricken from the Navy records on July 31, 1939. It was soon purchased by Bellanca Aircraft Corporation and later resold to private owners. Number 9241 was donated by its last owner, Ray Hyland of Rochester, New York, to the National Air and Space Museum in 1959. It is now on display in its former colors as plane number 21 of Marine Fighting Squadron VF-9M.

F. Robert van der Linden

Boeing P-26A

Wingspan: 8.52 m (27 ft. 11½ in.
Length: 7.26 m (23 ft. 10 in.)
Height: 3.18 m (10 ft. 5 in.)
Weight: Gross, 1,340 kg (2,955 lb.)
Empty, 996 kg (2,196 lb.)
Engine: Pratt and Whitney R-1340-25, 500 hp

The National Air and Space Museum's P-26A was received in these markings of the Guatemalan Air Force. It is exhibited in the colors of the U.S. Army Air Force's 34th Attack Squadron. (Photo: SI 75-11631)

Known affectionately as the "Pea-Shooter," Boeing's P-26 fighter has the distinction of being a turning point in military aircraft design, from the World War I type biplanes to the present-day monoplanes. The P-26 introduced the concept of the high performance, all-metal monoplane fighter. While representing a radical departure from previous design, the P-26 retained numerous features of its predecessors; it was the last open-cockpit fighter accepted by the U.S. Army Air Corps and the last with a fixed landing gear and external wing bracing. As Boeing's last production fighter, the P-26 served as America's first line of air defense in the mid- and late-1930s, until the advent of the more advanced Seversky P-35 and Curtiss P-36A aircraft.

Design of the P-26 was started in September 1931 as a joint Boeing/Army project. The new plane incorporated features proposed by both parties. Boeing was to construct the airframe with the Army providing the engines, instruments, and other necessary equipment. With almost the entire facilities of Boeing concentrated to insure success of the project, construction began on the first prototype in January 1932, and the first flight took place on March 20.

The continued success of the prototypes prompted the Army to contract for 111 improved production examples in January 1933 under the designation P-26A. The initial contract was increased by twenty-five new planes, which were B and C models. This brought total production for the Army to 136.

The structure of the P-26 was based to a great extent on experience gained in creating the Monomail and other Boeing all-metal designs. However, unlike the Monomail, the Pea-Shooter did not have cantilevered wings or retractable undercarriage. Boeing engineers opted for the lighter structure that external bracing allowed.

The P-26 prototype first flew March 20, 1932. (Photo: SI 75-11629)

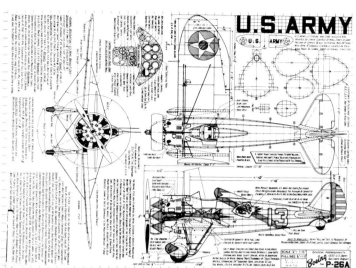

The P-26 was the first all-metal American fighter, the first production monoplane fighter, and the last U.S. Army fighter to feature an open cockpit, fixed undercarriage, and externally braced wings. (Photo: Courtesy Don C. Wigton)

While the streamlined fixed gear produced considerable drag, it greatly reduced weight and structural complexity.

The metal craft was of semimonocoque construction with aluminum bulkheads, bracers, longerons, and skin. The low wings were built of duraluminum with two main spars, supporting ribs, and skin, which were braced with external steel wires. The fully cantilevered tail surfaces were of single spar, dural skin construction.

Power was provided by a 600-hp, nine-cylinder Pratt and Whitney R-1340-27 Wasp aircooled radial, enclosed in a National Advisory Committee for Aeronautics cowling ring.

Maximum level speed was 234 mph at 7,500 feet, with a service ceiling of 27,400 feet. Armament consisted of either two .30-caliber machine guns or one .30-caliber and one .50-caliber weapon synchronized to fire through the propeller arc. Two 100-pound or five 30-pound bombs could be carried.

Originally, P-26As were built with streamlined headrests. Following the death of an Army pilot when his plane flipped over on landing, all P-26s were modified with a larger and strengthened headrest for increased protection.

After P-26 production had been completed, the Army sought to reduce the inordinately high landing speed by installing experimental flaps on one machine. The modification reduced the speed from 82.5 to 73 mph. Boeing retrofitted the flaps to all A models and equipped the B and C models under construction.

P-26Bs and Cs were identical to the P-26A with the exception of the installation of fuel injection R-1340-33 Wasp and modifications to the fuel system.

When the P-26 was removed from regular service, those aircraft stationed overseas were sold to the Philippines and Panama. Eleven P-26A versions were sold to China and one to Spain. Those serving with the air forces of China and the Philippines fought gallantly against the invading Japanese, scoring numerous successes before their destruction by the more numerous and modern adversaries.

The P-26A of the National Air and Space Museum was one of the aircraft originally based overseas and later sold to Panama in 1937. It was resold to Guatemala, where it flew in the Guatemalan Air Force from 1943 to August 2, 1954. In 1958 the government of Guatemala donated the P-26A to the Smithsonian Institution, where it is now on display. The aircraft was restored by the U.S. Air Force and is painted in the colors of the 34th Attack Squadron that was stationed at March Field, California.

F. Robert van der Linden

Bücker Bü-133 Jungmeister

Wingspan:	6.60 m (21 ft. 7½ in.)
Length:	5.90 m (19 ft. 4 in.)
Height:	2.25 m (7 ft, 4½ in.)
Weight:	Gross, 585 kg (1,290 lb.)
	Empty, 420 kg (925 lb.)
Engine:	Warner, 185 hp

An airplane that dominated the aerobatic scene for many years, the Bücker Bü-133 Jungmeister was a mass production aircraft built in Germany before World War II and in Spain during the war. Because of its agility and lightness on the controls, it was selected by a number of European flying clubs and air services as an advance trainer for aerobatics.

Among the great aerobatic pilots who chose Jungmeisters were Rumania's Alex Papana, Germany's Count Hagenburg, and in the United States, Beverly "Bevo" Howard and Mike Murphy.

One Jungmeister enjoys a rather interesting history. Having been acquired by Papana, the aircraft was airfreighted to the United States aboard the airship *Hindenburg*. During the Cleveland Air Races of 1937, the plane was flown in competition by both Papana, the owner, and Count Hagenburg after the latter's Jungmeister crashed while flying inverted a few inches above the ground. These two pilots had been engaging in a contest to prove their superiority in flying skill and daring. Papana had made a low level inverted pass in front of the grandstands. Hagenburg, not wishing to be outdone, repeated the maneuver at knee height but as he pushed forward to climb out, the vertical fin hit the ground, slowing him sufficiently to cause the plane to crash. Fortunately, Hagenburg was not injured seriously, and a few minutes later was back in the air completing his performance in Papana's plane.

A familiar sight at many an air show—"Bevo" Howard cutting a tape in his Jungmeister.
(Photo: International Aerobatic Club Collection; SI 73-5734)

The Jungmeister as it was marked when owned by Alex Papana. (Photo: Courtesy Stephen J. Hudek)

(Diagram by Björn Karlström, courtesy Model Airplane News)

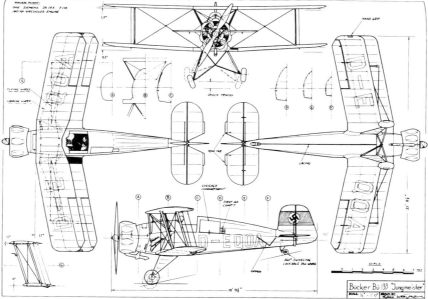

Bücker Bü 133 "Jungmeister"

This plane was acquired by Murphy, who flew it two of the three times he won the U.S. Aerobatic Championship—in 1938 and 1940–41. The plane was sold to Bevo Howard, also a former U.S. Aerobatic Champion, who flew it regularly in demonstrations around the United States, especially at graduation ceremonies for aviation cadets at Hawthorne Aviation Company Schools of Charleston, South Carolina, of which he was president. Howard took great pleasure in flying numerous weekend programs for his own enjoyment and for worthy causes. Unfortunately, while flying one of these shows he had a fatal accident, and the airplane was almost demolished. In recognition of his contribution to U.S. aviation, particularly in keeping alive aerobatic flying, the airplane has been rebuilt by his estate and friends, some of whom worked with him and maintained the Jungmeister during its flying career. It was given to the National Air and Space Museum under the terms of Howard's will.

A number of these aircraft still exist, both here and in Europe, and command high prices because of their scarcity and demonstrated maneuverability. After the war a limited number of the planes were produced near Munich; however, high labor costs made them almost prohibitively expensive. This situation and the growing enthusiasm for aerobatic flying led to the development of such planes as the Pitts Special, the Zlin 526A Trener Master, and the YAK 18 PS.

Some pilots of the prewar era contend that the only aircraft that matched the Jungmeister were the specially built Great Lakes trainers; others even question this comparison.

While the Jungmeister was designed to use either the Hirth HM 506, 160-hp inline air-cooled engine or the seven-cylinder radial air-cooled Siemens Sh-14A of 160 hp, the latter engine was used almost exclusively.

The Jungmeister's diminutive size, plus a high power-to-weight ratio, with ailerons on both upper and lower wings, insured its future as an aerobatic aircraft. It ranks high on the list of all-time greats in the world of aerobatics.

Louis S. Casey

Cessna 180
"Spirit of Columbus"

Wingspan:	10.97 m (36 ft.)
Length:	7.98 m (26 ft. 2 in.)
Height:	2.36 m (7 ft. 9 in.)
Weight:	Gross, 1,157 kg (2,550 lb.)
Engine:	Continental O-470-A, 225 hp

A National Aeronautic Association press release dated April 18, 1964, announced that Mrs. Geraldine Mock had become the first woman to pilot an aircraft around the world. Previous attempts by women, including the much-discussed flight by Amelia Earhart, were unsuccessful.

When success did come, it was accomplished by this tiny housewife from Columbus, Ohio, flying a 1953 Cessna 180 single-engine monoplane, the *Spirit of Columbus*. In 1953, the first year of production, 640 Model 180s were produced. The *Spirit of Columbus* was the 238th, bearing serial number 30238 and registration number N-1538C. After several owners and 990 flying hours, the plane was purchased by Mrs. Mock for her world flight attempt. Additional fuel tanks were custom-made to fit inside the cabin; personal equipment and survival gear were assembled and stowed aboard, and detailed flight planning was completed.

On March 19, 1964, at 9:31 a.m., Mrs. Mock

In the Cessna 180 Spirit of Columbus, Mrs. Geraldine Mock became the first woman to pilot an aircraft around the world. (Photo: SI 75-13710)

departed from Columbus on her history-making solo flight. Twenty-nine days, 11 hours, and 59 minutes later, she arrived back home, on April 17, 1964, after flying 23,103 miles around the world. The flight was monitored by the National Aeronautic Association and its Fédération Aéronautique Internationale-affiliated organizations around the world. The FAI certified Mrs. Mock's flight as a speed record around the world for aircraft weighing less than 3,858 pounds. On May 4, 1964, she was awarded the Federal Aviation Administration's Exceptional Service Decoration by President Lyndon B. Johnson.

The Model 180 was developed as one of a family of aircraft designs. Borrowing some features from the Army's L-19 Bird Dog liaison plane, the 180 is a rugged four-place plane. Variations on the basic airframe have made it a popular "bush" type aircraft, in use in most of the undeveloped parts of the world as well as in the United States. The 180 was successfully modified with the addition of a

The Spirit of Columbus *was fitted with additional fuel tanks and equipment for Mrs. Mock's flight. (Photo: SI 75-13711)*

tricycle landing gear to become the Model 182, which has enjoyed a long production run as a high performance workhorse in the general aviation category.

After completing her flight, Mrs. Mock never flew the *Spirit of Columbus* again. The manufacturer exchanged aircraft with her, giving her a later model plane. For a number of years the record-setting aircraft was suspended in the Cessna factory in Wichita, Kansas, until it was cleaned up for its trip to the National Air and Space Museum in 1975.

Louis S. Casey

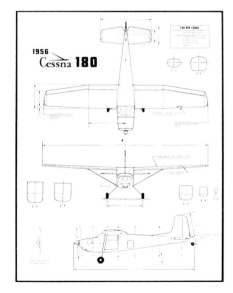

The Cessna 185 is identical to the 180, except that it has a 285-hp engine. (Photo: SI 75-13712)

Curtiss D

Wingspan:	26 ft. 3 in.
Length:	25 ft. 6 in.
Engine:	Curtiss 4-cyl. 40 hp for training; Curtiss 8-cyl. 60-75-80 hp for exhibition

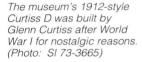

The museum's 1912-style Curtiss D was built by Glenn Curtiss after World War I for nostalgic reasons. (Photo: SI 73-3665)

The Curtiss D-III Headless biplane was the standard airplane used by the early Curtiss Exhibition Team and many embryo pilots. Powered by the 60-75-80-hp V-8 Curtiss engines, these aircraft gave excellent performance for their day, especially in the hands of such skilled pilots as Lincoln Beachey. His machine was specially constructed, incorporating double cable for all landing and flying wires. This special addition made it reasonably safe for Beachey to perform the "loops" and "death dives" for which he was famous. His continuous flirtation with disaster made him popular, and his services were in great demand at air shows of 1910-12. Others trying to imitate him contributed to the high rate of fatal crashes during this early period of aviation.

The Curtiss D and E aircraft were specially suited to exhibition flying, not only because of their maneuverability but also because they were easily disassembled and assembled for shipment between exhibition dates. This feature also made it easy to replace wing panels or other components broken during performances or bad landings. Another feature, incorporated for safety purposes, was the bamboo structure that linked the tail surfaces to the wings. Unlike other woods, bamboo has a hollow tubular cross section with nodules at frequent (8–12 in.) intervals. Both of these features contributed to the aircraft's high strength in relation to weight. Furthermore, bamboo will not splinter when cracked, with the high probability of impaling the pilot. Bamboo, especially if taped at intervals— as it was—will bend and crack but remain intact.

The D and E were closely related in design—the

major difference being the slightly greater wing area of the E. Engines were interchangeable.

A number of famous exhibition pilots used D and E model aircraft, among them Eugene Ely, John McCurdy, and Glenn H. Curtiss himself. The Curtiss Exhibition Company, managed by Jerome Fanciulli, ranged far and wide across the length and breadth of North America and, on occasion, Europe and other continents including Asia. Such activity was bound to attract many students and potential purchases of Curtiss planes. Among the former were U.S. Army and Navy student-pilots, and others from India and Japan. The first aircraft purchased by the Navy was a Curtiss E Hydro, which differed from the landplane mainly in having a central float and outrigger floats instead of wheeled undercarriage.

Louis S. Casey

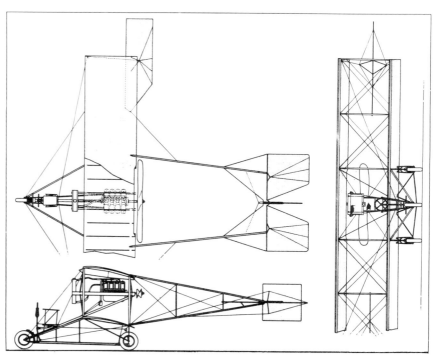

Curtiss F9C-2 Sparrowhawk

Wingspan: 7.75 m (25 ft. 5 in.)
Length: 6.28 m (20 ft. 7 in.)
Weight: Gross, 1,246 kg (2,770 lb.)
Empty, 948 kg (2,089 lb.)
Engine: Wright R-975-E3, 438 hp

*The museum's Sparrowhawk is pictured during its operational days with the airships. Lt. Harold B. Miller skillfully guides the fighter onto the U.S.S. Macon's trapeze somewhere off the Pacific coast on November 9, 1933. Hook-on speed was about sixty-five knots, ten knots above the fighter's stalling speed.
(Photo: National Archives 80-G-424788)*

The tiny Sparrowhawks that operated from the dirigible aircraft carriers during the 1930s will always occupy a special place in the annals of aviation. These colorful Navy fighters, petite and pleasing in design, with interesting gadgetry, captured the imagination of all who were exposed to them. Some regarded their aerial trapeze hook-on operations as stunts, but these parasite aircraft, assigned to protect and scout for the Navy's giant helium-filled airships, had potential and real value during that great period of aerial experimentation.

In the years between the world wars, American military policy was purely defensive. Two new airships, U.S.S. *Akron* and *Macon*, were to be airborne coastal defense scouts, keeping watch over the approaches to the United States. These airships had greater visual search capability than the surface fleet. Aircraft carried aboard could be used for attack, for defense of the airship itself, and to greatly increase the search range.

The Curtiss F9C-2 Sparrowhawks were assigned to the lighter-than-air (LTA) unit of the Navy. Originally designed for surface carrier operations, the Sparrowhawks failed at first to win Navy acceptance. When the need for an airshipbased fighter became apparent, however, the small size and light weight of this airplane made it a natural.

Eight Sparrowhawks were produced for this mission at the Buffalo plant of the Curtiss Aeroplane Company. The first production model of the F9C-2 arrived at Lakehurst, New Jersey, Naval Air Station in June 1932. This was the home base for the airship *Akron* for its sea patrol duties off the East Coast. Air tactics were developed during these patrol missions. The fighters would simulate attacks against the airships, while gunners on board would fire back with gun cameras. As airborne scouts, two Sparrowhawks would fly abreast of the dirigible, reporting various sightings by radio.

When the scouting mission was concluded, the huge airship would accelerate to full speed, which

The dirigible U.S.S. Macon *was photographed on July 7, 1933, just two weeks after her commissioning. A Sparrowhawk prepares to begin hook-on maneuvers over New Jersey, before the big craft took up its assigned station at Sunnyvale, California.*
(Photo: National Archives 80-G-428444)

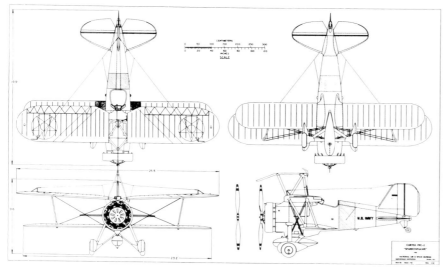

Rolled outdoors for the first time after restoration on August 13, 1974, forty-two years after its initial debut, the Sparrowhawk appears ready for flight. The colorful "Men on the Flying Trapeze" insignia was the official heavier-than-air unit emblem, assigned to the lighter-than-air branch of the Navy.
(Photo: SI 74-8399)

was slightly above the Sparrowhawks' stalling speed. This would provide a sufficient margin of maneuvering speed for the Sparrowhawks as they approached for the recovery operation. The pilot would skillfully guide the overhead hook on his fighter to the horizontal bar of the extended recovery trapeze. Once hooked on, the engine of the fighter would be stopped and the trapeze with fighter attached would be raised into the open belly of the dirigible and stored in special racks. As many as four could be recovered in successive hook-ons. The fighters were launched in the reverse of this procedure.

There is much to be told of these few short years of LTA operations, as it was a time of experimentation and development of aerial surveillance. All ended too quickly, however, when first the *Akron* on the East Coast and then the *Macon* on the West were lost at sea. Prior to these tragedies, there had not been a single operational loss of a Sparrowhawk. Now, with only three remaining, and no dirigible from which to operate, the aircraft were relegated to utility flying. In this capacity, they were not well liked by the pilots who flew them.

By 1939 the last and aging Sparrowhawk was retired and transferred by the Navy to the Smithsonian Institution. In its final years the aircraft had been rebuilt from the best parts of the surviving F9C-2s and carried the bureau number 9056. For exhibit purposes, it was marked with the unit colors of the U.S.S. *Akron* and attracted the interest of many museum visitors.

Recognizing the significance of this little fighter in later years, the Potomac Chapter of the Antique Airplane Association, under the supervision of National Air and Space Museum personnel, undertook the restoration of the airplane as a group project. In 1974 the fighter emerged like new in the elaborate colors of the U.S.S. *Macon* unit to which 9056 had been assigned.

The insignia of the "Men on the Flying Trapeze" on the side of its fuselage symbolizes those exciting days of the great airships and the spectacular launch and recovery method that was used. The dirigibles are gone, and this one Sparrowhawk is the best remaining evidence of their existence.

Robert C. Mikesh

Curtiss P-40E Warhawk

Wingspan:	11.37 m (37 ft. 4 in.)
Length:	9.49 m (31 ft. 2 in.)
Height:	3.23 m (10 ft. 7 in.)
Weight:	Gross, 3,756 kg (8,280 lb.)
	Empty, 2,880 kg (6,350 lb.)
Engine:	Allison V-1710-39, 1,150 hp

The Curtiss P-40 is one of the best known U.S. fighters of World War II. P-40s were first-line fighters at the start of the war, and scored victories over Japanese aircraft both at Pearl Harbor and in the Philippines. However, the Warhawk's greatest fame was achieved by the shark-mouth P-40s of the Flying Tigers.

The P-40 design originated with the installation of an Allison V-1710-19 inline engine in a P-36A in place of the Pratt and Whitney R-1830 radial engine. The P-40 was first flown in October 1938. Its design was evaluated at Wright Field in 1939 along with those of several other proposed fighters, or pursuit planes, as they were called then. The P-40 won this competition, and a large order for them was placed with the Curtiss-Wright Corporation. The armament included two .50-caliber machine guns in the fuselage and four .30-caliber machine guns in the wings.

P-40s were improved with each successive model by the addition of armor plate, better self-

sealing tanks, more powerful engines, and a change in armament to six wing-mounted, .50-caliber machine guns. The P-40E was the first model with this armament.

Since the Warhawk's high-altitude performance was poor with the unsupercharged Allison engine, a Packard-built Rolls Royce V-1650-1 Merlin with a supercharger was used in the P-40F. The P-40K, which was in production along with the P-40F, used the more powerful Allison V-1710-73 engine.

The last model of the P-40 to be produced in quantity was the P-40N. Its weight was reduced by the use of a light-weight structure and wheels, removal of two guns, and removal of the front wing tank. The two machine guns were restored in later versions of the P-40N.

In addition to the U.S. Army Air Forces, P-40s were used by many of the Allied powers, including France, China, Russia, Turkey, Australia, Canada, New Zealand, South Africa, and Great Britain. The early P-40s were called Tomahawks, and the later

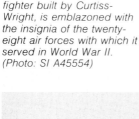

This P-40N, the 15,000th fighter built by Curtiss-Wright, is emblazoned with the insignia of the twenty-eight air forces with which it served in World War II. (Photo: SI A45554)

models Kittyhawks, by the British. They were used in Africa, the Middle East, and the Far East by British forces. Royal Air Force and Royal Australian Air Force squadrons in Africa were the first to paint shark mouths on their P-40s.

The USAAF used P-40s in North Africa, Iceland, Alaska, the Pacific, and the China-Burma-India area. It was in China and Burma that the P-40s achieved fame. The American Volunteer Group (AVG), the Flying Tigers, flew their P-40s, with the shark mouths painted on the engine cowling, against the Japanese with devastating effect. Led by Gen. Claire Chennault, in just over six months they destroyed 286 Japanese aircraft while losing only eleven planes in air-to-air combat. When the AVG was disbanded on July 4, 1942, the AAF 23d Fighter Group replaced them. The 23d, known as the Flying Tiger Fighter Group, was part of the 14th Air Force, commanded by General Chennault. It became one of the highest-scoring fighter groups in the AAF and played a significant role in enabling the 14th Air Force to maintain air superiority over the Japanese in China for the remainder of the war.

Although its performance did not match that of its contemporaries, the P-40 was a rugged, effective fighter that remained in production from 1939 to the end of 1944. Almost 14,000 P-40s were produced during this period.

The National Air and Space Museum's P-40E is actually a Kittyhawk 1A built in Buffalo and delivered to Canada for service in the Royal Canadian Air Force. After the war it came to the United States in civil status. In 1964 it was donated to the National Aeronautical Collection by the Meridian, Mississippi, Exchange Club in memory of Kellis Forbes, a man devoted to the development of Boys Club activities in Meridian. The P-40 is painted to represent an aircraft of the 75th Fighter Squadron, 23d Fighter Group, 14th Air Force.

Donald S. Lopez

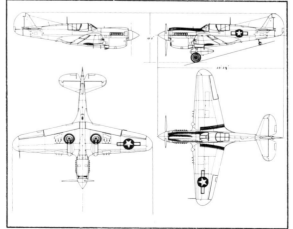

The P-40 was a deadly adversary even when parked, as evidenced by the P-51 wing tip in its "mouth." Actually, the P-51 hit the P-40 with its wing tip while taking off from the fighter strip at Kweilin, China. (Photo: SI 74-1155)

Curtiss R3C-2

Wingspan:	Upper, 6.71 m (22 ft.)
	Lower, 6.10 m (20 ft.)
Length:	6.01 m (19 ft. 8½ in.)
Height:	2.46 m (8 ft. 1 in.)
Weight:	Gross, 1,152 kg. (2,539 lb.) Empty, 975 kg. (2,150 lb.)
Engine:	(1925) Curtiss V-1400, 610 hp
	(1926) Curtiss V-1400, 665 hp

Piloted by Lt. James H. "Jimmy" Doolittle, the Curtiss R3C-2 captured the Schneider Cup for seaplanes in 1925, achieving 232 mph.
(Photo: SI A43532)

Early in the development of aviation a spirit of sporting and competition became a major aspect of its ever-growing appeal. Air races began to enjoy a worldwide popularity, and two of the most coveted prizes were the Pulitzer Trophy and the Schneider Cup.

In 1912 a wealthy French aviation enthusiast, Jacques Schneider, established a trophy to be awarded annually to the winner of a race to be flown over water in seaplanes. The Pulitzer Trophy Race, on the other hand, was sponsored by an American newspaperman, Ralph Pulitzer, to promote high speed in landplanes.

In 1925 the U.S. Army and Navy ordered from the Curtiss Aeroplane and Motor Company aircraft of basically the same design but with individual variations. These airplanes ran away with first place in both trophy races in that same year. One of them also established a straightaway speed record for seaplanes.

This airplane was the R3C-1/R3C-2 (the -1 is the landplane and the -2 the seaplane version).

The R3C-1, piloted by Lt. Cyrus Bettis, won the Pulitzer Trophy Race on October 12, 1925, at a speed of 248.9 mph. On October 25, fitted with streamlined single-step wooden floats and redesignated the R3C-2, it was piloted to victory by Army Lt. James H. "Jimmy" Doolittle in the Schneider Cup Race held at Bay Shore Park, Baltimore. The average speed was 232.57 mph. On the day after the Schneider Race, Doolittle flew the R3C-2 over a straight course at a world record speed of 245.7 mph.

In the Schneider Cup Race of November 13, 1926, this same airplane, piloted by Lt. Christian F. Schilt, USMC, and powered by an improved engine, won second place with an average speed of 231.4 mph.

The R3C-1 was similar in dimensions and plan to the R2C-1 of 1923 but had a more powerful Curtiss V-1400 610-hp engine (665 hp in the 1926 racer).

The R3C-1 was a single-seat, single-bay, wire-

Lt. Cyrus Bettis, winner of
the Pulitzer Trophy in 1925,
stands next to his R3C-1
(Photo: SI A53865)

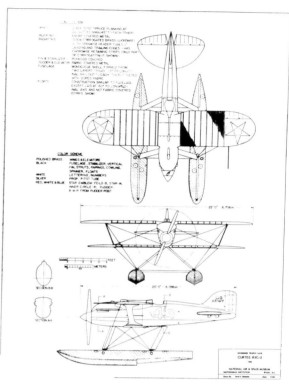

braced biplane. The wings were covered with two-ply spruce planking, 3/32-inch thick, forming a box structure that required no internal bracing. Among the interesting features were the low-drag wing radiators made of corrugated brass sheeting, .004-inch thick, covering much of the surface of both upper and lower wings with the corrugations running chordwise. The upper wing was flush with the top of the fuselage, permitting the pilot to see over the wing. All ribs were of spruce, conforming to the Curtiss C-80 airfoil section, and the ailerons, made of metal, were fabric-covered. The cantilever vertical fin and horizontal stabilizer were of wood.

An ingeniously fabricated streamlined monocoque structure, the fuselage consisted of a shell of two layers of spruce over which fabric was doped for added strength and protection. This shell was formed over seven birch plywood bulkheads that were connected by four ash longerons, making a rigid structure.

The unbalanced movable controls were metal. Only necessary navigation and engine instruments were installed. They consisted of gauges for water temperature, oil temperature, oil pressure, and fuel quantity, as well as a tachometer and an airspeed indicator.

The fixed landing gear in the R3C-1 was a tripod configuration. A laminated hickory tail skid was

added to protect the rudder.

As a landplane, the R3C-1 carried only 27 gallons of fuel, which gave 48 minutes flying time at full throttle. In the R3C-2, the fuel capacity was increased to 60 gallons, enough for 1.3 hours at full throttle, by installing fuel tanks in the floats.

The wings and elevators were painted gold; the fuselage, stabilizer, fin, struts, fairings, cowling, pontoons and/or wheels were all black.

Contemporary star cockades were painted on the right and left sides of the upper surface of the top wing and the lower surface of the bottom wing, outboard of the wing radiators. The rudder was painted with red, white, and blue vertical stripes, the blue stripe being next to the rudderpost. Both sides of the vertical fin were lettered "U.S. Army," in white. On both sides of the fuselage aft of the cockpit a large numeral 43 was painted in white. This was the number used in the Pulitzer Race. When flown in the 1925 Schneider Race, the aircraft carried the number 3, and in the 1926 Schneider Trophy Race it was numbered 6.

It was on loan for several years to the Air Force Museum, where it was restored by Air Force personnel. It now hangs in the Pioneers of Flight gallery at the National Air and Space Museum.
Claudia M. Oakes

Curtiss Robin J-1 Deluxe "Ole Miss"

Wingspan:	12.5 m (41 ft.)
Length:	7.7 m (25 ft. 6 in.)
Height;	2.44 m (8 ft.)
Weight:	Gross 1,145 kg (2,523 lb.)
	Empty 760 kg (1,675 lb.)
Engine:	Wright J-6-5 Whirlwind, 165 hp

Designed for the civil market by the Curtiss Aeroplane and Motor Company, the Robin was a slender airplane of modest performance. This three-seat monoplane flew in the spring of 1928 with a 90-hp Curtiss OX-5, the engine that had powered Curtiss JN-4 Jenny trainers in World War I. Robins offered flight characteristics as straightforward as their appealing lines. A distinctive feature (shared with Fairchild cabin monoplanes of the period) was side cockpit windows that ran almost to the floor.

The biplane dominated aviation until Charles Lindbergh's historic 1927 flight from New York to Paris showed the world that the era of the monoplane was truly at hand. His *Spirit of St. Louis*—like the Stinson SM, Bellanca *Columbia*, and Ford Tri-motor—all featured a single high wing and fully enclosed cabin. The Robin, built to the same formula, was conventional in structure with a welded fuselage built of rugged steel tubing that was rectangular in cross section. Except for the cowling, the plane was entirely fabric-covered. Orange with black trim was a common factory color scheme. More than 300 Robins were fitted with the surplus OX-5 and sold to the civil market at $4,000. Others were powered by the 170-hp Curtiss Challenger (a six-cylinder, twin-row radial

engine that was less than satisfactory) and the excellent 165-hp Wright J-6-5 Whirlwind. These later versions, with the added expense of new engines, sold for almost twice the price of the lethargic OX-5 Robin, but offered substantially better performance.

Robin production took place in St. Louis, Missouri, in association with the Robertson Aircraft Corporation, a local fixed-base operation that ran the contract air mail route between St. Louis and Chicago (Major William B. Robertson had been one of Lindbergh's financial backers). Some 750 Robins were built by the Curtiss-Robertson Airplane Manufacturing Corporation before the Depression and competition from newer types called a halt to production late in 1930.

One of aviation's most delightful records was set in a Curtiss Robin by Douglas "Wrong Way" Corrigan. He left New York for California in July 1938 and touched down in Ireland 28 hours later, claiming he accidentally read his compass backward. The plucky pilot—who had been denied official permission to fly the Atlantic—thus earned his nickname and delighted the world.

Aviation's exuberant adolescence was also marked by a penchant for endurance records. In July 1929, Dale Jackson and Forest O'Brine set an

The Curtiss Robin of 1928 was a popular three-seat general aviation transport. This Robin was powered by a 90-hp Curtiss OX-5 engine. (Photo: SI 83-9874)

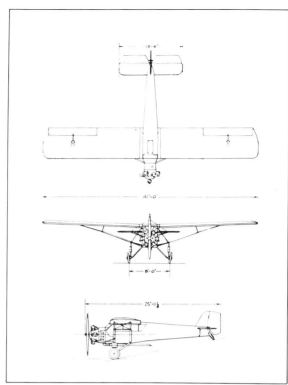

The Gilbert & Barker Manufacturing Company of Springfield, Massachusetts, was one of many companies to operate Curtiss Robins as corporate aircraft.
(Photo: SI 84–8597)

Piloted by brothers Fred and Algene Key, the National Air and Space Museum's Robin J-1 Ole Miss stayed aloft from June 4 to July 1, 1935, setting a refueled endurance record of 653 hours (27 days). Food, fuel, and supplies were passed from another Robin in more than 400 aerial contacts.
(Photo: SI 79–5022)

impressive record in the Challenger-powered *St. Louis Robin*. With the help of aerial refueling, they remained aloft 420 hours and 17 minutes. When their mark was bested by a Stinson monoplane the following June, they took off again in the *St. Louis Robin* on July 21, 1930, and set a new mark of 647 hours and 28 minutes.

The greatest record for sustained flight was set five years later in a Whirlwind-powered Curtiss Robin J-1 Deluxe named *Ole Miss*. After two unsuccessful attempts in 1934, brothers Fred and Algene Key took off from Meridian, Mississippi, on June 4, 1935, and landed again 27 days later. There to greet the exhausted fliers on the evening of July 1 were 35,000 wildly cheering spectators. The Key brothers' total flight time was 653 hours and 34 minutes. Among the dangers they had faced were severe thunderstorms and an electrical fire.

During the flight, Fred and Al Key took turns manning the controls and sleeping on the extra fuel tank behind them in the cabin. They received food, fuel, and supplies 432 times through a sliding roof hatch from another Robin. A metal catwalk made in-flight maintenance and lubrication of the engine possible. Their Wright Whirlwind engine consumed 6,500 gallons of gasoline, at a rate of 10 gallons per hour, and 300 gallons of oil. Their estimated ground track was 52,320 miles, or more than twice the circumference of the earth.

Almost twenty years after its famous flight, *Ole Miss* was offered to the National Air Museum by the Key family. On July 2, 1955, Fred Key flew the famous Robin, now fully restored, to National Airport in Washington, D.C., where it was formally presented to the Smithsonian Institution.
Jay P. Spenser

Curtiss Robins had pleasing but utilitarian lines. The 170-hp Curtiss Challenger engine powered this Robin C-1.
(Photo: SI 84–8958)

Fred Key serviced the Wright J-6-5 engine flight from a special catwalk. The Key brothers took turns sleeping atop a fuel tank in the cabin.
(Photo: 76–17446)

Dassault Falcon 20

Wingspan:	16.3 m (53 ft. 6 in.)
Length:	17.2 m (56 ft. 4 in.)
Height:	5.7 m (17 ft. 7 in.)
Weight:	Gross 13,000 kg (28,660 lb.)
	Empty 7,230 kg (15,940 lb.)
Engines:	2 General Electric CF700-2D
	1,930 kg (4,250 lb.) thrust each

The Dassault Falcon is a French executive jet aircraft, originally developed as the commercial version of the famous Mystère fighter aircraft. In its ten-seat executive role, the Falcon 20, originally known as the Mystère 20, has shared an elite market with such aircraft as the Learjet, the Hawker-Siddeley (now British Aerospace) 125, and the North American Sabreliner. In the United States, it was marketed as the Fan Jet Falcon by Pan American Airways through its subsidiary, the Falcon Jet Corporation, established in 1972 for the specific purpose of selling this fine aircraft in the highly specialized U.S. market.

When Fred Smith of Federal Express sought a small jet aircraft to carry loads consisting exclusively of air express packages, the Dassault Falcon won the competition as the ideal aircraft for the purpose. It was fast, with a top speed of 535 mph; it could be converted for Federal Express's very specialized needs; and it was small enough to reduce the risk of carrying uneconomical loads during the initial, highly sensitive period, when the new airline risked its entire future on the right choice of aircraft.

The first Dassault Falcon made its maiden flight on May 4, 1963. It is a well-porportioned, all-metal low-wing monoplane, with full cantilever wing and tail surfaces, pressurized fuselage, and retractable tricycle dual-wheel landing gear. It is powered by two aft-mounted General Electric CF-700-2D turbofan engines. For cargo use, the Series 20 was

modified by several basic changes, the success of which is a tribute to the inherent soundness of the design.

Most important of these changes was the installation of a cargo door, measuring 55 inches × 74.5 inches. This is located on the left side of the forward fuselage and is operated by a closed-circuit electrohydraulic system that utilizes the aircraft batteries to operate an electric motor and hydraulic pump. Control of the door is independent of the aircraft's hydraulic and battery master systems and may be operated in all aircraft electrical configurations, provided that a battery is connected.

The door is impressively large when seen in relation to the fuselage diameter. This advantage is supplemented by a strengthened floor that can accept loads of concentrated weight. The passenger windows are plugged. Other modifications include the relocation of emergency controls (a consequence of the redesign of the floor); installation of forward escape hatches; removal of the Auxiliary Power Unit (APU); and increased travel of the "all-flying" tail. The nose-wheel is slightly larger, and the disc brakes are of a higher performance, as are the batteries. All these changes have increased the all-up weight of the Cargo Falcon 20 to 28,660 pounds, compared with the 25,300 pounds of the standard executive Falcon.

The inauguration of Federal Express Cargo

The Federal Express Falcon 20 inaugurated the world's first airline devoted exclusively to air express. (Photo: SI 76–3151)

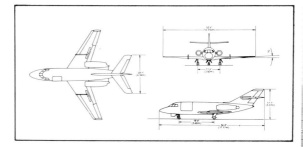

Falcon service was a new milestone in the history of air transport in the United States. Fred Smith created a new category of airline when he launched his package distribution system from a centralized clearing house at Memphis, Tennessee. The first two Falcons were delivered in June 1972, and cost $1.2 million each. One of these, N8FE— the very aircraft now in the National Air and Space Museum—carried the first Federal Express air express package on April 17, 1973. The service was an immediate success. Within a few months, more Falcons had been ordered, and by the end of 1974, no less than thirty-three of the French aircraft were flying on the spokes of the Federal Express network.

Success breeds success. The Falcons had done their job so well that the airline had to buy larger aircraft to cope with the booming demand for overnight air express service. A fleet of Boeing 727-100Fs gradually supplemented and then finally replaced the Falcons, and by 1982, less than a decade after N8FE inaugurated the new service, Federal Express's front-line aircraft were McDonnell Douglas DC-10Cs—whose cargo holds were big enough to carry several Falcons each.

The inclusion of the Federal Express Falcon 20 in the collection of the National Air and Space Museum is important for a number of reasons. First, it is representative of a new category of airline, the exclusive air express carrier. Several other enterprising individuals and corporations, recognizing the essential logic of Fred Smith's innovative idea, have gone into business with similar hub-based systems. The Falcon therefore reminds us that the development of air transport is as dynamic today as in previous decades, and that history is concerned with today's events as well as yesterday's.

Second, the Falcon was the first commercial jet to be placed in the Air Transportation gallery. Previous candidates for inclusion were too large to go into the building on the Mall. The Falcon, therefore, was a welcome addition, and makes a fascinating contrast with the Douglas M-2 mailplane. The M-2 inaugurated air mail service almost half a century before Federal Express took wing.

Third, the Falcon is a French design, built by Avions Marcel Dassault, headquartered at Vaucrosson, France. Most foreign aircraft are rare and difficult to obtain, and until recently the Museum has been unable to include a foreign-built commercial aircraft in its collection.

One of the customs at Federal Express is to

name each aircraft after a child of one of the airline employees. The name is now chosen at random, but the Falcon in the National Air and Space Museum was the first, and is named *Wendy*, after Fred Smith's daughter. The tail number, N8FE, does not mean that it was the eighth in the line. In fact, it was the first one delivered, but Smith felt that no harm would be done if the public assumed that the number on the tail indicated that Federal Express already had a fleet of eight aircraft when his enterprise first got under way.

Dassault Falcon 20, number N8FE, was donated to the National Air and Space Museum by Federal Express in 1983.

R. E. G. Davies

Dayton-Wright
(de Havilland) DH-4

Wingspan:	12.9 m (42 ft. 5-1/2 in.)
Length:	9.2 m (30 ft. 1-1/4 in.)
Height:	3.2 m (10 ft. 6 in.)
Weight:	Empty: 1,200 kg (2,647 lb.)
	Gross: 1,911 kg (4,214 lb.)
Engine:	Liberty V-12 400 hp

The de Havilland DH-4 in the National Air and Space Museum collection was the first American-built version of Geoffrey de Havilland's famous World War I bomber. Although this particular plane did not see combat during the war, it was a testbed for what was to become America's first bomber and the only American-built aircraft to serve with the U.S. Army Air Service.

Upon America's entry into the Great War on April 6, 1917, the Aviation Section of the Signal Corps did not possess any combat-worthy aircraft. So that a viable air arm could be created in the shortest possible time, a commission was established under the direction of Colonel R. C. Bolling to study current Allied aircraft designs being used at the front and to arrange for their manufacture.

Several European aircraft were chosen for American manufacture, including the French SPAD XIII, the Italian Caproni bomber, the British SE-5, the Bristol Fighter, and the Airco DH-4. The DH-4 was selected because of its comparatively simple construction and adaptability to mass production. It was also well-suited for the American 400-hp Liberty V-12 engine. Designed to be produced by American automotive production lines, the Liberty

was efficiently manufactured in large numbers. However, considerable engineering changes from the original British design were required to meet mass production standards.

The DH-4 was not without problems. The pilot and observer found themselves separated by the 67-gallon main fuel tank. This dangerous feature not only made communication between crew members difficult, but also proved to be quite hazardous in the event of a crash. The highly acclaimed Liberty engine was also cause for concern. Built in the record time of six weeks, the Liberty engine—not surprisingly—had some teething problems.

After initial testing in October 1917, production contracts were placed for the DH-4, "Liberty Plane." By the time of the armistice on November 11, 1918, three manufacturers were building DH-4s. The largest producer was the Dayton-Wright Company of Dayton, Ohio, which built a total of 3,106 aircraft; the Fisher Body Division of General Motors Corporation of Cleveland, Ohio, produced 1,600 aircraft; and the Standard Aircraft Corporation of Patterson, New Jersey, built 140 machines. Plans were under way to produce an additional 7,500 DH-4s, but orders were cancelled

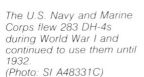

The U.S. Navy and Marine Corps flew 283 DH-4s during World War I and continued to use them until 1932.
(Photo: SI A48331C)

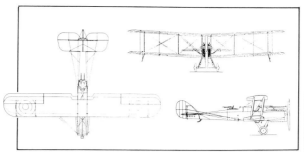

after the armistice, at which time a total of 4,346 aircraft were delivered to front-line service with the U.S. Army Air Service. Included in this number were 283 aircraft that were transferred to the U.S. Navy and Marine Corps to equip four squadrons operating along the channel coast. The U.S. Army Air Service had a total of thirteen squadrons equipped with the DH-4 by the time of the Armistice.

Although the DH-4 was in combat for just under four months, it proved equal to other combat aircraft on the western front. The American-built DH-4, powered by the Liberty, was a very serviceable and potent adversary, capable of outrunning all but the fastest German fighters. Of the six Medals of Honor awarded to aviators during the First World War, four were awarded to pilots and observers flying DH-4s. One such action took place on October 8, 1918, when Lt. Harold Goettler and 2nd Lt. Erwin Bleckley of the 50th Aero Squadron, flew repeated missions over enemy lines to drop much-needed supplies to the survivors of the "Lost Battalion" of the 77th Division. At the cost of their lives, they accomplished the first successful American combat airlift operation. The other DH-4 Medal of Honor recipients were 2nd Lt. Ralf Talbot and Gunnery Sgt. Robert Robinson of the First Marine Aviation Force.

After the war, the DH-4 continued its illustrious career in the United States; the U.S. Army Air Service and Army Air Corps continued to operate the DH-4 until 1932 despite its obsolescent design because of the large number of available aircraft that had never been used in the big spring offensives planned for 1919.

In the postwar period, the DH-4 demonstrated its versatility by replacing the converted Curtiss JN-4N Jenny trainers and antiquated Curtiss R-4 biplanes that were being used by the U.S. Government for air mail service. The L.W.F. (Lowe-Willard-Fowler) Company of College Point, New York, converted the DH-4 to a single seat mail plane with a 500-lb mail compartment in the front seat. For night flying, special flame-surpressing exhaust stacks were fitted to prevent night blindness. The rugged DH-4 proved to be ideally suited for the task of delivering mail throughout the United States. After 1927, a number of air mail DH-4s were modified or rebuilt as forest fire patrol aircraft to fly long-range patrols over the great western wilderness.

When the immense number of government-surplus aircraft became available in the 1920s, innovative pilots also modified the versatile DH-4

for use as crop dusters, budding commuter airliners, and air ambulances; and they were flown at county fairs as barnstorming crowd pleasers.

The DH-4 in the National Air and Space Museum collection was built in Dayton, Ohio, by the Dayton-Wright Aeroplane Company. It was completed and flown on October 29, 1917. This airplane was used in more than 2,600 experiments including engine, propeller, and control experimentation until its retirement in April 1919.

The museum's DH-4 carries the complete military equipment used on American DH-4s in World War I: six 25-lb Mark II bombs, two DeRam DR-4 cameras, a wireless transmitter, and two Holt wing-tip flare holders. Defensive armament consists of two fixed, forward-firing .30-caliber Marlin machine guns, and the observer's position is armed with two flexible .30-caliber Lewis machine guns on a Scarff ring mount.

The color scheme is typical of the early American DH-4s. The wings and tail are covered by a natural Irish muslin painted with a clear dope. The fuselage is finished in a cream yellow color, the top surface being dark brown. The star wing markings were placed on the early DH-4s, but upon their arrival in France these markings were changed to roundels to conform with the markings used by the Allies.

Karl S. Schneide

"Double Eagle II" (gondola)

Envelope dimensions:
Height: 34.14 m (112 ft.)
Diameter: 19.81 m (65 ft.)
Weight: 510 kg (1170 lb.)
Capacity: 4,800 cu m (160,000 cu. ft.) helium

Gondola dimensions:
Height: 1.37 m (4½ ft.)
Length: 4.57 m (15 ft.)
Width: 2.13 m (7 ft.)
Weight: 345 kg (760 lb.)

When the *Double Eagle II* balloon touched down in a wheatfield near Miserey, France, about sixty miles northwest of Paris, on August 17, 1978, a century-old dream had been realized, the crossing of the Atlantic by balloon.

Ben Abruzzo, Maxie Anderson, and Larry Newman, all of Albuquerque, New Mexico, made the 3,100-mile flight from Presque Isle, Maine, in 137 hours, 6 minutes. Lift-off had been at 8:42 p.m. on August 11. Their helium-filled balloon, the *Double Eagle II*, was 112 feet high, 65 feet in diameter, and had a capacity of 160,000 cubic feet. Abruzzo, Anderson, and Newman rode in a 15 × 7 × 4½-foot gondola named *The Spirit of Albuquerque*, equipped with a twin-hulled catamaran that would float in case of an emergency water landing. Also carried along by Newman, a hang-glider pilot and owner of a hang-glider manufacturing company, was a glider which was attached to the gondola with the idea of using it for the descent at the end of the flight. It had to be cast off to lighten the balloon, however, before the crew reached their goal.

Before this successful crossing, seventeen attempts had been made to cross the Atlantic by balloon with the loss of seven lives. The earliest known serious attempt was in 1873, when *The Daily Graphic*, sponsored by the well-known Civil War balloonist John Wise, took off from New York City but got no farther than the Catskills when it was forced down in a storm. The most recent attempt before that of the *Double Eagle II* was in July 1978 by two Englishmen who took off from Saint John's, Newfoundland. They fell short of their goal, Brest, France, by only 103 miles. Abruzzo and Anderson themselves had made an unsuccessful attempt in September 1977, being

forced down by bad weather off the coast of Iceland. Their balloon for that try was the *Double Eagle*.

The *Double Eagle II* was constructed by Ed Yost of Tea, South Dakota, who had himself made a transatlantic attempt in 1976. The gondola was equipped with computers for navigation and radio gear for communication with land monitoring stations. Included were a VHF radio, two single sideband HF radios, an ADF beacon transmitter, an amateur band radio, a maritime radio, and a hookup to the Nimbus 6 satellite, which transmitted their latitude and longitude to Goddard Space Flight Center in Maryland.

Officially, the Atlantic crossing was attained at 10:02 p.m. on August 16, when the *Double Eagle II* crossed the Irish coast. But the goal of the three pilots was Le Bourget Airfield near Paris, where Lindbergh had landed. However, late in the afternoon of the 17th, with ballast low and daylight fading, the pilots reached the decision to land in the French province of Normandy. Thus at 7:48 p.m. they came down in a wheatfield near Miserey and were immediately surrounded by crowds who had been following the balloon's path.

During the crossing, the altitude of the *Double Eagle II* had varied from a heart-stopping low point of 3,500 feet on August 13 when clouds screened the sun and cooled the gas, causing the balloon to sink, to a high point of 24,950 feet on August 16.

The success of the *Double Eagle II*, after so many others had failed, can be attributed to twentieth-century technology, better understanding of weather patterns, and the skill and experience of the pilots.

Claudia M. Oakes

The gondola and part of the balloon on the Double Eagle II *are on exhibit in the Balloons and Airships gallery. The heads of the mannequins were made from life masks of the three balloonists. (Photo: SI 81–1342)*

Douglas A-4C Skyhawk

Wingspan:	8.39 m (27 ft. 6 in.)
Length:	12.23 m (40 ft.)
Height:	4.58 m (15 ft.)
Weight:	Gross, 10,215 kg (22,500 lb.)
	Empty, 4,367 kg (9,619 lb.)
Engine:	Wright J65-W-16A, 3,496 kg (7,700 lb.) thrust

The Douglas A-4 Skyhawk is a very versatile light attack-bomber that has been a U.S. Navy first-line aircraft for many years. Despite its relatively small size, it is able to carry a large and varied assortment of aerial weapons. Throughout the entire conflict in Vietnam, it was noted for its unusual accuracy in attacking selected ground targets.

In the early 1950s some of the aircraft design group at the Douglas Aircraft Company became concerned by the trend toward increasing complexity and weight in combat aircraft. The group, led by Ed Heinemann, whose design philosophy is "Simplicate and Add Lightness," proposed a new attack plane with a gross weight of about half the official specification weight of 30,000 pounds. The design was accepted by the Navy, and an initial contract was let in June 1952. The designation A4D was later changed to A-4 when the Defense Department revised its aircraft designation system in 1962.

The National Air and Space Museum's A-4C is shown on the deck of the U.S.S. Bon Homme Richard off the coast of Vietnam in 1967. It was part of Navy Attack Squadron VA-76. (Photo: SI 75-12075)

Unlike most other carrier aircraft, the A-4, with its relatively small wingspan, does not have folding wings. The elimination of this feature allowed a much simpler, lighter wing, which in turn allowed a much lighter aircraft.

The A-4, or "Heinemann's Hotrod" as it was sometimes called, was first flown on June 22, 1954. The first Skyhawks were powered by 7,200-pound-thrust Curtiss-Wright J65-W-2 engines, but production models, A4D-1s (A-4As), used 7,700-pound-thrust J65-W-4 engines. The first Skyhawks were delivered to Navy Attack Squadron VA-72 in October 1956.

During the test program, Navy Lt. Gordon Grey, set a new world speed record over a 500-kilometer closed course of 695.163 mph. The Skyhawk was the first attack plane to hold this record.

The next model of the Skyhawk was the A4D-2 (A-4B), which included provisions for inflight refueling (both as a receiver and as a tanker), a powered rudder, and some structural

An A-4 Skyhawk of VA-94 lands on the U.S.S. Hancock. A second Skyhawk is just starting its final approach for landing. (Photo: USN 1123399)

strengthening. The A4D-2N (A-4C), first flown in 1959, incorporated radar in the nose and an improved ejection seat.

The next model, the A4D-5 (A-4E), was powered by the 8,500-pound-thrust Pratt and Whitney J-52-P-2 engine. This engine's lower fuel consumption improved the Skyhawk's range by about 25 percent. A two-seat version of the A-4E was produced for use as a Navy advanced trainer.

The A-4F used a 9,300-pound-thrust J-52-P-8A engine and was equipped with a zero-zero ejection seat (safe ejection possible at zero altitude and zero airspeed) and new electronic gear mounted under a fuselage hump behind the cockpit.

One outstanding feature of the Skyhawk is the ability to carry a variety of external stores. The early A-4s could carry some 5,000 pounds of bombs, missiles, fuel tanks, rockets, and gun pods on three stations, while the A-4E and subsequent models could carry 8,200 pounds on five stations. The standard armament: two 20-mm machine guns.

The A-4 was widely used by both the Navy and Marines, and played a major combat role in Southeast Asia. The A-4 is also used by several foreign nations, including Argentina, Australia, and Israel.

The National Air and Space Museum's A-4C was received from the Navy in July 1975. Just prior to its transfer, it was repainted in the markings it carried while assigned to VA-76 (Navy Attack Squadron) on the U.S.S. *Bon Homme Richard* when it was operating off the coast of Vietnam from March to June 1967.

Donald S. Lopez

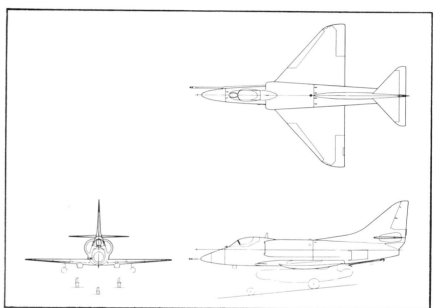

A fully loaded A-4 of VA-94 is being moved into place on the catapult of the U.S.S. Hancock. (Photo: U.S. Navy)

Douglas D-558-2 Skyrocket

Wingspan:	7.62 m (25 ft.)
Length:	12.80 m (42 ft.)
Height:	3.86 m (12 ft. 8 in.)
Weight:	Launch, 7,161 kg (15,787 lb.)
	Landing, 4,673 kg (9,421 lb.)
Engine:	Reaction Motors, Inc., XLR-8-RM-6 (Model A6000C4) 4-chamber rocket engine rated at 2,721 kg (6,000 lb.) thrust

On the morning of November 20, 1953, A. Scott Crossfield became the first pilot to fly at twice the speed of sound, Mach 2. He accomplished this feat while flying the experimental air-launched rocket-propelled Douglas D-558-2 #2 Skyrocket. This sweptwing research plane attained Mach 2.005 (1,291 mph) while in a shallow dive at an altitude of 62,000 feet. Seconds afterward, the plane's XLR-8 rocket engine exhausted its fuel supply and shut down. Crossfield glided earthward to a smooth dead-stick landing on Muroc Dry Lake, at Edwards Air Force Base, California.

The D-558-2 #2 was just one of six different D-558 research airplanes ordered by the U.S. Navy from the Douglas Aircraft Company for obtaining aerodynamic information at transonic and supersonic speeds. The Navy issued a letter of intent to Douglas on June 22, 1945, for construction of six Model D-558 aircraft, having straight, thin wing and tail surfaces, and turbojet propulsion. Development of the aircraft began

under the direction of chief engineer Edward H. Heinemann. Subsequent analysis of captured data on wartime German sweptwing research, combined with sweptwing studies by American scientist Robert T. Jones, caused Douglas and the Navy to modify the D-558 contract by deleting three of the planned aircraft and replacing them with three sweptwing vehicles powered by both turbojet and rocket engines. The first three aircraft, each powered by a single General Electric TG-180 turbojet, became known as the D-558-1 Skystreak series. The last three, powered initially by a Westinghouse J-34 turbojet for low-speed flight plus a Reaction Motors, XLR-8 rocket engine for high-speed research, became known as the D-558-2 Skyrocket series.

The D-558-1 and D-558-2 greatly differed from one another in detail design and there was little commonality between them. Both took off from the ground. Because of its engine type and airframe design, the D-558-1 was limited to approximately

The D-558-2 #2 drops away from its Boeing P2B-IS (B-29) Superfortress and its XLF-8 rocket engine begins to ignite. (Photo: Douglas Aircraft Co., ES 82553)

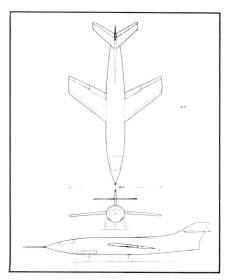

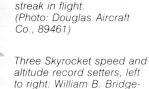

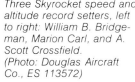

Mach 1, the speed of sound. The more powerful D-558-2, using its 6,000-pound-thrust rocket engine fueled with liquid oxygen and diluted ethyl alcohol, could easily exceed Mach 1. The safety hazards of operating a heavily loaded rocket-propelled airplane from the ground later caused Douglas to modify the D-558-2 #2 and #3 for air launching from the bomb bay of a converted Boeing P2B-1S (Navy B-29) Superfortress. At the same time, Douglas modified the D-558-2 #2 to all-rocket propulsion, utilizing the space formerly taken up by its turbojet engine for additional rocket fuel. Thus modified, the D-558-2 #2 was capable of reaching Mach 2, which it did while being flown in a special high-speed flight research program by the National Advisory Committee for Aeronautics (NACA).

The first D-558-1 Skystreak, bureau number 37970, completed its maiden flight on April 14, 1947, piloted by Eugene F. May. On August 20, 1947, Navy Cmdr. Turner F. Caldwell set a new world air-speed record of 640.663 mph while flying the D-558-1 #1. Five days later, on August 25, 1947, Marine Corps Maj. Marion Carl, while flying the second D-558-1, bureau number 37971 (NACA 141), broke Caldwell's record by reaching 650.796 mph. The NACA utilized the third D-558-1, bureau number 37972 (NACA 142), for extensive investigations of transonic aerodynamic phenomena and aircraft behavior, retiring this Skystreak in 1953. The D-558-1 #1 did exceed Mach 1 on September 29, 1948, while piloted by Eugene F. May and flown in a 35-degree dive. One Skystreak, the D-558-1 #2, crashed on May 3, 1948 during a takeoff accident following engine failure, killing Howard C. Lilly, a NACA research pilot.

The first D-558-2 Skyrocket, bureau number 37973 (NACA 143), completed its initial flight on February 4, 1948, piloted by John F. Martin. The second Skyrocket, bureau number 37974 (NACA 144), went to the NACA, which used it to investigate the behavior characteristics of sweptwings. During this program, before its conversion to all-rocket propulsion, the D-558-2 #2 revealed the tendency of sweptwing aircraft to pitch up under certain aerodynamic conditions. After modification in 1950 to all-rocket configuration, the D-558-2 #2 attained Mach 1.88 and an unofficial altitude record of 79,494 feet, while flown by Douglas test pilot William B. Bridgeman. Following delivery to the NACA, this Skyrocket extended its unofficial record altitude to 83,235 feet, while flown by Marine test pilot Marion Carl on August 21, 1953. Shortly afterward, NACA research pilot A. Scott Crossfield exceeded Mach 2 in the plane. The NACA utilized the third D-558-2, bureau number 37975 (NACA 145), in a program evaluating the effectiveness of wing slats and leading edge devices, and examined its behavior with external stores mounted beneath its wings. All three Skyrockets were retired from flight operations in 1956. At one point, Douglas considered developing a D-558-3 hypersonic research aircraft, upon request of the Office of Naval Research, but this aircraft remained a paper study.

The D-558-1 and D-558-2 were of mixed aluminum and magnesium construction. Both types featured jettisonable nose sections to serve as emergency escape capsules, and both were designed to carry heavy instrumentation payloads for flight research purposes. The first two D-558-1 Skystreaks were bright glossy red overall, but the D-558-1 #3 and later D-558-2 Skyrockets were glossy white, which proved more desirable for optical tracking purposes. The historic Douglas D-558-2 #2, NACA 144, the first Mach 2 airplane, is in the collection of the National Air and Space Museum.

Richard P. Hallion

Douglas DC-3

Wingspan:	28.95 m (95 ft.)
Length:	19.66 m (64 ft. 6 in.)
Height:	5 m (16 ft. 11 in.)
Weight:	Gross, 11,430 kg (25,200 lb.)
Cruising Speed:	297.65 km/hr (185 mph)
Engines:	Two Wright SGR 1820-71, 1200 hp

Eastern Air Lines' Douglas DC-3 #344 is in the Smithsonian collection. In operation from December 7, 1937, through September 1952, this plane accumulated 56,782 hours, the greatest number of any in Eastern's DC-3 fleet. (Photo: SI A43662)

The development of the Douglas DC-3 was brought about by the commercial airlines' demand for an economical passenger-carrying airplane. Up to 1934, airline passenger craft were too slow and carried too few passengers to be really profitable. United Air Lines had ordered sixty of the new Boeing 247s, the first truly modern airliners and had effectively tied up production. The 247 carried ten passengers at 160 mph and made all other transports obsolete. The other carriers were thus forced to find another plane if they wished to be competitive in the passenger-carrying business.

In 1933 the Douglas Aircraft Company designed a new passenger plane, as ordered by Transcontinental and Western airlines, to compete with the Boeing 247. The first model, the DC-1, was soon succeeded by the DC-2 and the start of quantity production. American Airlines, at the time, was using the slow Curtiss Condor, which was fitted with sleeper berths. American needed a new airplane able to compete with the DC-2 and the Boeing 247, but one with sleeping accommodations.

In 1935 C. R. Smith, president of American Airlines, made a direct request of Douglas to build a "larger, more comfortable plane which could lure the luxury trade." On December 17, 1935, the Douglas Sleeper Transport (DST) made its first flight.

The original plane was designed as a luxury sleeper with seven upper and seven lower berths and a private forward cabin. The day plane version, known as the DC-3, had twenty-one seats instead of fourteen berths. The design included cantilever wings, all-metal construction, two cowled radial engines, retractable landing gear, and trailing edge flaps. The controls included an automatic pilot and two sets of instruments. The original design was so satisfactory that the basic specifications were never changed.

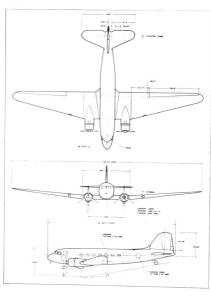

This United Air Lines Douglas DC-3 Mainliner had twin Wasp 1,250-hp engines. (Photo: SI 75-11811)

A Delta Air Lines Douglas DC-3 is shown in flight. (Photo: SI 75-11812)

This U.S. Air Force C-47 with combat markings was used as a gunship. (Photo: SI 75-4492)

American Airlines initiated DST nonstop New York-to-Chicago service on June 25, 1936, and in September started service with the DC-3. A year later, with the DC-3 in service, Smith stated, "It was the first airplane in the world that could make money just by hauling passengers." This was the beginning of an immortal airplane known the world over. As the success of the DC-3, with its larger capacity for passengers, its speed, and its economical operation, was realized, airlines throughout the world began placing orders with Douglas.

In the United States the big three transcontinental lines were very competitive. With the advent of DST coast-to-coast service by American Airlines, Trans World Airlines obtained DSTs and DC-3s for such flights also. When United Airlines, with its Boeing 247s, saw that the Douglas plane was outclassing its own service, the company purchased ten DSTs and five DC-3s, and began flights on January 1, 1937. In July of that same year United introduced sleeper service between New York and California.

By 1938, 95 percent of all U.S. commercial airline traffic was on DC-3s. Two hundred sixty DC-3s, 80 percent of the number of airliners, were in service in 1942 on domestic carriers. As of December 31, 1969, thirty DC-3s were still being used by U.S. airlines.

Foreign companies also began to order the economical Douglas-built plane. KLM was the first European airline to own and operate DC-3s, in 1936, followed by companies in Sweden, Switzerland, France, Belgium, and elsewhere. By 1938 DC-3s were flown by thirty foreign airlines, and by 1939, 90 percent of the world's airline traffic was being carried by these aircraft.

The impact of the DC-3 was felt the world over. In July 1936 President Franklin D. Roosevelt presented Donald W. Douglas, head of Douglas Aircraft, with the Collier Trophy. Recognizing the DC-3 as the "outstanding twin-engined commercial plane," the citation read, "This airplane, by reason of its high speed, economy, and quiet passenger comfort, has been generally adopted by transport lines throughout the United States. Its merit has been further recognized by its adoption abroad, and its influence on foreign design is already apparent."

In 1939 the DC-3 was called on to aid the military fleets of the world. Many commercial carriers in Europe put their DC-3s to use as military transports. The United States ordered new versions of the DC-3 modified for troop transport and cargo carrying. These were designated as C-47s and C-53s. As military versions were built, they were put into operation in European and Pacific theaters during World War II. C-47s initiated the Berlin Airlift in 1948. In military service since 1941, the C-47 proved most useful in many endeavors.

Many names and numbers were assigned to the DC-3. England labeled it the "Dakota" or "Dak." American pilots, during World War II, called it the "Skytrain," "Skytrooper," "Doug," or "Gooney Bird." The U.S. military's official titles were C-47, C-53, C-117, and R4D. The airlines called it "The Three." Of all the names the affectionate title "Gooney Bird" lingers on.

The normal gross weight for the aircraft was 25,200 pounds, with twenty-one passengers. Many times these weights were exceeded as conditions required. The normal range was 1,500 miles, but this could be extended by adding fuel tanks. The cruising speed varied from 155 mph to 190 mph depending on the load carried and the power used. The DC-3's safety record was better than that of most airplanes, primarily because of its great structural strength and efficient single-engine performance.

Since 1935, 803 commercial transports and 10,123 military versions have been built. In addition, about 2,000 have been constructed under license in Russia (Li-2) and about sixty in Japan. In service since 1936, the DC-3 is still in use today throughout the world.

Melinda Scarano

Douglas M-2

Wingspan:	12.09 m (39 ft. 8 in.)
Length:	8.81 m (28 ft. 11 in.)
Height:	3.07 m (10 ft. 1 in.)
Weight:	Gross, 2,253 kg (4,968 lb.)
	Empty, 1,320 kg (2,910 lb.)
Engine:	Liberty 12, 400 hp

On April 17, 1926, Western Air Service, Inc., commenced operation on Contract Air Mail Route 4 (CAM-4) between Los Angeles and Salt Lake City, via Las Vegas. For service over this route, a distance of about 660 miles, Western selected the Douglas M-2 aircraft, a mailplane version of the O-2 observation plane produced by the Douglas Company to replace the U.S. Army DH-4 aircraft.

The Douglas M-2 was selected because it was far superior in strength, construction, performance, and flying characteristics to other aircraft entered in the Post Office Department's competition for airmail airplanes. The M-2 was a single-bay biplane with the conventional form of axleless undercarriage. The fuselage, a truss of steel tubes and tie rods, was made in two detachable sections. The engine section was detachable at the station at the front wing beam and the engine cowling was hinged to facilitate inspection. The fuselage aft of the firewall was covered with fabric. The wings, vertical fin, and horizontal stabilizer

were of standard wood beam and built-up rib construction, with the elevators and rudder made of Duralumin tubing. The power plant was a 400-hp, Liberty water-cooled engine, with nose radiator. Two main fuel tanks, each of sixty gallons capacity and made of sheet aluminum, were so mounted in the lower wing that they could be jettisoned by the pilot. A small 10-gallon gravity tank was located in the upper wing.

A design detail of particular interest was the location and construction of the M-2 mail compartment. It was situated in front of the pilot's cockpit, sealed from the engine by a fireproof bulkhead, and lined with reinforced Duralumin. It was six feet long, had a capacity of 58 cubic feet, and could carry up to 1,000 pounds of mail. A unique feature was the provision of two removable seats that permitted carrying passengers or reserve pilots from one field to another. The passengers were seated well down in the compartment and protected by suitable

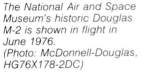

The National Air and Space Museum's historic Douglas M-2 is shown in flight in June 1976.
(Photo: McDonnell-Douglas, HG76X178-2DC)

The Douglas M-2 as it appeared prior to installation of long collective exhaust pipes in 1926. (Photo: SI A5314)

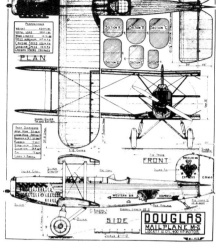

Western Air Express's Douglas M-2 (right) at Salt Lake City in 1926 transfers mail destined for New York. (Photo: SI 76-15553)

windshields. Access was provided by the use of aluminum covers over the top, arranged and constructed so that, with passengers aboard, the roof door could be folded down, providing a cockpit opening.

Flights were scheduled daily in both directions on the Los Angeles-to-Salt Lake City run, with one-way flight time averaging slightly in excess of six hours. The record time for the route was 4 hours, 12 minutes. The schedule was maintained by four regular pilots, two reserve pilots, eight mechanics, and three radio operators at the fields. Although transporting the mail remained the airlines' chief concern, Western Air Express invited passenger traffic, and invaluable experience was gained flying passengers in the M-2 over the same rugged territory of eastern California, southern Nevada, and western Utah traveled many years before by the Mormons.

The M-2 performed remarkably well during the early years on the CAM-4 route. Its load-carrying capability, remarkable stability, and rugged construction contributed to a perfect safety record and profitable operation. Government and airline experiences with the Douglas mailplanes and the O-2 led to modifications of the basic design. Relatively minor changes in cockpit layout, engine accessories, and airframe construction led to the M-3 mailplane, which differed little in physical appearance from the M-2 version. A subsequent addition of five feet to the wingspan resulted in the final version, the M-4, which realized considerable gain in payload at a negligible loss in performance. While Western eventually added two M-4s to its fleet of six M-2s, the M-4 saw more extensive service with National Air Transport (later United Air Lines) from 1927 to 1930 on the Chicago-New York route. National Air Transport modified all of its M-3s into the M-4 configuration and eventually had twenty-four Douglas mailplanes on its roster, to

become the largest operator of this type in commercial service.

The M-2 of the National Air and Space Museum is believed to be the last Douglas mailplane in existence. This machine is actually an M-4 model originally purchased by Western from the Post Office Department in June 1927 and registered as NC 1475, serial number 338. The aircraft saw considerable service on Western's mail route until 1930, when it crashed and was sold to Continental Air Map Company of Los Angeles. The airplane had a series of corporate and private owners until it was reacquired by Western Air Lines in April 1940 and subsequently registered with the Federal Aviation Administration as M-2 NC150, Western's first M-2. The first substantial restoration took place in 1946, although no attempt was made to make it flyable. For the next twenty-two years, the M-2 made its home in a corner of Western's hangar at Los Angeles International Airport. In 1974 an intensive, large-scale restoration effort commenced, under the impetus of retired Western Captain Ted Homan.

Volunteers from Western Air Lines, McDonnell-Douglas Corporation, Goodyear Tire Company, and many other organizations completely rebuilt the aircraft and its Liberty engine, returning the machine to flyable condition. The M-2 flew for the first time in thirty-six years on June 2, 1976, and after a series of test flights was recertified airworthy by the Federal Aviation Administration. After a successful transcontinental journey in May 1977, the venerable M-2, resplendent in the silver and red colors in which it flew the old Mormon Trail, is displayed as a lasting tribute to the men and women who pioneered the mail-passenger service during the formative years of commercial aviation in the United States.

E. T. Wooldridge, Jr.

Douglas SBD–6 Dauntless

Wingspan:	12.66 m (41 ft. 6 in.)
Length:	10.06 m (33 ft.)
Height:	4.15 m (13 ft. 7 in.)
Weight:	Gross, 4,940 kg (10,882 lb.)
	Empty, 2,967 kg (6,554 lb.)
Engine:	Wright Cyclone R-1820-52, 1,000 hp

Designed in 1938 and accepted by the U.S. Navy in February 1939, six months before the start of World War II, the Douglas SBD (for Scout Bomber Douglas) represented prewar technology. Fortunately, its design was quite adaptable to changes dictated by combat experience, such as increased armor protection for the crew and self-sealing fuel tanks. Above all, it was a compact, rugged dive-bomber that could take a lot of punishment.

Although a contract for fifty-seven SBD-1s was negotiated during the first week of April 1939, the SBD had barely passed its teething period when war broke out. This order was then substantially increased, with successive model changes indicating responses to lessons and tactics learned in the European phase of the war. Among the improvements to the original design was the change to a more powerful engine, a Wright Cyclone R-1820-52, which delivered 1,000 horsepower to maintain the performance in spite of

added weight of the modifications. The attack on Pearl Harbor added new urgency to the production lines, and an additional 500 SBDs were ordered. By this time the armament had changed; two .50-caliber machine guns had replaced the .30-caliber guns fitted to the earlier planes in the series. A second .30-caliber gun was added to the flexible mount in the rear cockpit. The SBD-3s produced under this expanding program, plus the remaining SBD-2s, played a major role in the crucial battles of the Coral Sea and Midway. In the Battle of Midway on June 4, 1942, the first telling attack was made by the SBDs from the U.S.S. *Yorktown* on the Japanese carrier *Kaga*. This was followed almost immediately by the SBDs from the *Enterprise* as they attacked the *Akagi* and the *Soryu*. In the ensuing fighting the Japanese lost four large aircraft carriers, the *Kaga*, the *Akagi*, the *Hiryu*, and the *Soryu*, and with them the majority of their well-trained, experienced naval pilots. The SBD losses were moderate, under the circumstances.

The National Air and Space Museum's SBD-6 is painted in the markings of a Daunt-less that served on the U.S.S. San Jacinto. (Photo: National Archives 80-G-234651)

*An SBD-5 on twilight patrol over Wake Island.
(Photo: SI 75-11350)*

amounting to thirty-five Navy and eight Marine planes. The Battle of Midway is regarded by most historians as the turning point of the Pacific War, since Japan's losses in ships, planes, and experienced pilots, in addition to those previously lost in the Battle of the Coral Sea, were never replaced. More and more, the Japanese were forced to operate from land bases with younger, less experienced pilots.

The SBDs gave a good account of themselves in every engagement in which they participated, and they served longer than intended, for their successor, the Curtiss SB2C, was long delayed by modifications required to make them acceptable for carrier service. All told, the SBDs accounted for most of the damage from the air sustained by the Japanese carriers and other lesser ships during the war.

Ordnance for the SBD could consist of a variety of loads, including a 1,600-pound bomb mounted on the center rack and two 100-pound bombs on wing-mounted racks, all externally mounted. The bomb carried on the center rack was dropped clear of the propeller by a displacing gear, which insured adequate clearance. In scouting configuration, drop-tanks could be attached to the wing mounts for greater endurance. Unlike most of its contemporaries, the SBDs did not have folding wings to improve its shipboard stowage ability. Instead, they had the same basic wing construction as their forerunners, the Northrop XBT-2, the Northrop Gamma, and the Douglas DC-3.

The National Air and Space Museum's SBD-6, bureau number 54605, was the last of its type in active service with the Navy, and was the sixth and last modification of the SBD series. It was accepted by the Navy on March 30, 1944, and delivered on April 7, 1944. Its entire service life of four years was with Flight Test at Patuxent River Naval Air Station, Maryland. It was put in storage at Weeksville, North Carolina, in May 1948, and transferred to the Smithsonian in 1961.

The colors and markings of the exhibited aircraft are representative of the SBD in combat. They are of aircraft 109 of VS-51, which served on the U.S.S. *San Jacinto*.

Louis S. Casey

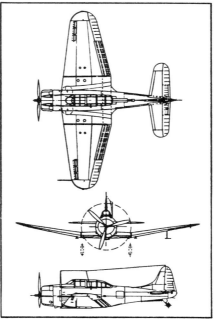

*An SBD from the U.S.S. Enterprise was the first carrier-based aircraft lost in World War II, shot down by a Zero on its way to Pearl Harbor.
(Photo: SI A43573C)*

Douglas World Cruiser "Chicago"

Wingspan:	15.24 m (50 ft.)
Length:	20.66 m (35 ft. 6 in.)
Height:	4.15 m (13 ft. 7½ in.)
Weight:	Gross, 3,348 kg (7,380 lb.) landplane; 3,710 kg (8,180 lb.) seaplane
	Empty, 1,987 kg (4,380 lb.) landplane; 2,350 kg (5,180 lb.) seaplane
Engine:	Liberty V-12, 420 hp

In 1924 powered, manned flight had just passed its twentieth birthday. In World War I the airplane had proven itself able to play a vital military role, and it was currently providing entertainment in barnstorming, air racing, and speed and altitude record flights. But it was necessary to prove somehow that the airplane was a valuable and viable method of transportation and could therefore have a great impact on the world's future. To prove this, the U.S. Army Air Service decided to attempt a round-the-world flight. Though no less than five other nations tried, the United States was the first to succeed—April 6 to September 28, 1924.

The Douglas Aircraft Company was commissioned by the Army Air Service to build an aircraft for the flight. The result was an open-cockpit, two-place biplane of tubular steel and wood framework with fabric covering. It was powered by a twelve-cylinder water-cooled Liberty engine of 420 horsepower. This prototype was tested at McCook Field, Dayton, Ohio, and accepted by the Air Service at Langley Field, Hampton, Virginia.

Four more aircraft were then built, numbers 1, 2, 3, and 4. They were respectively named *Seattle*, *Chicago*, *Boston*, and *New Orleans*, and their crews were as follows:

Seattle—Maj. Frederick L. Martin (pilot and flight commander) and Sgt. Alva L. Harvey;
Chicago—Lt. Lowell H. Smith (pilot) and Lt. Leslie Arnold;
Boston—Lt. Leigh Wade (pilot) and Lt. Henry H. Ogden;
New Orleans—Lt. Erik H. Nelson (pilot) and Lt. Jack Harding.

Director of the flight was Maj. Gen. Mason M. Patrick, chief of the Air Service. He headed a

The Douglas World Cruiser Chicago, now in the collection of the National Air and Space Museum, is shown on an over-water leg of its world flight.
(Photo: SI A48828)

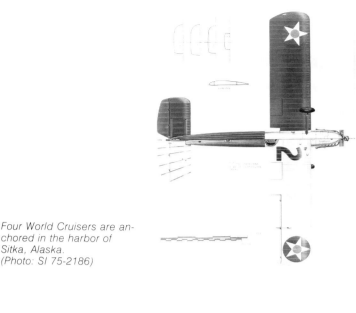

(Diagram by Björn Karlström, Courtesy National Aeronautic Association)

DOUGLAS D.W.C. "WORLD CRUISER" 1924

Four World Cruisers are anchored in the harbor of Sitka, Alaska.
(Photo: SI 75-2186)

President Coolidge and Navy Secretary Weeks (third and fourth from the left) pose in front of the Chicago with five of the world flyers.
(Photo: USAF 11671A.S.)

logistics and planning operation unparalleled for that time. Under the supervision of Lt. St. Clair Streett, advance divisions of mechanics and technicians were sent to bases along the route the aircraft would take. Special crates of spare engines, parts, and tools were readied for shipment. At several bases throughout the route, the planes would use facilities of the Royal Air Force. Also, the U.S. Navy would stand by to assist on the overwater legs of the trip.

The four aircraft had no radios, navigational aids, or weather-forecasting equipment. Their only instruments were a compass, an altimeter, and a turn-and-bank indicator.

On April 6, 1924, the flight took off from Seattle and immediately encountered bad weather. The *Seattle*, which had been delayed by a forced landing caused by engine trouble, was trying to catch up to the others when the weather forced it off course. It crashed near Chignik, Alaska.

The other three continued without mishap, however, across the Pacific to Japan. Lieutenant Arnold, in his diary of the flight, described flying over Japan's Mount Fuji on June 1: "For the first hour the trip was delightful and the weather perfect. Midway in Yokahama Bay we passed the volcano O Shima which was putting out great clouds of steam, and soon afterwards thru a rift in the clouds we could see Japan's famous Fujiyama with the sun shining on its snow capped dome

some 12,400 feet above sea level—a truly beautiful sight."

After leaving Japan, the three aircraft continued across China, Indo-China, Siam, Burma, India, Persia, Asia Minor, the Balkans, and France. From Strasbourg, they were escorted to Paris by the French Air Force, and there they received a tumultuous welcome from cheering crowds on Bastille Day. The next day they left Paris and landed in London.

Disaster again occurred between the Orkney and Faroe islands, when the *Boston* suddenly lost oil pressure and had to land at sea. Although the landing was successful, the *Boston* was damaged beyond repair during an attempt to hoist it on board a Navy ship. At Pictou, Nova Scotia, the prototype aircraft arrived to join the remaining two and became the *Boston II*. From there the planes flew on for a triumphal journey across the United States, arriving in Seattle on September 28, having accomplished the 27,553-mile flight in 175 days or 371 hours, 11 minutes flying time, with an average speed of 70 mph.

Two of the World Cruisers still survive. The *New Orleans* (#4) is in the Air Force Museum at Dayton, Ohio. The *Chicago* (#2), in the collection of the National Air and Space Museum, has been restored and is on exhibit.
Claudia M. Oakes

Ecker Flying Boat

Wingspan:	12.8 m (42 ft.)
Length:	7.9 m (26 ft.)
Height:	4.3 m (14 ft.)
Engine:	Roberts 6-cylinder, 60 hp

Most of the aircraft in the National Air and Space Museum collection achieved fame in their own right or represent an important aircraft type of technical or historical significance. The Ecker Flying Boat adequately meets these criteria, but it deserves a place in the national collection for another equally noteworthy reason. The Ecker represents that vast, largely unknown, wholly uncelebrated population of pioneer aviators who built flying machines in their backyards out of bits and scraps from the local hardware store. Their efforts helped to carry the burgeoning technology of heavier-than-air flight out of infancy.

Herman A. Ecker, a native of Syracuse, New York, was gripped and inspired by the excitement of the daring displays put on by the acclaimed aviators of his day such as the Wright brothers and Glenn Curtiss. In short order he joined the growing ranks of early pilots, learning to fly at Belmont Park, New York, most likely in 1911. After honing his skills as a pilot and an airplane builder with several other machines, possibly as many as four, Ecker built the

flying boat now in the NASM collection probably in 1912 or early 1913. The exact date of construction is uncertain, as are a good many of the details regarding Ecker's flying activities and his aircraft.

Ecker patterned his craft closely after the highly successful and popular Curtiss Models E and F flying boats. Indeed, the Ecker is essentially a copy of the famous Curtiss design. Despite the similarity in general appearance with the commercially produced Curtiss flying boat, the Ecker machine bears the hallmarks of a lone builder, long on enthusiasm and ingenuity, but short on resources and access to the latest technology.

Ecker, for example, attached the airplane's muslin covering with ordinary carpet tacks and tightened and sealed the fabric with wallpaper sizing glue. This sufficed on clear days, but when it rained the water-soluble glue dissolved. Ecker dealt with this problem by applying a coat of varnish over the glue. The spruce wing structure was simple, with little internal bracing, even by 1912 standards. Basic aircraft hardware was largely improvised. Strut

Herman A. Ecker (right) and his mechanic, Al Just, in the cockpit of the Ecker Flying Boat, probably in 1912. (Photo: SI 45252-A)

fittings were handmade from sheet steel, and the turnbuckles used to put tension in the bracing and control wires were refashioned motorcycle spokes.

As with the rest of the airplane, the engine was somewhat makeshift. Ecker converted a Roberts six-cylinder marine engine for aeronautical use. He removed several unnecessary components to save weight and added an automobile-type radiator for cooling. Later a second radiator was fitted to cure continual overheating problems. There were two carburetors feeding fuel into a unique rotary-valve intake that in turn redistributed the fuel to the individual cylinders. The six-gallon fuel capacity provided for twenty to thirty minutes of flying time. The engine had no exhaust pipe. Hot exhaust simply spewed out of each cylinder under the wing, requiring a protective aluminum sheath on the upper center-section fabric. There were no engine instruments; all adjustments were based on engine sound.

Like many of the one-off aircraft built and flown by lesser-known pioneers, the basic configuration of the Ecker Flying Boat changed several times during its operational life. Initially it was fitted with a wheeled landing gear. Later, pontoons replaced the wheels to allow flying off water. In its final and present form, the Ecker features an actual boat hull made of spruce, oak, and ash, sealed internally with oil and externally with a hand-rubbed grey enamel finish. The hull reportedly had beaching gear to move the aircraft from water to land and vice versa, but no information on the size and style of the wheels exists.

The flying record of the Ecker is as hazy as the history of its construction. By the time the aircraft in the NASM collection took to the air, Ecker had built a modest local reputation as a pilot and an exhibitionist in his home territory of western New York State. In a pontoon-fitted hydroaeroplane (possibly an earlier configuration of the NASM aircraft), Ecker was the first to fly in his hometown of Syracuse, New York, making a successful takeoff from nearby Onondaga Lake in 1911. By 1912, he was taking passengers aloft and doing exhibitions at fairs and other public gatherings. Some of this exhibition flying was certainly done with the aircraft in the NASM collection, but it is unknown exactly when and where or in which of its many configurations, the airplane appeared. The only direct reference to the flight history of this airplane is a vague statement made by Ecker in a 1930s newspaper interview in which he said he flew it extensively for a period of three years and then placed it in storage. The Ecker Flying Boat emerged one more time before it came to NASM when it was displayed at the 1930 New York State Fair.

The story gets murky again until the somewhat tattered airframe of the Ecker was discovered in the upper loft of a downtown Syracuse TV sales and repair shop in 1958. The components of the now ancient flying boat were gingerly hoisted out of a fourth-floor window and transported to the proud new owner's home to await restoration. Before long, news of the find reached the aircraft's original builder and pilot, Herman Ecker, who was by then

The Ecker Flying Boat just after restoration in 1982 at NASM's Garber Facility. (Photo: SI 82-8329)

The Ecker on display at the 1930 New York State Fair. (Photo: SI 81-16762)

living out a happy retirement in Florida. Ecker prevailed upon the discoverer of his long-lost airplane to donate the flying boat to the Smithsonian Institution. In 1961 the Ecker arrived at NASM and was stored until its restoration in 1981–1982.

The Ecker Flying Boat holds a place of honor in the NASM collection as one of the oldest flying boats in existence. Perhaps more important, however, it stands as a monument to those determined early aeronautical pioneers whose names may be lost to history, but whose perseverance, achievements, and sheer daring undergird the modern aerospace establishment.

Peter L. Jakab

Designer, builder, and pilot of NASM's pioneer flying boat, Herman A. Ecker, behind the wheel of a Curtiss-type pusher, probably in 1911. (Photo: NASM)

Fairchild FC-2

Wingspan:	13.5 m (44 ft.)
	Folded, 3.98 m (13 ft.)
Length:	8.68 m (30 ft. 11 in.)
Height:	2.73 m (9 ft.)
Weight:	Gross, 1,630 kg (3,600 lb.)
	Empty, 930 kg (2,050 lb.)
Engine:	Wright J-4, 220 hp

The "All-Purpose Monoplane" of Sherman Mills Fairchild, despite its unassuming appearance, was designed for aerial photography. It was such a success that it was also used as a light transport in the Canadian bush country, in the jungles and mountains of South America, and on the Antarctic continent.

Sherman Fairchild was an important designer, builder, and user of aerial cameras in the early 1920s. None of the aircraft then available met the requirements of his work. His criteria for a usable airplane included a wide field of view for the pilot and photographer and stability for high-altitude camera work. The ability to operate out of small, rough fields and the space to accommodate the bulky contemporary cameras were also important.

Norm MacQueen was Fairchild's engineer. Fred Weymouth, Professor Alexander Klemin, Fairchild chief pilot Dick Depew, and chief photographer E. P. Lott assisted in the design.

The resulting aircraft was the Fairchild FC-1,

The museum's exhibit aircraft NC6853 is shown here fully restored in the markings of Pan American-Grace Airways (Panagra). (Photo: SI A1830)

which first flew on June 14, 1926, for twenty-three minutes. It was powered by the then standard Curtiss OX-5 engine. The airplane had a closed, heated cabin, which was unusual for the time. The fuselage narrowed at the pilot's window, and V-shaped struts supported a semicantilever wing. An unusual three-longeron structure gave rise to the "razor back" nickname; later models with a more conventional four-longeron structure were called "turtle back."

A unique feature of the Fairchild monoplane, however, was that the wings folded for easier storage and road mobility. The folding operation was simple—two men in two minutes could fold the 44-foot span into a 13-foot compact unit. Unfolding took about the same amount of time. A large Yale padlock hung down in clear view of the pilot to show that the wings were locked in place.

The criteria that produced a fine camera plane also produced an aircraft adaptable for a number of other purposes. The FC-1 flew in the Ford

Reliability Tour in 1926 and attracted attention. Casey Jones, veteran airman and proprietor of the Curtiss Flying Service, ordered several Fairchilds for his operation. His interest in the Fairchild was regarded as significant by aircraft buyers.

The first production model of the Fairchild was the FC-2. The Curtiss OX-5 was replaced by the more powerful Wright J-4 engine, which became a major factor in the success of the FC-2.

The first FC-2 off the production line was procured by the U.S. Department of Commerce and was used to accompany Lindbergh on his goodwill tour of the United States in the *Spirit of St. Louis*.

Float-equipped FC-2s were used extensively in the demanding Canadian bush country. In the United States, Colonial Air Transport flew FC-2s.

A number of Fairchilds were used in significant and record-breaking flights. The Fairchild FC-2 *La Niña*, piloted by Cy Caldwell, delivered Pan American's first contract airmail by proxy. The *City of New York*, piloted by Charles Collyer and carrying J. H. Mears, made an around-the-world trip in 1928. The plane flew over the land areas, but was carried across the oceans by ship. Another FC-2 made the first New York-Miami nonstop flight in January 1928.

The most famous individual Fairchild, however, was the FC-2W *Stars and Stripes*, which was the first airplane to fly on the continent of Antarctica. It was left in the ice at the end of the first expedition, but was recovered, refurbished, and flown four years later by the second expedition. Much of the aircraft was later used to supply parts for other FC-2s, but portions of it are now in the collection of the National Air and Space Museum.

The museum's FC-2, NC6853, represents the first service airplane of Pan American-Grace Airways (Panagra) in 1929. Aircraft of this type, possibly the museum specimen, flew the first Peruvian Airway flight from Lima to Talara, Peru, on September 13, 1928. This same plane is also thought to have made the first international airmail and passenger flight between Lima and Guayaquil, Ecuador. It was sent to the National Air and Space Museum in 1949, from Lima, by Panagra.
Michael E. Dobson

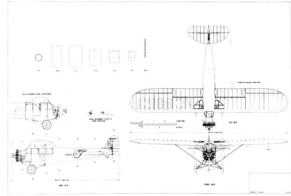

Focke-Achgelis Fa-330

Rotor diameter: 7.32 m (24 ft.)
Length: 4.09 m (13 ft. 5 in.)
Weight: Gross, 170 kg (375 lb.)
Empty, 80 kg (180 lb.)

In the fall of 1941, heeding the pleas of U-boat commanders to develop a method to aid their long-range visibility when surfaced, the Focke-Achgelis company began construction of a type of rotary wing glider. This new aircraft was designed to carry one observer/pilot, and was pulled along behind the submarine by a cable. It was equipped with a telephone communication system to the boat.

Construction took place at the Weser Flugzeugwerke at Delmenhorst, Germany. The first test flight was made in the spring of 1942, with experimental flights from ships following that summer. By early fall, production began; some 200 Fa-330s were constructed before the end of World War II. Their use was restricted in the later years of the war, however, because it was discovered that they could be detected by radar.

The collapsible little aircraft was constructed of steel tubing with a rudder extending from the rear of the airframe. A three-bladed rotor was mounted on a pylon behind the pilot's seat. The pilot had a brake to control the speed of the rotor and a foot pedal to operate the rudder.

The rotor was started with a rope or, if there was enough wind, by hand. Normally, only two men were needed to assist with takeoff. Once aloft, the aircraft's velocity was determined by the speed of the wind plus the speed of the U-boat. Information and directions were relayed back and forth through the telephone system.

The U-boat carried enough cable to raise the Fa-330 to a height of 700 feet; most often it flew at between 200 and 500 feet.

To bring the aircraft back down, seamen turned a winch that brought in the cable. In case of an emergency, the pilot could operate a lever that released the entire rotor assembly. This action pulled free the parachute stored on the pylon behind the pilot. The latter then released his seat belt, and the fuselage followed the rotor assembly into the sea.

The Fa-330 could be easily dismantled and assembled by a very few men. When not in use, it was stored in a special watertight hatch.

Pilots of these aircraft were U-boat seamen, who had never flown before. They were trained in a wind tunnel at Chalais-Meudon, France.

The National Air and Space Museum's Fa-330 was received as a transfer from the Department of the Air Force on July 7, 1950.
Claudia M. Oakes

This Focke-Achgelis 330 is being towed into flight for a test over land.
(Photo: SI 74-2175)

Easily seen in this close-up photograph are the parts of the FA-330.
(Photo: SI 74-2695)

The National Air and Space Museum's FA-330 is assembled and ready for exhibit.
(Photo: SI 76-16035)

Fokker D.VII

Wingspan:	Upper, 8.93 m (29 ft. 3½ in.)
	Lower, 6.86 m (22 ft. 10 in.)
Length:	7.01 m (23 ft.)
Height:	2.82 m (9 ft. 3 in.)
Weight:	Gross, 878 kg (1,936 lb.)
	Empty, 700 kg (1,540 lb.)
Engine:	Mercedes, 160 hp, or BMW, 185 hp

In January 1918, late into World War I, a competition of single-seat fighter designs was held at Johannisthal Aerodrome near Berlin to select an aircraft that would lead Germany's planned 1918 offensive. The winner of the competition was the Fokker Flugzeugwerke's D.VII, which earned the reputation of being the best German fighter of the war.

The D.VII, designed by Reinhold Platz, was a clean, simple-looking biplane, equipped with two Maxim 08/15 7.92mm-machine guns, manufactured at Spandau. The wings had fabric-covered plywood ribs and plywood leading edges, with no external bracing wires. The fuselage was wire-braced steel tubing, completely fabric covered except for the cowling. Mercedes 160-hp and BMW 185-hp engines proved to be the most successful for the aircraft.

Speed, however, was not a factor in its success, as even with the 185-hp BMW its top speed was only 124 mph. But it had the capability of holding a steep climb without stalling, making it lethal in a rear attack from below, and it could attain and maintain high altitudes from which to drop down on unsuspecting Allied aircraft.

Because of the great demand for D.VIIs at the

The Fokker D.VII U.10, which was captured November 9, 1918, is now in the National Air and Space Museum's collection. (Photo: SI A9852K)

front, they were manufactured not only by the Fokker factory at Schwerin but also by the Albatros Werke and the Ostdeutsche Albatros Werke.

In May 1918 the first D.VIIs were delivered to the front and were assigned to Jagdgeschwader (Jasta) Nr. I, the Von Richthofen "Circus," in time for their use in the Second Battle of Aisne. Most of the Jastas were equipped with the new aircraft by the fall, and their overwhelming success was proven by the increase in the number of victories in 1918—from 217 in April to 565 in August. The Allies so greatly esteemed and feared the D.VII that the surrender of all these aircraft was part of their Armistice terms.

The National Air and Space Museum's specimen, the U.10, has an interesting history. On November 9, 1918, two days before the Armistice, this D.VII had landed on a small airstrip that had been reopened by the U.S. Air Service just the week before, behind the front lines to the east of Verdun. The three American airmen there, Capt. Alex H. McLanahan, Lt. Edward P. Curtis, and Lt. Sumner Sewall, rushed out and apprehended the pilot, Lt. Heinz von Beaulieu-Marconnay, before he could burn the airplane. The mood of the captured pilot seemed one of hopelessness about the war,

The D.VII is the featured aircraft in the museum's World War I Aviation gallery.
(Photo: SI 80–2085)

Armament for NASM's D.VII consists of two Maxim 08/15 7.92-mm machine guns.
(Photo: SI 71-2317)

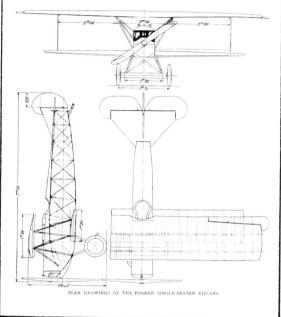

PLAN DRAWINGS OF THE FOKKER SINGLE-SEATER BIPLANE

Hermann Goering flew an all-white D.VII in World War I.
(Photo: SI A44862)

possibly because his brother, a German ace, had died of wounds only a few days earlier. Nevertheless, the American SPADs had been hangared out of sight, and the pilot's claim that he had landed by mistake was plausible.

The Fokker had been manufactured a few months earlier in the Albatros plant at Schneidemuhl. To its factory finish had been added a cryptic marking—a large "U.10" on the side. It is believed that the U.10 represented Lieutenant von Beaulieu-Marconnay's former cavalry unit, the Tenth Uhlans. The "kicking mule" insignia of the U.S. 95th Aero Squadron was painted on the aircraft after its capture.

The Smithsonian acquired the aircraft from the War Department in 1920.

Claudia M. Oakes

Fokker T-2

Wingspan:	24.26 m (79.57 ft.)
Length:	15.00 m (49.20 ft.)
Height:	3.71 m (12.17 ft.)
Weight:	Gross, 4,922 kg (10,850 lb.)
Engine:	Liberty V-12, 420 hp

In 1920 travel across the continental United States was usually by train, occasionally by automobile, or possibly even by a series of short flights in open-cockpit biplanes. The nonstop transcontinental flight was still in the future, but not far in the future. The plane that was to accomplish this feat was built in the Netherlands in 1921, designed by Reinhold Platz, chief constructor for the Netherlands Aircraft Company (Fokker) of Veere, Netherlands. The Fokker F.IV transport monoplane was the third successful transport built by Fokker following World War I. The name Fokker was, of course, well known, because of the success of the Fokker fighters built for Germany during that war.

Only two F.IVs were built, both purchased in 1922 by the U.S. Air Service. One, the A-2, was fitted out as an ambulance plane, and in addition competed in a few races; the other, the T-2, was fitted as a transport. During the engineering tests of these planes at McCook Field, Dayton, Ohio, the project test pilot, Lt. Oakley G. Kelly, proposed that the T-2 be modified to enable it to fly nonstop across the United States. This had never been successfully accomplished despite several attempts.

After the proposed transcontinental flight had been approved, Lt. John A. Macready, another test pilot, was chosen as copilot, and the T-2 was modified for the flight. The wing center section was strengthened by the addition of plywood face plates on the spars. The normal 130-gallon fuel tank, located in the leading edge of the wing, was retained and supplemented by a 410-gallon tank in the wing center section and a 185-gallon fuselage-mounted fuel tank.

The original four-wheel landing gear was modified by fitting wheels and tires from a Martin MB bomber, and a bench type seat and an auxiliary set of controls were installed at the rear of the cabin. The single 400-hp Liberty V-12 engine was mounted off-set to the right of the center line of the aircraft, which enabled the pilot and the controls to be placed next to the engine on the left side of the fuselage nose. All engine controls were mounted directly on the engine.

The first two attempts started from San Diego to take advantage of prevailing winds and to use the California refined fuel, which had a higher natural octane rating than other fuels then available. On the first flight, fog conditions in the mountain passes 50 miles east of San Diego forced Kelly and Macready to turn back. They remained aloft, however, for an unofficial endurance record, and at the same time checked the performance of the

The National Air and Space Museum acquired the T-2 in 1924 from the War Department.
(Photo: SI A45288B)

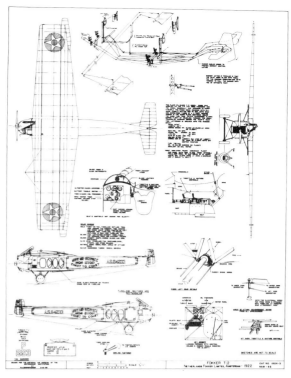

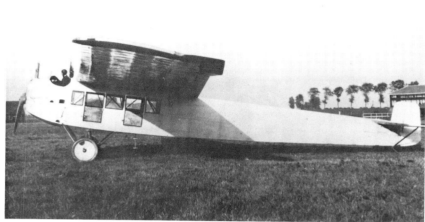

The great army Monoplane T-2, piloted by Lieutenants Kelly and Macready, landed in San Diego in the record-breaking time of 26 hours and 50 minutes from the time they left Hempstead, Long Island. A speed of more than 100 miles an hour was maintained in the first successful non-stop transcontinental flight. That Lieutenants Kelly and Macready chose PENNZOIL for safe lubrication of their Liberty 12 is the unanswerable testimonial for its SUPREME PENNSYLVANIA QUALITY.

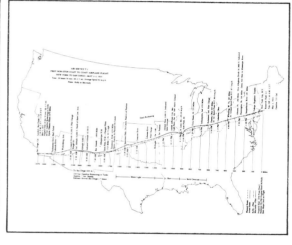

The original version of the T-2, the F.IV, was intended as a commercial transport. The T-2 itself was built in late 1921 in the Fokker factory at Veere, Island of Walchern, Netherlands, and was one of two F.IVs delivered to the U.S. Army on June 30, 1922.
(Photo: SI A47482)

This map shows the route followed by Kelly and Macready on their flight.
(Photo: SI A49911)

After the T-2's record flight, the Pennzoil Company used this poster in its advertising campaign. (Pennzoil was used in the aircraft.) Inset, Lt. Oakley G. Kelly at right and Lt. John A. Macready at left.
(Photo: SI A45789F)

aircraft and the fuel and oil consumption. The second flight ended at Fort Benjamin Harrison, near Indianapolis, when a cracked water jacket caused the engine to seize.

The third flight began at Roosevelt/Hazelhurst Fields, Long Island, on May 2, 1923. Using California refined fuel shipped to Roosevelt Field for this flight, they made a precarious takeoff, followed by a low level flight until they had climbed to reasonable flight altitudes. Mechanical problems with the voltage regulator threatened to cancel the flight soon after takeoff; however, Lieutenant Kelly disassembled the regulator and repaired it in flight. At the same time, Lieutenant Macready held the plane on course, using the rear controls, though the awkward positioning of these auxiliary controls made it difficult to fly for any length of time. Kelly was pilot until they reached McCook Field, at

which time he crawled back to the rear of the cabin, past the cabin fuel tank, after which Macready reversed the procedure, moving forward to take over the pilot's controls. There were five such transfers during the 2,470-mile flight.

The plane droned steadily, but slowly, westward through the night and passed through solid overcast and light rain, making navigation very uncertain. At daylight they were delighted to discover that they were almost directly on their planned course. Shortly after noon on May 3, the T-2, now piloted by Macready, made a diving turn over San Diego and headed directly for Rockwell Field, landing at 12:26 after 26 hours, 50 minutes, and 38 ⅖ seconds enroute, flying at an average speed of 92 mph.
Louis S. Casey

Ford 5-AT Tri-motor

Wingspan:	23.71 m (77 ft. 10 in.)
Length:	15.18 m (49 ft. 10 in.)
Height:	4.16 m (13 ft. 8 in.)
Weight:	Gross, 5,738 kg (12,650 lb.)
	Empty, 3,470 kg (7,650 lb.)
Engines:	Pratt and Whitney Wasps, 420 hp

One of the most important events in the selling of aviation to the general public was the entry of Henry Ford into aircraft manufacturing. The Ford automobile was at the time the symbol of reliability, and it followed in the minds of a good many people that a Ford airplane would be safe to fly. And it was. The Ford Tri-motor was a rugged, dependable transport airplane, which won a permanent place in aviation history.

The story of the Ford Tri-motor begins with William B. Stout, an engineer who had previously designed several aircraft using principles similar to those of Professor Hugo Junkers, the famous German manufacturer.

Stout, a bold and imaginative salesman, sent a mimeographed form letter to leading manufacturers, blithely asking for $1,000 and adding: "For your one thousand dollars you will get one definite promise: You will never get your money back." Stout raised $20,000, including $1,000 each from Edsel and Henry Ford.

The two Fords became very interested in air transportation, and in April 1925 the Ford Motor Company started an experimental air freight service between Detroit and Chicago. In August of that year, Ford purchased the Stout Metal Airplane Company.

Up to this point, Stout airplanes used a single engine. The introduction of the lightweight Wright air-cooled radial engine, however, set Stout and his design team onto a new course: a three-engine airplane.

The first Ford Tri-motor was retroactively designated 3-AT (for Air Transport). It was an unsightly airplane, which could not be landed power-off because of the terrible air-flow patterns generated by its unusually positioned engines. A mysterious fire broke out in the factory in January 1926, after the third flight of the 3-AT, destroying that airplane and others of Stout's. The 3-AT was dropped from further development, and proved to be Stout's last major design effort with Ford.

The National Air and Space Museum's Ford Tri-motor is a 5-AT-B, shown here taking off during its public relations career.
(Photo: SI A268E)

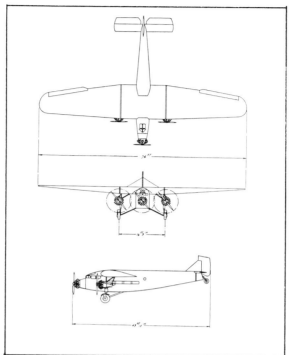

The first production version of the Ford Tri-motor was the 4-AT.
(Photo: SI A48737C)

Ford Tri-motors were used on the first transcontinental route. Transcontinental Air Transport (TAT) later became TWA.
(Photo: SI A531A)

The 3-AT was the first Ford Tri-motor. Note the unusual position of the engines.
(Photo: SI A48738E)

(Diagram: Courtesy Aerospace Industries Association of America, Inc.)

A team of engineers began work on the 4-AT, which was the prototype for the classic Ford Tri-motor design. While it bore more than a superficial resemblance to contemporary Fokker products, the Ford had two overwhelming advantages for the domestic market: the Ford name and all-metal construction.

The first 4-AT made its maiden flight on June 11, 1926. By the time Ford stopped producing aircraft in 1933, 199 Ford Tri-motors had been built. More than one hundred airlines flew the Ford in the United States, Canada, Mexico, Central and South America, Europe, Australia, and China.

Increasing airline use and the availability of the new Pratt and Whitney 420-hp Wasp engine led to the 5-AT model in the summer of 1928. The 5-AT became the most famous of the Ford Tri-motor designs. Two other types, the 8-AT and 14-AT, did not go beyond prototype status.

The Ford Tri-motor is an inherently stable airplane, designed to fly well on two engines and to maintain level flight on one. Its rugged construction and ability to operate from grass and dirt airstrips have kept the Tri-motor in operation. Island Airlines of Port Clinton, Ohio, still flies a Ford in its daily operation on scheduled sight-seeing trips.

The museum's Ford Tri-motor is a 5-AT-B, NC9683, donated by American Airlines. Its long and varied history began when it was sold to Southwest Air Fast Express (SAFE) on April 12,

1929, the thirty-ninth 5-AT built by Ford. It sold for $55,475 in cash. American Airlines bought out SAFE the following year, acquiring the Tri-motor in the process. During 1931, NC9683 flew the routes of Colonial Air Transport, a division of American. Later, it flew on the transcontinental route between Cleveland and Los Angeles. In May 1934 it was transferred to the Chicago base until it was retired from American in 1935.

In 1936 the airplane was sold to TACA International Airlines, and operated in Nicaragua for several years. In 1946 NC9683 was sent to Mexico, where it was used for passenger and cargo hauling until 1954, When it was resold to a crop-dusting company in Montana.

During its operations with the crop-dusting company the airplane also flew a cargo route in Alaska until it was resold in Mexico. It finally ended up beside a small airfield in Oaxaca, in use as someone's living quarters. A wood-burning stove had been installed, and a chimney stuck through the aluminum roof.

Reacquired by American Airlines, NC9683 was fully restored and was flown on public relations tours throughout the country, including the first regular flight departing from Dulles International Airport, Virginia, in November 1962. At the close of its public relations career, it was donated to the National Air and Space Museum, where it hangs in the Air Transportation gallery.
Michael E. Dobson

Gates Learjet Model 23

Wingspan:	10.80 m (35 ft. 7 in.)
Length:	13.20 m (43 ft. 3 in.)
Height:	3.80 m (12 ft. 7 in.)
Weight:	Gross, 5,783 kg (12,750 lb.)
	Empty, 2,790 kg (6150 lb.)
Engines:	2 General Electric CJ 610-1 turbojets, 1293 kg (2850 lb.) thrust each

Airliners powered by jet engines had just begun to establish their value to airline transport service in 1959, as William P. Lear, Sr., initiated the development of the Learjet. Under his direction, this small, fast airplane was built, flown, and demonstrated to have the combination of form and function that makes an outstanding performer and a masterpiece of aviation design.

The first Learjets were pioneers in the entirely new field of business and personal jet aviation. These were the Model 23 Continentals, the founding products of the original Learjet Corporation and subsequently, after April 1967, of the Gates Learjet Corporation, as the company is known today. The Learjet that is in the collection of the National Air and Space Museum, with federal registration number N802L, is the second aircraft of this type built, and the first of the production model 23s.

On October 7, 1963, the first flight of a Learjet was made by the prototype Model 23, N801L. This original airplane flew 194 hours during 167 separate flights until it was unfortunately destroyed following a test flight in June 1964.

N802L completed its maiden flight of 1 hour, 30 minutes on March 5, 1964, and was retained by the factory for continued testing and modification

analysis until it was retired from flight on June 17, 1966. Throughout this period, a total of 1,127 flying hours were logged during 864 flights. Although a significant phase in the working life of this aircraft had come to an end, N802L continued to perform as a full-scale wind-tunnel model with the National Aeronautics and Space Administration. Following this, the aircraft was returned to the factory at Wichita, Kansas, and restored for donation to the National Air and Space Museum, where it was received on October 11, 1977.

With the cross-continent flight of a Model 23 on May 21, 1965, Learjets began to set formally recognized performance records. On this particular flight, pilots John M. Conroy and Clay Lacey, flying with five observers, covered 5,005 statute miles from Los Angeles to New York and back in 11 hours, 36 minutes.

On December 14, 1965, another Model 23, flown by Henry Beaird and Ronald G. Puckett, with five other persons on board, left Wichita to climb to and reach an altitude of 40,000 feet in 7 minutes, 21 seconds. With an engine thrust-to-weight ratio of 1:2.2 pounds, a Model 23 can outclimb an F-100 Super Sabre to 10,000 feet, and this aircraft can be just as impressive on the way down.

Both the success of the basic Model 23 design

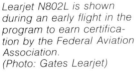

Learjet N802L is shown during an early flight in the program to earn certification by the Federal Aviation Association.
(Photo: Gates Learjet)

Learjet Model 23 prototype
(N801L) and the second
Learjet N802L share air-
space over Kansas during
test program.
(Photo: Gates Learjet)

(Diagram: Courtesy Gates
Learjet)

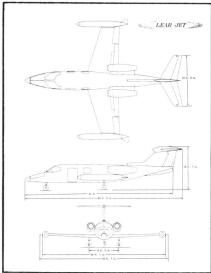

Learjet Model 24 is shown
during the May 1966 re-
cord-setting around-the-
world flight. This is a refueling stop at Santa Maria, the
Azores, 10 hours after takeoff from Wichita.
(Photo: Gates Learjet)

and the expansion of the corporate and personal jet market inspired a number of derivative models with increased range, size, and speed.

Between May 23–26, 1966, the first Model 24 flew around the world to set or break eighteen international aviation records. With Henry Beaird as pilot-in-command, Rick King and John O. Lear as alternates, and John Zimmerman as an observer, the flight of this aircraft covered a straight line distance of 22,992.8 statute miles in 50 hours, 39 minutes of flight. This was the one-hundred-fifth production Learjet built.

Between May 17–19, 1976, during the American Bicentennial year, Arnold Palmer and James Bir flew a Model 36 from Denver, Colorado, to set a speed record around the world. The flight time over a specifically recognized course was 48 hours, 48 minutes for an average speed of 400.23 mph.

Flying a Model 28 on February 19–20, 1979, Neil Armstrong set five world speed records for an aircraft of this class. Two of them for altitude achieved, two for sustained flight at 51,000 feet, and one for high-altitude time-to-climb.

Performance is a direct result of design and construction, and the design of the Model 23 was based on the known structural quality of a Swiss strike-fighter, the AFA P-16. The cabin of this smallest model seats up to nine persons, including pilots, and may be fully pressurized. The windshield and cabin windows are formed of stretched, laminated acrylic plastic. The ailerons, elevators, and rudder are mechanically connected to the cockpit controls, while all trim surfaces are

electrically operated. There is a small tab on the left aileron for roll and one on the rudder for yaw. The incidence angle of the horizontal stabilizer is changed for pitch trim control. The aircraft has spoilers for speed control on the upper surface of each wing panel forward of the flaps. These are actuated by hydraulic pressure, as is the fully retractable landing gear and multiple disc brakes on the dual mail wheels.

As a matter of aerodynamic design the fuselage narrows at each side as the wing and engine nacelles extend outward. This is a design concept known as "area rule" and is used to smooth the flow of air around these projections during high-speed flight.

Construction of N802L began on October 23, 1964, with work on the tail group. This was sixteen days after the first flight of the prototype. Just 135 days later N802L had been assembled and flown. On June 15, 1966, during testing of an experimental control-system modification, this aircraft encountered severe vibrations, which brought the decision to retire it from flight.

N802L was a technological advance and a research tool significantly involved in the creation of business jet aviation. As an example of this transportation mode, it represents the ability to cruise above most weather, over long distances, and at high speed. Whether the business jet operates as a small airliner or as a more personal, independent aircraft, it permits the movement of passengers and articles to airports both large and small around the world.

Garry L. Cline

Goodyear "Pilgrim" (gondola)

Width:	Envelope, 12.03 m (39 ft. 6 in.)
	Car, 1.14 m (3 ft. 9 in.)
Length:	Envelope, 33.37 m (109 ft. 6 in.)
	Car, 4.42 m (14 ft. 6 in.)
Height:	Envelope, 13.64 m (44 ft. 9 in.)
	Car, 1.75 m (5 ft. 9 in.)
Diameter:	Envelope, 9.59 m (31 ft. 6 in.)
Weight:	987 kg (2,175 lb.)
Engine:	Lawrence L-4, 60 hp

In the mid-1920s the Goodyear Tire and Rubber Company of Akron, Ohio, built a fleet of small airships that were used to demonstrate lighter-than-air flight and to train future airship pilots. Among these airships was the first ever designed for inflation with helium—the *Pilgrim*.

The *Pilgrim* was completed May 15, 1925, made its first flight June 3 with Jack Yolton as pilot, and was christened on July 18 by Mrs. P. W. Litchfield, wife of the president of Goodyear. It was constructed of magnesium-coated steel-tube framework covered with two-ply, rubberized, aluminum-coated fabric. The envelope had a helium capacity of 55,000 cubic feet. It was powered by a single, Lawrence L-4 60-hp, three-cylinder, air-cooled, engine with a four-blade Reed propeller. Its 40-gallon fuel capacity gave it a range of 525 miles at a speed of 40 mph.

The gondola, which was attached snugly to the envelope, could accommodate one pilot and two passengers in the comfort of blue mohair velour upholstered seats with mahogany finished veneer.

By the time the *Pilgrim* was retired on December 30, 1931, it had made 4,765 flights, carried 5,355 passengers, flown a total of 2,880 hours, and covered 94,974 miles.

The Smithsonian acquired the *Pilgrim* gondola from Goodyear in 1933.

Claudia M. Oakes

The Goodyear Pilgrim *was the first commercial airship designed to use helium. (Photo: SI A46989)*

The Pilgrim *lands atop the M. O'Neil department store in downtown Akron, Ohio, on June 28, 1928. (Photo: Courtesy Goodyear Aerospace Corp.)*

Grumman F6F-3 Hellcat

Wingspan:	13.06 m (42 ft. 10 in.)
Length:	10.24 m (33 ft. 7 in.)
Height:	3.99 m (13 ft. 1 in.)
Weight:	Gross, 6,991 kg (15,413 lb.)
	Empty, 4,152 kg (9,153 lb.)
Engine:	Pratt and Whitney R-2800-10W
	Double Wasp, 2,000 hp

In the first two years of the United States' involvement in World War II, the U.S. Navy did not have an aircraft in its inventory that was as maneuverable as the Japanese Zero fighter. During this time, the Navy and Marine Corps depended on the Grumman F4F Wildcat to bridge this gap until a replacement aircraft could be produced. Earlier, on June 30, 1941, the Navy had placed an order with Grumman Aircraft Company in Bethpage, New York, to produce a new prototype carrier fighter. Two years later, the design efforts of Grumman's engineers resulted in one of the war's most potent fighter aircraft—the Hellcat.

The lines of the little Wildcat provided the foundation for the Hellcat's design. However, Grumman engineers abandoned the round fuselage cross section of the Wildcat and adopted a teardrop-shaped cross section for the Hellcat. This streamlined fuselage would surround the large Pratt and Whitney R-2800-10W Double Wasp engine. The increased load from the engine dramatically increased the wing area of the plane. The Hellcat's backward-rotating folding wing had the largest wing area (334 square feet) of any U.S. fighter aircraft produced during the war. This large square-panel wing was mounted at the minimum angle of

incidence to obtain the least drag in level flight. However, a relatively large angle of attack was required so the Double Wasp engine was mounted with a negative thrust line. The combination of all of these design factors resulted in a tail-down flight attitude.

On June 26, 1942, within a year of the Navy's initial request, Robert L. Hall tested the XF6F-1 equipped with the Wright R-2600 Cyclone. One month later, the second prototype, the XF6F-2, flew powered by the Pratt and Whitney R-2800-10. The Hellcat's design proved an immediate success. Few modifications were made to the production Hellcats from these early prototypes.

The Hellcat first entered combat on August 31, 1943, in a series of raids on Marcus Island. Lt. Richard Loesch was the first pilot to claim an air-to-air victory in the F6F. American pilots now had an aircraft that was faster and almost as maneuverable as their Japanese opponents. The Hellcat's most successful day in combat came on June 19, 1944, during operations in the Mariana Islands. During this air battle that became known as "the Great Marianas Turkey Shoot," the Japanese lost over 270 aircraft compared with 26 lost by the United States. The Hellcat also saw combat in Europe. Hellcats of

A patrol of Hellcats. Note the tail-down flight attitude. (Photo: SI 43541-H)

the Royal Navy's Fleet Air Arm escorted Fairey Barracudas during raids on the German battleship *Tirpitz*, hidden in a Norwegian fjord. They also were flown by American pilots over the invasion beaches in southern France during Operation Anvil. During the war pilots flying Hellcats destroyed over 5,100 enemy aircraft, compared with 270 Hellcats lost in combat—a ratio of 19:1.

The Air and Space Museum's Hellcat, Bureau Number 41834, rolled off the Grumman assembly line on February 4, 1944. The airplane's service life began on February 27, 1944, when it was assigned to VF-15 in San Diego, California. No. 41834 and VF-15 departed San Diego on *U.S.S. Hornet* on February 29, 1944, for Pearl Harbor. Here the Museum's Hellcat served as a training and patrol aircraft. Because of the wear and tear placed on the Hellcat by the rigorous training schedule, the aircraft was sent to the Navy's Assembly and Repair Department at the Alameda Naval Air Station. Following the war the aircraft served as an unmanned target drone in a training and maintenance unit. One of the Hellcat's last flights occurred on July 1, 1946, when the plane monitored radioactivity over the Bikini Island nuclear test sight. On November 3, 1948, the Navy transferred Hellcat No. 41834 to the Smithsonian.

The staff and volunteers from the Grumman Aerospace Company restored the Hellcat for the Smithsonian. The plane was painted with the markings of an F6F that served in VF-5 off the *U.S.S. Yorktown*. The aircraft was painted in the Navy's tricolor camouflage, sea blue, intermediate blue, and insignia white, with the U.S. insignia enclosed in a red border.

Smithsonian's Hellcat. The F6F of the National Air and Space Museum on display in 1984.
(Photo: SI 85-16191-17)

The Hellcat was one of the most successful U.S. fighters to serve during the war. Stable flight characteristics made it extremely popular with its pilots. By the war's end, 12,275 Hellcats had been built. During its short but successful career, the Hellcat was flown by 305 aces, more than any other operational American fighter during the war.
Alex M Spencer

Hellcat ready for launch. Deck handlers prepare to remove the chocks as a Hellcat runs up its engine for takeoff.
(Photo: U.S. Navy)

Grumman FM-1 (F4F-4) Wildcat

Wingspan:	11.58 m (38 ft.)
Length:	8.77 m (28 ft. 9 in.)
Height:	4.52 m (9 ft. 2½ in.)
Weight:	Gross, 3,607 kg (7,952 lb.)
	Empty, 2,612 kg (5,758 lb.)
Engine:	Pratt and Whitney R-1830-86, 1,200 hp

When war broke out in the Pacific, the Grumman F4F Wildcat was the basic fighter aircraft of the U.S. Navy and Marine Corps. By 1942 all American fighter squadrons were equipped with the F4F-4, as the folding-wing version of the Wildcat was designated. These planes held the line in the Pacific for the first two years of World War II, although often outnumbered and pitted against aircraft of superior performance.

The Wildcat's basic opponent was the Japanese Zero, a fighter that could outmaneuver and outperform it, but the Wildcat's heavy armament and solid construction gave it an advantage in the hands of skilled pilots.

The original design of the new F4F series was a cleaned-up version of its predecessor, the chunky F3F biplane fighter. This newer biplane never left the drawing board, however, since there was a rapid appreciation of the superiority of monoplane design. Brewster Aeronautical Corporation came forward in the Navy's 1938 fighter design competition with a carrier-based monoplane, the F2A Buffalo. Competing against Grumman's first single-wing fighter design, the Brewster entry won the Navy contract for the new carrier-based fighter.

Still having confidence in their basic design, Grumman engineers reworked the F4F and came up with a greatly improved model superior in performance to the Brewster F2A. The Grumman design was accepted, and quantity production contracts from the Navy were awarded.

Production models were not only provided to the U.S. Navy and Marine Corps but also to the French, who were in dire need of aircraft of all kinds. When France capitulated, its production contracts were taken over by the British Purchasing Commission. The F4F, called the Martlet by the British, served with the Fleet Air Arm. The Martlet gained the distinction of becoming the first U.S. aircraft in British service to shoot down a German aircraft in World War II, its victim being a Junkers JU.88.

In the Pacific, the Wildcat first drew blood in the defense of Wake Island in December 1941. When the attack on the island began on December 8, Marine Fighter Squadron VMF-211 lost eight of its twelve F4F-3 Wildcats on the opening day. The remaining four were flown continuously, fighting

This Grumman-designed FM-1 is about to be catapulted from the deck of the escort carrier U.S.S. Breton somewhere in the Pacific in mid-1943. The camouflage and markings of the National Air and Space Museum's Wildcat are patterned after this operational fighter.
(Photo: National Archives 80-G-82593)

In 1975 volunteers at the Grumman Aerospace Corporation restored the museum's Wildcat to factory freshness and nearly flyable condition.
(Photo: Grumman, 751774)

heroically for two weeks, breaking up many air attacks and sinking a cruiser and a submarine with 100-pound bombs before the last two Wildcats were destroyed on December 22, the day the Japanese landed on Wake.

Despite similar losses throughout the Pacific, this tough little fighter had a kill average for the war of nearly seven-to-one.

A new Grumman fighter, the F6F Hellcat, loomed as the replacement, but the Navy still needed the Wildcat to equip the small escort carriers, for which it was well suited in size and weight.

To make room for production of the Hellcat at the Grumman plant, Wildcat manufacture was transferred to the Eastern Aircraft Division of General Motors. These fighters emerged with the designations FM-1 and FM-2.

The Wildcat in the National Air and Space Museum, bureau number 15392, is the four-hundredth FM-1 built in Linden, New Jersey. It was accepted by the Navy on July 21, 1943. Most of its operational life was spent at Norman, Oklahoma, and after thirteen months of service it was placed in storage and deleted from Navy records to await future museum needs.

In 1974 the Grumman Aerospace Corporation accepted the task of restoring the Wildcat for exhibit in the new National Air and Space Museum. Former and active members of the company, many of whom had built Wildcats for Grumman during the war, voluntarily worked on the project. Early in 1975 the fighter once again emerged like new and in nearly flyable condition. Its new paint coating duplicated the Navy blue-gray camouflage used early in the war; the markings were patterned after an FM-1, number E-10, that operated from the CVE U.S.S. Breton in the Pacific in mid-1943.

A major component missing from this FM-1 when it emerged from storage was its engine ring-cowl. Since a spare could not be located, the Marine Corps Museum loaned the cowling from the Wake Island Memorial, which was disassembled around 1965. Although smoothed over on the outside, battle damage is still very evident on the inside of this assembly. This historic cowling from a Wildcat that had the earliest encounter with the enemy adds even greater significance to the museum's airplane by perpetuating the Wake Island Memorial, "dedicated to the gallant Marine, Naval, Army, and Civilian personnel who defended Wake against overwhelming Japanese invasion armadas, 8 thru 23 December 1941."

Robert C. Mikesh

This F4F, called the Martlet by the British, roars down a carrier deck for takeoff.
(Photo: SI A3641)

This engine ring cowl, formerly part of the Wake Island Memorial, now serves as a replacement for the one missing from the museum's Wildcat. It is a lasting memorial to the gallant defenders of that island in December 1941.
(Photo: U.S. Marine Corps)

Wildcats were the exclusive carrier-based fighter aircraft for the U.S. Navy in the first years of the war in the Pacific. Grumman was noted for its stubby fighter designs.
(Photo: Smithsonian Institution)

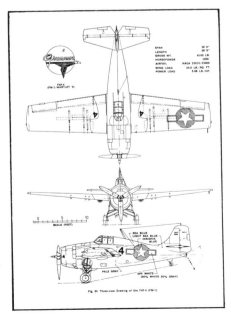

Grumman G-21 Goose

Wingspan:	15 m (49 ft.)
Length:	11.7 m (38 ft. 4 in.)
Height:	3.7 m (12 ft.)
Weight:	Gross, 3,630 kg (8,000 lb.)
	Empty, 2,486 kg (5,475 lb.)
Engines:	Two Pratt and Whitney Wasp Jr. SB-2s, 450 hp each

Affectionately nicknamed "Goose," the G-21 was Grumman's first monoplane to fly, its first twin-engined aircraft, and its first aircraft to enter commercial airline service. This remarkably versatile amphibian has served for over fifty years in a variety of roles that have confirmed the strength and durability of its original design.

The inspiration for the G-21 came from a syndicate of ten wealthy New York businessmen and aviators led by Wilton Lloyd-Smith who were seeking a replacement for the Loening Air Yacht they used to commute from their Long Island homes to their offices in Manhattan. In 1936 they approached Grover Loening, who declined but suggested that the syndicate contact the Grumman Aircraft Engineering Corporation, for which Loening consulted and which he had helped finance. Leroy Grumman accepted and immediately went to work with designer and company cofounder William Schwendler, as well as hydrodynamicist Ralston Stalb to build the new G-21 amphibian "air yacht."

The outline of the new design emerged quickly, revealing a stubby yet graceful aircraft. Constructed of 24ST Alclad aluminum, the G-21 was an all-metal, high-winged monoplane powered by two 450-horsepower Pratt and Whitney Wasp Jr. nine-cylinder, air-cooled radial engines mounted on the leading edge of the high-set wings. The deep fuselage served also as a hull and was equipped with hand-cranked retractable landing gear. Inside the cabin was room for four to six passengers and a flight crew of two. Depending on the level of comfort desired by the individual customer, the G-21 could be fitted with a galley and a lavatory. Floats were suspended beneath each wing and a conventional cruciform tail section installed.

On May 29, 1937, the G-21 completed its first test flight, piloted by Robert L. Hall and Bud Gillies from Grumman's Bethpage, New York, factory. Flight trials went smoothly and after a lengthening of the hull step to improve the aircraft's performance on the water, the aircraft was readied for production. The performance of the G-21 was praiseworthy for its time and rivaled commercial airliners in service. With a cruising speed of 290 kilometers per hour (180 miles per hour), the G-21 possessed a range of 1,300 kilometers (800 miles).

On July 3, just five weeks after its maiden flight, the first of twelve G-21s ordered was delivered to its initial customers, Wilton Lloyd-Smith and department store heir Marshall Field III. Soon other wealthy owners were enjoying the exemplary flight

NASM's G-21 during its installation in the Hall of Air Transportation. (Photo: SI 89-19032-28)

characteristics and handling of the G-21 Goose. Among those customers were financiers Henry H. Morgan and E. Roland Harriman, C. W. Deeds of United Aircraft, Colonel McCormick of the *Chicago Tribune*, Boris Sergievsky, test pilot for Sikorsky Aircraft, and Britain's Lord Beaverbrook. In addition, two were purchased by Asiatic Petroleum. Soon these aircraft were modified to G-21A standards with Wasp Jr. SB-2 engines, an increase in certificated gross weight from 7,500 to 8,000 pounds, and a slightly modified hull to reduce water spray.

The popularity of the G-21 spread as its versatility became well-known throughout the aviation community. Soon orders came in to Grumman from airlines, the military, and foreign customers, impressed by the G-21's potential. Lloyd Aereo Boliviano (LAB) was the first airline to purchase the G-21 but did not put it into service. KNILM, the Dutch East Indies subsidiary of KLM, acquired two G-21's and operated them from 1940 until early 1942 when the last one was shot down by the invading Japanese. The coming of World War II prevented the adoption of the Goose on a wider scale by airlines until after the cessation of hostilities.

In 1938, the Royal Canadian Air Force was the first military service to recognize the abilities of the Goose when it ordered one in June of that year, followed soon by orders from the U.S. Army and Navy, as well as the Peruvian Air Force and the Portuguese Navy. During World War II, the Army was the first to order a substantial quantity, operating 26 as OA-9s and OA-13s. The U.S. Navy and Coast Guard operated 169 "Gooses" designated as JRFs in utility, transport, and anti-submarine duty. In total, the air forces and navies of eleven nations have flown the Goose. France flew at least fifteen in combat in Indochina where several JRFs were armed with bombs and machine guns. A total of 345 G-21s were produced by October 1945 when production ended.

While most of the G-21s were quickly phased out of military service after World War II, the Goose renewed its career as an airliner in earnest. Uniquely adapted for travel in virtually any environment, the Goose saw widespread service with small airlines in the Caribbean, California, and Alaska. Among those flying the G-21 were Reeve Aleutian Airways, Alaska Coastal Airlines, Chalk's Flying Service, and Mackey Airlines. Antilles Air Boats was particularly noted for flying the Goose around the Caribbean from their base in St. Croix in the Virgin Islands. Avalon Air Transport (later Catalina Airlines) competed for a while with Catalina Seaplanes, connecting southern California with Catalina Island.

The Goose still flies today, in its original form and also modified with turboprop engines for increased performance. For over fifty years the rugged and versatile G-21 has performed its daily tasks providing much needed service carrying passengers and freight throughout the world.

The Grumman G-21A, c/n 1048, in the National Aeronautical Collection of the National Air and Space Museum was built in 1938 for the Venezuela Oil

Development Branch of the Asiatic Petroleum Company. It was delivered on December 10 without luxury appointments but with special cactus-proof tires for operation in remote areas. It was later sold and flown in Ecuador until 1951 when it was returned to Grumman, refurbished with soundproofing and a camera door, and repainted. In 1954 this aircraft was acquired by Chalk's Flying Service and flown out of Miami, Florida, to the Bahamas. On February 22, 1977, it was acquired by Catalina Airlines. In December 1982, the aircraft was transferred to Warbirds West and eventually acquired by the Naval Aviation Museum, which in turn transferred title of the aircraft to the National Air and Space Museum on June 30, 1983. The aircraft was then restored by Buehler Aviation Research of Fort Lauderdale, Florida, and placed on display in the Hall of Air Transportation in 1989.

F. Robert van der Linden

The G-21 was a rugged aircraft whose portly appearance belied its excellent flying characteristics. (Photo: SI 85-12757)

The U.S. Coast Guard operated the JRF version of the Goose. (Photo: NASM, Arnold Collection A-1064)

The versatility of the G-21 is evident as it is shown here emerging from the water. (Photo: SI 84-18024)

Grumman G-22 "Gulfhawk II"

Wingspan:	Upper, 8.72 m (28 ft. 7 in.)
	Lower, 8.18 m (26 ft. 1 in.)
Length:	7.01 m (23 ft.)
Height:	3.05 m (10 ft.)
Weight:	Cross-country, 1,903 kg (4,195 lb.)
	Aerobatic, 1,625 kg (3,583 lb.)
Engine:	Wright Cyclone R-1820-G1, 1,000 hp

The Grumman Gulfhawk II *was one of the most exciting and versatile aerobatic aircraft of all time.*
(Photo: SI A43509)

One of the most exciting aerobatic aircraft of all time was the Grumman *Gulfhawk II*, built by Grumman in Bethpage, Long Island, for the Gulf Oil Companies. It was delivered to Roosevelt Field, Long Island, in December 1936, to be used by Maj. Alford "Al" Williams, former naval aviator and Marine, who at the time was head of Gulf's aviation department.

This sturdy little biplane nearly matched the F3F standard Navy fighter that was operational at that time. The *Gulfhawk II* was powered by a Wright Cyclone R-1820-GI 1,000-hp engine equipped with a three-blade Hamilton-Standard propeller. The wings, of unequal span and like those of the earlier F2F-1, were constructed of aluminum spars and ribs and were fabric-covered. The fuselage was monocoque construction covered with a 0.032-inch aluminum alloy, and could accommodate only the pilot. Modifications were made in the construction to withstand the high-load factors encountered

The Gulfhawk II *was also used to demonstrate aerial maneuvers to aviation cadets in World War II. (Photo: SI A45297)*

during aerobatics, and the aircraft was equipped for inverted flying for periods of up to half an hour.

The *Gulfhawk II* was painted bright orange, the fuselage having blue trim and the wings black-edged white stripes radiating rearward and outward on the top surface of the upper wing and the bottom surface of the lower wing.

For twelve years, from 1936 to 1948, the plane thrilled many an air show spectator throughout the United States and Europe. It was a feature attraction at such meets as the Cleveland Air Races, the Miami All-America Air Show, and the New York World's Fair, demonstrating percision aerobatics and the then-new technique of "dive bombing."

In 1938 the *Gulfhawk II* was crated and shipped to Europe. Aviation enthusiasts in England, France, Holland, and Germany were treated to Major Williams's daring maneuvers in the colorful little biplane. During this overseas visit the only other person ever to fly the *Gulfhawk II*, the famous German World War I ace Ernst Udet, piloted the aircraft over Germany. In exchange, Major Williams became the first American to fly the vaunted Messerschmitt 109.

The *Gulfhawk II* was also used as a "flying laboratory." A new, pilot's throat microphone was tried out in it in 1937, and during World War II the *Gulfhawk II* was used to test oils, fuels, and lubricants under extreme operating conditions.

Many aviation cadets viewed the aircraft during its three-month tour of flight-training fields in 1943. Major Williams made the tour at the request of Gen. H. H. Arnold to demonstrate airmanship and precision aerobatic flying.

On October 11, 1948, the *Gulfhawk II* made its last flight. At Washington National Airport, Major Williams took his plane through a demonstration of aerobatics, and then taxied to a strip adjacent to the airport administration building, where he shut off the engine and removed the stick, formally decommissioning the historical airplane. It was presented to the Smithsonian Institution, and became part of the National Air and Space Museum's collection.

Claudia M. Oakes

Major Al Williams and the Gulfhawk II. (Photo: SI 73-3245)

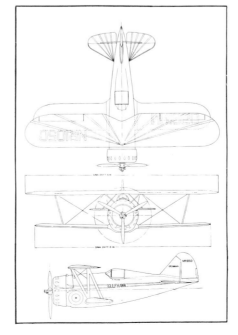

Hawker XV-6A Kestrel

Wingspan:	6.98 m (22 ft. 11 in.)
Length:	12.93 m (42 ft. 5 in.)
Height:	3.28 m (10 ft. 9 in.)
Weight:	Gross, 6,804 kg (15,000 lb.)
	Empty, 4,536 kg (10,000 lb.)
Engine:	Rolls Royce Bristol Engine Div.
	Pegasus 5, 15,500-lb. static thrust

The National Air and Space Museum's Kestrel was donated by NASA in 1974 after having been used in tests at Langley Research Center, Hampton, Virginia. (Photo: NASA)

Designed by Hawker Aviation, Ltd., of Great Britain (now Hawker Siddeley Aviation, Ltd.), the vertical and short takeoff and landing (V/STOL) Kestrel F.G.A. Mk. 1 was an outgrowth of the earlier pioneer Hawker P.1127, whose development began in 1957, and which made its first flight in 1960. The P.1127 was the product of Sir Sidney Camm and Ralph Hooper of Hawker and Dr. Stanley Hooker of the Bristol Engine Company (now Rolls Royce, Bristol Engines Division). It represented a highly innovative and successful approach to vertical flight. While other vertical-flight aircraft utilized rotors (such as helicopters and convertiplanes) or direct jet thrust (such as the "tail-sitting" Ryan X-13 Vertijet), the P.1127 used a special "vectored thrust," turbofan engine in which air from the front fans of the engine was directed through two rotating nozzles, and the exhaust gas from the engines was directed through two additional rotating nozzles. The "cold" nozzles were mounted on the fuselage sides in line with the leading edge, and the "hot" nozzles were also mounted on the fuselage sides, but further back under the midpoint of the wings. By operating a special nozzle control "VTO throttle" in the cockpit,

the pilot could rotate the four nozzles downward, so the exhaust was vectored vertically, and the Kestrel lifted off the ground straight up. The nozzles could also be placed in any intermediate position, so that the aircraft could make a short takeoff. To provide stability during its vertical takeoffs, the Kestrel had a reaction control system whereby compressor bleed air was vented through special shutter valves located in the nose, tail, and wingtips. Once aloft, the pilot manipulated the nozzle control so that the nozzles faced aft, and the Kestrel moved in horizontal flight.

A total of nine Kestrels were built. The National Air and Space Museum's Kestrel contains portions of two of them. The fuselage and tail surfaces are from XS 689, the second Kestrel, and the wing is from XS 694, the seventh Kestrel built. This particular aircraft, NASA 521 (Air Force serial 64-18263), was test flown from 1968 through 1974 by the National Aeronautics and Space Administration (NASA) at Langley Research Center, Hampton, Virginia, under the designation XV-6A. It completed a total of 210 flights. During its NASA test program, test pilots explored the Kestrel's vertical takeoff and landing performance, stability and control

Kestrels of the Tripartite Evaluation Squadron fly over England in 1965. (Photo: Hawker-Siddeley Aviation, Ltd.)

Tests of the Kestrel led to the development of the world's first VTOL jet fighter, the Hawker Harrier. (Photo: NASA)

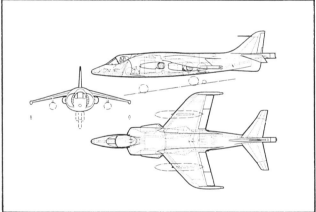

characteristics, and methods of vectoring thrust from the rotating engine nozzles to enhance the airplane's maneuverability while in forward flight.

The first Kestrel made its initial flight on March 7, 1964. The nine Kestrels originally served with a special experimental tripartite Evaluation Squadron at West Raynham, England, composed of American, British, and West German flight-test personnel, who evaluated the aircraft for possible military service. The successful demonstration of the Kestrel led directly to the development of the Hawker Siddeley Harrier G.R. Mk. 1, the world's first operational VTOL jet fighter. This aircraft, the Harrier, is now in service with the Royal Air Force and the U.S. Marine Corps.

Richard P. Hallion

Hiller Flying Platform

The Flying Platform was almost literally a flying carpet, which the pilot controlled principally by shifting his weight instead of using manual or mechanical flight controls.

This small circular vehicle on which the pilot stood used the ducted fan for lift and propulsion. Two engines separately turned two counter-rotating propellers inside a common duct ring to counteract the tendency of the craft to turn. To change heading, the reduction in speed of one engine and propeller caused the craft to turn. Other controls and instruments were virtually unnecessary. To move forward, the standing pilot merely shifted his weight forward, which tilted the craft and propelled it in that direction.

This unorthodox craft was built as a test vehicle by Hiller Helicopters of Palo Alto, California, under the direction of the Office of Naval Research. It had the potential, however, for a number of military applications. Among these were artillery spotting,

scout patrols over otherwise inaccessible terrain, and, if used in large numbers, greater freedom of movement for assault troops.

Designers of the craft hoped that volume production of advanced models would put the "air motorcycle in every family garage."

Control problems associated with this lift principle prevented prolonged travel in a constant direction, for the craft had an inherent tendency to right itself.

Consequently, when the Flying Platform had completed its Office of Naval Research and Army Air Mobility Division test program, it was transferred to the National Air Museum in 1960.

Further development of this propulsion method continued in other forms of aircraft, but the Hiller Flying Platform was the first ducted fan type of VTO (vertical takeoff) aircraft to fly, carrying a man in untethered free flight.

Robert C. Mikesh

*The Hiller Flying Platform, once exhibited in the Vertical Flight gallery, as shown here, is now on display at the museum's Paul E. Garber Preservation, Retoration, and Storage Facility in suburban Maryland.
(Photo: SI 77–6386)*

*The Flying Platform was designed to be an airborne motorcycle for both civil and military use.
(Photo: Hiller Helicopters)*

Hiller XH-44
Hiller-Copter

Rotor diameter:	7.62 m (25 ft.)
Length:	4.06 m (13 ft. 4 in.)
Height:	2.39 m (7 ft. 10 in.)
Weight:	Gross, 640 kg (1,410 lb.)
	Empty, 545 kg (1,200 lb.)
Engine:	Original, Franklin, 90 hp
	Later, Lycoming, 125 hp

It was in December 1942 that seventeen-year-old Stanley Hiller, Jr., started work on his first helicopter, the XH-44. By the time Hiller was nineteen, he was making frequent demonstration flights with a machine of his own design. More significantly, however, this Hiller XH-44 was acclaimed as the first successful helicopter in the United States with twin coaxial counter-rotating blades.

On May 14, 1944, the first untethered successful flight of the XH-44 took place in the University of California stadium. Up to this time, successful helicopters usually had a small tail rotor used for directional control and for counteracting the torque of the main rotor.

Hiller's design was quite different in control principle. The need for the tail rotor was eliminated by the two coaxial blades rotating in opposite directions, which canceled out each other's torque. So successful was his design that Hiller frequently demonstrated the craft's stability with his hands off

Stanley Hiller, Jr., hovers in the XH-44 at the University of California stadium, Berkeley, in 1944. (Photo: Hiller Helicopters)

the controls and extended out the window. Some onlookers dubbed the craft the "Flying Bathtub," since the new craft was so compact in comparison to the gangly appearance of earlier types.

The construction and development of the Hiller-Copter, as it was more properly called, was not a mere home project based on considerable luck, however. Hiller's early interest in model airplane building turned to model cars. Seeing the sales potential in engine-powered model cars, Hiller manufactured a toy car of his design with the backing of his father.

It was while Hiller was involved in operating his company, Hiller Industries, that he became interested in helicopters. Inspired by motion pictures and photographs of recent developments in this type of air vehicle, he bought all the books on helicopter development that he could find. They were extremely few.

Then, Hiller decided to build his own helicopter. His ambition was to eliminate the need for a tail

Six persons made up the original staff of Hiller Aircraft when it was organized in 1942. Stanley Hiller is fourth from left; third from left is Harold Sigler, Hiller's oldest associate. (Photo: Hiller Helicopters)

rotor. He believed it robbed the lifting rotors of too much engine power, estimated at 40 percent, that otherwise could be used for direct lift. He also wished to eliminate the excessive vibration that he believed existed in the conventional helicopters, increasing the control problem and demanding considerable pilot skill.

Young Hiller found that Harold Sigler of his own company's engineering staff was interested in these new concepts. Taking Hiller's ideas, Sigler put them on paper, made them feasible from an engineering standpoint, and contributed much to furthering the helicopter's design.

By December 1943 the craft was completed and had made several tethered experimental flights, but the first free-flight attempt ended in a minor crash. Repairs and corrections were made in the design, and, having achieved success, Hiller gave the first public demonstration of the Hiller-Copter on August 30, 1944, at San Francisco's Marina Green.

In 1945 Hiller formed United Helicopters, Inc., to continue research toward his original goal of producing a practical, simplified low-cost rotary-wing aircraft. From Berkeley, California, he and his growing staff moved to Palo Alto, where they designed and manufactured a number of successful twin- and single-rotor helicopters.

Only one XH-44 was ever built, as follow-on models were of improved design. But the XH-44 Hiller-Copter is unique in other respects besides those already mentioned. It was the first helicopter to be built and successfully flown in the western United States, and it is believed to be the first to use all-metal rotor blades. This bright yellow craft logged more than one hundred hours flying time before it was retired in 1946.

For several years the XH-44 was displayed in Hiller's main production plant in Palo Alto, hanging from the ceiling. In early 1953 this historic "first" in a long line of other successful Hiller helicopters was renovated, and presented to the National Air and Space Museum on May 28. In addition to the craft's historic significance, it serves as an inspiration to the young of challenges that can be met and successes that can be achieved.
Robert C. Mikesh

Success had its setbacks with this mishap in the early stages of free-flight trials of the Hiller-Copter. (Photo: Hiller Helicopters)

A backyard swimming pool serves as a landing spot for the float-equipped XH-44. (Photo: SI 74-4493)

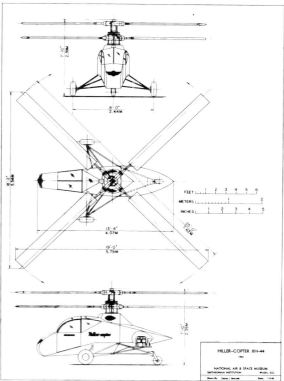

Hughes H-1

Wingspan:	9.67 m (31 ft. 9 in.)
Length:	8.23 m (27 ft.)
Weight:	Gross, 2,495 kg (5,500 lb.)
Engine:	Pratt and Whitney Twin Wasp, Jr., 700 hp

The Hughes H-1 racer was developed to be the fastest landplane in the world. It was designed by Howard Hughes and Richard Palmer and built by Glenn Odekirk. On September 13, 1935, Hughes achieved the design goal by flying the H-1 to a new world speed record of 352.322 mph. The record was set over a specially instrumented course near Santa Ana, California.

Since Hughes did not require a sponsor for the aircraft, the H-1 had no markings except the license number NR258Y (later NX 258Y) in chrome yellow against the dark blue background of the wings, and in black against the doped aluminum rudder. The fuselage was left in its natural polished aluminum finish. The H-1 was powered by a Pratt and Whitney Twin Wasp Junior radial piston engine, which was rated at 700 horsepower at 8,500 feet but which could deliver 1,000 horsepower for high-speed flight. A wind tunnel model of the aircraft was exhaustively tested in the

Howard Hughes stands be-side his airplane, in which he set a world-speed re-cord of 352.322 mph on September 13, 1935, at Santa Ana, California. (Photo: SI A4127OB)

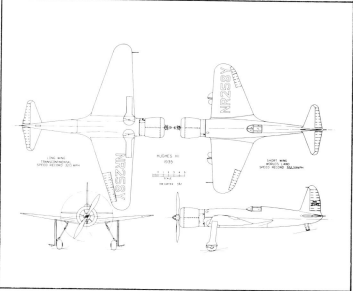

(Diagram by D. W. Carter, Courtesy Racing Planes, vol. 3, by Reed Kinert, by permission of Aero Publishers)

*Piloted by Hughes, the H-1 set a transcontinental speed record of 7 hours, 28 minutes, and 25 seconds on January 20, 1937.
(Photo: SI 41270)*

200-mph wind tunnel at the California Institute of Technology's Guggenheim Aeronautical Laboratory. Actual performance figures for the aircraft closely matched the predicted design performance.

The H-1 had two sets of wings. The wings Hughes used to break the landplane speed record were of a low aspect ratio and shorter than those with which it is now fitted. The wings now fitted on the aircraft span 31 feet, 9 inches, have a moderate-aspect ratio, and were used when Howard Hughes broke the transcontinental speed record in the H-1 on January 19, 1937. Hughes departed Los Angeles before dawn and arrived at Newark Airport, outside New York City, 7 hours, 28 minutes, and 25 seconds later. His average speed over the 2,490-mile course was 332 mph, and this nonstop flight was truly an outstanding accomplishment.

The Hughes H-1 was designed for record-setting purposes, but it also had an impact on the design of high-performance aircraft for years to come. Some of the outstanding design features of the H-1 were:

A closefitting bell-shaped engine cowling to reduce airframe drag and improve engine cooling;
Gently curving wing fillets between the wing and the fuselage to help stabilize the airflow, reduce drag, and prevent potentially dangerous eddying and tail buffeting;
Retractable landing gear to reduce drag and

increase speed and range (typical of everything on the H-1, the landing gear was so perfectly fitted that the gear fairings and doors are difficult to see without looking closely);
All rivets and joints flush with the aircraft's skin and flathead and counter-sunk screws on the plywood wings;
Ailerons designed to droop 15 degrees when the flaps are fully extended to improve lift along the full length of the wing during landing and takeoff;
The pilot sitting in a smoothly faired and totally enclosed cockpit, which had an adjustable canopy windscreen to permit easy entry and exit from the aircraft.

The Hughes H-1 racer was a major milestone aircraft on the road to such radial engine-powered World War II fighters as the American Grumman F6F Hellcat and Republic P-47 Thunderbolt, the Japanese Mitsubishi Type O (Zero), and the German Focke-Wulf FW 190. It demonstrated that properly designed radial-engine aircraft could compete with the lower-drag inline designs despite having larger frontal areas because of their radial engine installations.

The H-1 was kept in the Hughes factory at Culver City, California, until it was donated to the Smithsonian Institution in 1975. It is now exhibited in the Flight Technology gallery of the National Air and Space Museum.

Richard P. Hallion and Claudia M. Oakes

Kellett XO-60

Length:	Blades folded, 7.90 m (25 ft. 11 in.)
Height:	3.09 m (10 ft. 2 in.)
Weight:	Gross, 1,198 kg (2,640 lb.)
Engine:	Jacobs R-915-3, 300 hp

It is not surprising that the military quickly realized the tremendous potential of the autogiro. Such a stable, slow-flying aircraft with the ability to take off and land almost vertically, and the capability of staying close to the ground at slow speeds, made the autogiro almost ideal for observation and liaison missions.

In 1942 the Kellett Autogiro Corporation designed for the Army Air Force an aircraft that would fill such a need. Designated the YO-60, this new aircraft was a "blow-up" of an earlier Kellett autogiro, the YG-1B, which in turn had been based on the Kellett KD-1.

The YO-60 featured two-place tandem seating with the pilot in front and the observer in the rear seat, which could be swiveled to face in either direction. The cockpit was enclosed with transparent sheeting, so designed to give the pilot and observer downward visibility over the fuselage sides while their heads remained within the enclosure. There were also windows in the floor of the fuselage for observation.

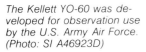

The Kellett YO-60 was developed for observation use by the U.S. Army Air Force. (Photo: SI A46923D)

Several design changes were made in the earlier models to improve stability and performance. Most noticeable were two vertical fins installed on the horizontal stabilizer, which improved directional control over the single fin arrangement. A modified rotor head provided cleaner design and eliminated the need for the interblade cables. The rotor head pylon was shortened and externally braced to the fuselage. This was prompted by a near-fatal accident after a hard landing, when the entire overhead assembly broke loose, causing the rotor blades to strike the autogiro's occupants. The newer blades were thicker and had a constant taper in plan form to improve efficiency and add strength. A change in landing-gear strut length also aided in near-vertical takeoffs by changing the angle of attack for ground takeoff roll.

The YO-60 was powered by a 300-hp Jacobs R-915-3 engine. The rotor blades were driven by the engine prior to takeoff, but were disengaged from the engine during flight.

Seven of these aircraft were built and delivered

The YO-60 had near-vertical takeoff and landing capability.
(Photo: SI A46923A)

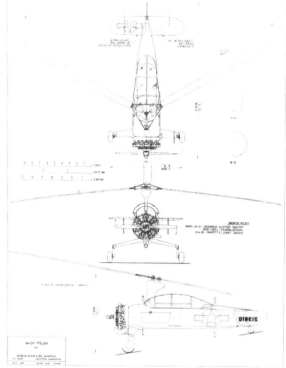

The blades of the YO-60 could be folded back for easier storage and transport.
(Photo: SI A46923C)

to the Army Air Force. Six were accepted in 1943, and went to such diverse bases as Orlando, Florida; Robins, Georgia; Thermal, California; Albuquerque, New Mexico; and Wright Field, Ohio. None, however, were assigned to operational reconnaissance units.

The seventh, designated XO-60, was delivered to Wright Field on December 6, 1944, for test and evaluation at the Wright Air Development Center. From there the aircraft went to Freeman Field, Indiana, a repository for aircraft that would later go into museums. When Freeman Field was closed, the plane was moved to Chicago, where, at the Park Ridge storage depot, it was earmarked for the Smithsonian's National Aeronautical Collection. The Smithsonian officially received it on May 1, 1949.
Claudia M. Oakes

Langley Aerodrome No. 5

Wingspan:	4.2 m (13 ft. 8 in.)
Length:	4.03 m (13 ft. 2 in.)
Height:	1.25 m (4 ft. 1 in.)
Weight:	11.25 kg (25 lb.)
Engine:	Langley, approx. 1 hp

The Langley Aerodrome No. 5 was launched from a houseboat on the Potomac River near Quantico, Virginia, on May 6, 1896. (Photo: SI A18870)

Professor Samuel Pierpont Langley (1834–1906), third Secretary of the Smithsonian Institution, was one of the first major aeronautical figures in the United States.

He started serious investigations in flight in 1887 with rubber band-powered models; however, their short and erratic performances led him to seek other types of propulsion. Unsuccessful experiments were conducted with engines powered by gunpowder, hot water (fireless boiler), compressed air, electricity, and carbon dioxide.

In 1892 Langley began experimenting with large tandem-winged models powered by steam engines, and on May 6, 1896, his Aerodrome No. 5 made the first successful flight of any engine-driven heavier-than-air craft.

It was launched from a spring-actuated catapult mounted on top of a houseboat on the Potomac River near Quantico, Virginia. Two flights were made during the afternoon, one of 3,300 feet and

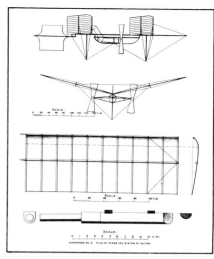

This rare photograph of the Aerodrome in flight was taken by Alexander Graham Bell, who witnessed the proceedings. (Photo: Columbia Historical Society)

one of 2,300 feet. On both occasions the Aerodrome landed in the water, as planned, because, in order to save weight, it was not equipped with landing gear.

A distinguished observer, Dr. Alexander Graham Bell, wrote about these flights in *Nature* on May 28, 1896:

On the occasion referred to, the aerodrome at a given signal, started from a platform about 20 feet above the water and rose at first directly in the face of the wind, moving at all times with remarkable steadiness, and subsequently swinging around in large curves of, perhaps, a hundred yards in diameter and continually ascending until its steam was exhausted, when at a lapse of about a minute and a half, and at a height which I judge to be between 80 and 100 feet in the air, the wheels ceased turning, and the machine, deprived of the aid of its propellers, to my surprise did not fall but settled down so softly and gently that it touched the water without the least shock, and was in fact immediately ready for another trial.

In the second trial, which followed directly, it repeated in nearly every respect the actions of the first except that the direction of its course was different. It ascended again in the face of the wind afterwards moving steadily and continually in large curves accompanied with a rising motion and a lateral advance. Its motion was, in fact, so steady that I think a glass of water on its surface would have remained unspilled. When the steam gave out again, it repeated for a second time the experience of the first trial when the steam had ceased, and settled gently and easily down. What height it reached at this trial I cannot say, as I was not so favourably placed as in the first, but I had occasion to notice that this time its course took it over a wooded promontory, and I was relieved of some apprehension in seeing that it was already so high as to pass the tree tops by twenty or thirty feet. It reached the water one minute and thirty-one seconds from the time it started, at a measured distance of over 900 feet from the point at which it rose.

On November 28, 1896, a similar model, Aerodrome No. 6, was flown for a distance of approximately 4,800 feet.

The power plant of Aerodrome No. 5 consisted of a single-cylinder steam engine equipped with a double-action piston with a slide valve, and a flash-tube boiler fired by a pressure burner that vaporized gasoline. The engine drove the propellers through a system of shafts and bevel gears.

Robert B. Meyer, Jr.

Secretary Langley had a workshop in a shed behind the Smithsonian, where he carried out his aeronautical investigations. (Photo: SI A18872)

The Aerodrome flew approximately 3,300 feet from this houseboat before landing in the Potomac. (Photo: SI A12583)

Lilienthal Standard Glider

Wingspan:	7.93 m (26 ft.)
Wing Area:	140 sq. ft.
Length:	4.19 m (13 ft. ¾ in.)
Height:	1.53 m (5 ft.)
Camber:	1-15/1-18

The men who built and flew hang gliders during the closing years of the nineteenth century laid the foundation for the design of the first successful flying machines. The German aeronautical pioneer Otto Lilienthal was the most influential member of this group of enthusiasts who sought to develop a stable glider as the first step toward powered flight.

Lilienthal was born in the Pomeranian village of Ankalm on May 24, 1848. He received a solid technical education and was employed by a number of German industrial firms prior to 1880, when he founded his own machine shop specializing in the production of marine signal devices and lightweight steam engines.

He began serious research in aeronautics in 1871 with a series of experiments designed to probe the physical principles that enabled birds to fly and that could also serve as a basis for the design of a successful airplane. The results of these tests, including important studies of the lift created by a curved surface in a moving stream of air, were published in 1889 under the title *Der Vogelflug als Grundlage des Fliegekunst (Birdflight As the Basis of Aviation)*. This volume greatly influenced the work of the Wright brothers and other aeronautical experimenters.

Lilienthal was not satisfied to restrict himself to

Lilienthal swings his legs to maintain control.
(Photo: SI A627B)

the exploration of aerodynamic theory, however. In 1891 he began work on a series of gliders that he hoped would demonstrate the practical applicability of the principles outlined in his book. By 1896 Lilienthal had developed eighteen different glider types, including both monoplanes and biplanes, and two unsuccessful powered machines.

The Lilienthal glider on exhibit at the National Air and Space Museum is a Normal-Sagelapparat (standard sailing machine), constructed by the German master in 1894. Lilienthal built at least eight machines of this type, which he considered to be the safest and most successful of his designs. The glider consists of a frame constructed of willow and bamboo. The wings and tail surfaces are covered with cotton cloth. A horizontal stabilizer is connected to the frame by a pivot at the front of the rudder. The wings are designed to fold to the rear for ease in transportation and storage.

As in all Lilienthal craft, the operator of the standard glider was suspended between the wings by bars that passed beneath his arms, which were placed in padded cuffs attached to the frame. Two padded wood braces were mounted with the pads in line with his ribs. The movement of the pilot's legs and torso altered the center of gravity and

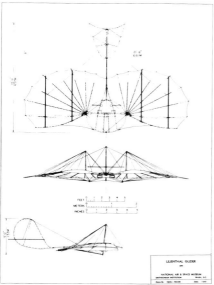

Many of Lilienthal's glides were made from an artificial hill constructed near his home in the Berlin suburb of Gross-Lichterfelde. (Photo: SI A45669)

Lilienthal makes a flight in a biplane glider. (Photo: SI A48094F)

The Heritage of
LILIENTHAL

Otto Lilienthal, 1848–1896. (Photo: SI A39013)

The 1894 standard glider is exhibited in the museum's Early Flight gallery. (Photo: SI 80–3702–5)

provided the primary means of control. Lilienthal made flights of up to 1,150 feet in gliders of this type.

The specimen on display was purchased from Lilienthal by the American newspaper magnate William Randolph Hearst in the spring of 1896. Hearst sponsored test flights of the glider on a Long Island estate in April and May 1896 in an effort to create publicity and boost the circulation of his newspaper, the *New York Journal*. Harry Bodine, a New Jersey athlete, made most of the flights, although *Journal* reporters and other spectators were also allowed to test their skill. Flights as long as 375 feet at altitudes of up to 50 feet were obtained with the machine.

Further flight testing of the glider ceased after Lilienthal's death in a similar machine on August 9, 1896. The German pioneer crashed after stalling his craft at an altitude of about 50 feet. He died the following day in a Berlin hospital.

The glider on exhibit was placed in storage until January 1906, when it was displayed at a New York Aero Club Show. It then passed into the hands of John Brisbane Walker, editor of *Cosmopolitan* magazine, who presented it to the Smithsonian Institution on February 2, 1906. Minor refurbishing was done in 1906 and 1928, and in 1967 the glider was completely restored. The horizontal stabilizer is not original to the machine.
Tom D. Crouch

Lockheed 5B Vega (Amelia Earhart)

Wingspan:	12.49 m (41 ft.)
Length:	8.38 m (27 ft. 6 in.)
Height:	2.49 m (8 ft. 2 in.)
Weight:	Gross, 1,315–1,450 kg (2,900–3,200 lb.)
	Empty, 748 kg (1,650 lb.)
Engine:	Pratt and Whitney Wasp D #3812, 450 hp

On May 20–21, 1932, Amelia Earhart became the first woman to make a nonstop solo flight across the Atlantic. The aircraft she used was a bright red Lockheed Vega 5B.

This particular Vega had been manufactured December 4, 1928, at Lockheed's Burbank, California, plant. It was used by Lockheed as a demonstrator until Earhart bought it on March 17, 1930.

In June 1928 Earhart had become the first woman to fly across the Atlantic, but she did so only as a passenger. She was frustrated at not having been at the controls even a minute of that 20-hour 40-minute flight, and was determined to prove she could do it on her own. She decided that a Lockheed Vega would be the plane she would use.

Her test flights began inauspiciously, however, when, during a flight at Langley Field, Virginia, in September 1930, a latch on her backrest gave way and she was thrown backward into the cabin. The plane nosed into a landing and had to be sent to Detroit Aircraft Corporation for repairs.

The repairs took almost a year. The wings, landing gear, and tail surfaces were all in good condition, but the fuselage had to be replaced.

Hating advance publicity for her flights, Earhart turned the Vega over to Bernt Balchen, her technical advisor. It was generally assumed that Balchen was planning an Antarctic flight; her secret was safe.

Balchen took the Vega to the old Fokker Aircraft Company plant at Hasbrouck Heights, New Jersey. There, he and mechanics Frank Nagle and Eddie Gorski reconditioned the plane for the upcoming flight. The fuselage was strengthened to take the extra fuel tanks that were added to provide a 420-gallon capacity; additional instruments were also installed.

On May 20, 1932, Earhart set off alone from Harbor Grace, Newfoundland. The weather was a problem from the start, and at one point in the

Amelia Earhart's bright red transatlantic Lockheed Vega is exhibited in the Pioneers of Flight gallery. (Photo: SI 80–2082)

In 1937 Earhart disappeared while attempting a round-the-world flight in this Lockheed Electra.
(Photo: SI A45874)

Earhart's first "first" was her 1928 transatlantic flight as a passenger in the Fokker Friendship, making her the first woman ever to fly across the Atlantic. She followed that up in 1932 when she made the first solo transatlantic flight by a woman.
(Photo: SI A45276E)

(Diagram: Aerospace Industries Association of America, Inc.)

Amelia Earhart used another Lockheed Vega when in 1935 she became the first woman to fly solo from Hawaii to the U.S. mainland.
(Photo: SI 73-4032)

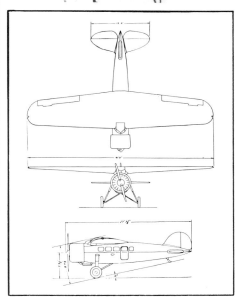

flight, ice on the wings forced her into a 3,000-foot, uncheckable descent. She finally managed to level off and, constantly fighting fatigue, she landed in a field near Culmore, Londonderry, Northern Ireland. She had made the 2,026-mile flight in 14 hours, 54 minutes.

She was greeted and praised enthusiastically upon her return to the United States, but she was never content to rest on her current laurels; there were always records to break and "firsts" to achieve. On August 24–25, 1932, in the same Vega, she flew from Los Angeles to Newark, covering the 2,448 miles in 19 hours, 5 minutes. This was the first solo nonstop transcontinental flight by a woman.

Amelia Earhart's Vega was one of 131 Lockheed Vegas manufactured. The Vega was an aesthetically pleasing aircraft with a spruce veneer monocoque fuselage and a spruce cantilever wing. The first Vega flew in 1927, and in an era of biplanes featured an advanced monoplane configuration in which the wing was completely braced internally, and the fuselage was of monocoque (shell) construction. The Vega was the first airplane built by Lockheed, and it established a tradition of Lockheed excellence in design that has continued to this day. The Vega was noteworthy in reintroducing the monocoque fuselage shape, which had first appeared on the Deperdussin monocoque racing airplane of 1913. This shape, wherein the fuselage is essentially a shell, maximizes both the load-carrying ability of the aircraft and its useful internal sapce. It subsequently became a standard design practice for transport aircraft. The Vega's wooden monocoque structure is a technological link on the road to the de Havilland Mosquito bomber of World War II, an eminently successful wooden aircraft having a monocoque fuselage design.

Amelia Earhart sold her Vega to the Franklin Institute in Philadelphia in June 1933. The aircraft was displayed there until it was transferred to the Smithsonian Institution on September 8, 1966.
Claudia M. Oakes

Lockheed 5C Vega "Winnie Mae"

Wingspan:	12.49 m (41 ft.)
Length:	8.38 m (27 ft. 6 in.)
Height:	2.49 m (8 ft. 2 in.)
Weight:	Gross, 2,041 kg (4,500 lb.)
	Empty, 1,177 kg (2,595 lb.)
Engine:	Pratt and Whitney Wasp C, serial no. 3088, 500 hp

The *Winnie Mae,* a special Lockheed Model 5C Vega flown by famed aviator Wiley Post, completed two around-the-world record flights and a series of special high-altitude substratospheric research flights. It was named for the daughter of its original owner, F. C. Hall, who hired Post to pilot the plane, which had been purchased in June 1930.

With the consent of his employer, Post entered the *Winnie Mae* in the National Air Races and piloted the plane to the first of its records, now inscribed on the side of its fuselage: "Los Angeles to Chicago 9 hrs. 9 min. 4 sec. Aug. 27, 1930."

On June 23, 1931, Post, accompanied by Harold Gatty as navigator, took off from New York to make a world circuit in record time. The first stop was Harbor Grace, Newfoundland. From there, the fourteen-stop course included England, Germany, Russia, Siberia, Alaska, Canada, thence to Cleveland, and finally to New York on July 1, 1931. The circuit was completed in 8 days, 15 hours, and 51 minutes. Hall's admiration for his pilot

Wiley Post stands beside his record-setting aircraft, the Winnie Mae.
(Photo: SI A5393A)

manifested itself in the gift of the *Winnie Mae* to Post.

Wiley Post spent the following year exhibiting the plane and conducting various flight tests. The airplane was groomed with an overhaul of the engine, and a radio compass and an auto pilot were installed. Both these instruments were at the time in their final stages of development by the Army and Sperry Gyroscope Company.

On July 15, 1933, Post left New York. Closely following his former route but making only eleven stops, he made a 15,596-mile circuit of the earth in 7 days, 18 hours, and 49 minutes.

Post next modified the *Winnie Mae* for long-distance, high-altitude operation. He recognized the need to develop some means of enabling the pilot to operate in a cabin atmosphere of greater density than the outside atmospheric environment. Because of its design, the *Winnie Mae* could not be equipped with a pressure cabin. Post therefore asked the B. F. Goodrich Company to assist him in

developing a full pressure suit for the pilot. Post hoped that by equipping the plane with an engine supercharger and a special jettisonable landing gear, and himself with a pressure suit, he could cruise for long distances at high altitude in the jetstream. On March 15, 1935, Post flew from Burbank, California, to Cleveland, Ohio, a distance of 2,035 miles, in 7 hours, 19 minutes. At times, the *Winnie Mae* attained a ground speed of 340 mph, indicating that the airplane was indeed operating in the jetstream.

Wiley Post died shortly afterward in the crash of a hybrid Lockheed Orion-Sirius floatplane near Point Barrow, Alaska, on August 15, 1935. His companion, humorist Will Rogers, also perished in the accident. The Smithsonian Institution acquired the *Winnie Mae* from Mrs. Post in 1936.

During its high-altitude flight research, the *Winnie Mae* made use of a special tubular steel landing gear developed by Lockheed engineers Clarence L. "Kelly" Johnson and James Gerschler. It was released after takeoff by the pilot using a cockpit lever, thus reducing the total drag of the plane and eliminating its weight. The *Winnie Mae* would then continue on its flight and land on a special metal-covered spruce landing skid glued to the fuselage. During these flights, Post wore a special pressure suit, the world's first practical pressure suit and an important step on the road to space. The suit was the third type developed by Post and Russell S. Colley of B. F. Goodrich Company. It consisted of three layers: long underwear, an inner black rubber air pressure bladder, and an outer cloth contoured suit. A special pressure helmet was then bolted on the suit. It had a removable faceplate that Post could seal when he reached a height of 17,000 feet. The helmet had a special breathing oxygen system and could accommodate earphones and a throat microphone. The suit could withstand an internal pressure of 7 psi. Bandolera-type cords prevented the helmet from rising as the suit was pressurized. A liquid oxygen container, consisting of a double-walled vacuum bottle, utilized the natural "boil off" tendencies of supercold liquid oxygen to furnish gaseous oxygen for suit pressurization and breathing purposes. This early full pressure suit is the direct ancestor of full pressure suits used on the X-15 research airplane and manned space voyages. The *Winnie Mae*, its special jettisonable landing gear, and Post's pressure suit are in the collection of the National Air and Space Museum.

Richard P. Hallion

Post was the first person to make a solo round-the-world flight, July 1933. (Photo: SI A32247F)

Wearing his pressure suit, Post enters the Winnie Mae *for a substratosphere flight. (Photo: SI A47511)*

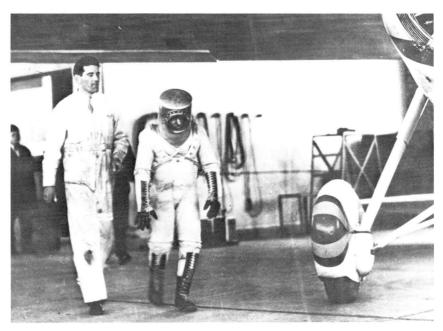

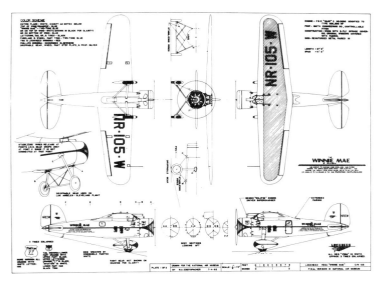

Lockheed 8 Sirius "Tingmissartoq"

Wingspan:	13.05 m (42 ft. 10 in.)
Length:	9.14 m (30 ft.)
Height:	4.50 m (14 ft. 9 in.)
Weight:	Gross, 3,502 kg (7,699 lb.)
	Empty, 2,082 kg (4,589 lb.)
Engine:	Wright Cyclone SR-1820-F2, 710 hp

A vacation flight with "no start or finish, no diplomatic or commercial significance, and no records to be sought." So Charles A. Lindbergh described the flight that he and his wife, Anne Morrow Lindbergh, were planning to make to the Orient in 1931. Their choice of route, however, showed the feasibility of using the great circle to reach the Far East.

The Lindberghs flew in a Lockheed Sirius low-wing monoplane, powered by a 680-hp Wright Cyclone. The Sirius had been designed in 1929 by John K. Northrop and Gerard Vultee, and this model was specially fitted with Edo floats, since most of the Lindberghs' flight was to be over water.

Their route took them from North Haven, Maine, to Ottawa, Moose Factory, Churchill, Baker Lake, and Aklavik, all in Canada; Point Barrow, Shismaref, and Nome, Alaska; Petropavlosk, Siberia; and on over the Kurile Islands to Japan. After receiving an enthusiastic welcome in Tokyo, they flew to China. They landed on Lotus Lake

near Nanking on September 19, thus completing the first flight from the West to the East by way of the North.

At Hankow, the Sirius, with the Lindberghs aboard, was being lowered into the Yangtze River from the British aircraft carrier *Hermes,* when the aircraft accidentally capsized. One of the wings was damaged when it hit a ship's cable, and the aircraft had to be returned to the United States for repairs.

Their next venture in the Sirius came as a result of the five countries' interest in the development of commercial air transport. In 1933 Pan American Airways, Imperial Airways of Great Britain, Lufthansa of Germany, KLM of Holland, and Air France undertook a cooperative study of possible Atlantic routes. Each was assigned the responsibility for one of the following areas: New Newfoundland to Europe via Greenland; Newfoundland via the great circle route to Ireland; Newfoundland southeast to the Azores and Lisbon;

The Lockheed Sirius in which the Lindberghs made their "north to the Orient" flight is now in the collection of the National Air and Space Museum. (Photo: SI A5172)

The Greenland Eskimo boy who named the Sirius Tingmissartoq painted the word on the aircraft's fuselage. (Photo: SI A45256D)

Miami, Bermuda, the Azores, and Lisbon; and across the South Atlantic from Natal, Brazil, to Cape Verde, Africa.

Pan American was to survey the Newfoundland to Europe via Greenland route. Ground survey and weather crews in Greenland were already hard at work when Lindbergh, Pan Am's technical advisor, took off from New York on July 9 in the rebuilt Lockheed Sirius, again accompanied by his wife, who would serve as copilot and radio operator. A Sperry artificial horizon and a directional gyro had been added to the instrument panel since the previous flight, and a new Wright Cyclone SR-1820-F2 engine of 710 horsepower was installed. Lindbergh's plan was not to set up a particular route but to gather as much information as possible on the area to be covered.

The *Jellinge*, a Danish ship, was chartered by Pan Am to maintain radio contact with the Lindberghs in the Labrador-Greenland-Iceland area. The ship also delivered advance supplies for them to Halifax, Saint John's, Cartwright, Greenland, and Iceland.

Every possible space in the aircraft was utilized, including the wings and floats, which contained the gasoline tanks. There was plenty of emergency equipment in case the Lindberghs had to make a forced landing in the frozen wilderness.

From New York, the Lindberghs flew up the eastern border of Canada to Hopedale, Labrador. From Hopedale they made the first major overwater hop, 650 miles to Godthaab, Greenland, where the Sirius acquired its name—*Tingmissartoq,* which in Eskimo means "one who flies like a big bird."

After crisscrossing Greenland to Baffin Island and back, and then on to Iceland, the Lindberghs proceeded to the major cities of Europe and as far east as Moscow, down the west coast of Africa, and across the South Atlantic to South America, where they flew down the Amazon, and then north through Trinidad and Barbados and back to the United States.

They returned to New York on December 19, having traveled 30,000 miles to four continents and twenty-one countries. The information gained from the trip proved invaluable in planning commercial air transport routes for the North and South Atlantic.

The aircraft was in the American Museum of Natural History in New York City until 1955. The Air Force Museum in Dayton, Ohio, then acquired it and transferred it to the Smithsonian in 1959.
Claudia M. Oakes

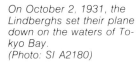

On October 2, 1931, the Lindberghs set their plane down on the waters of Tokyo Bay. (Photo: SI A2180)

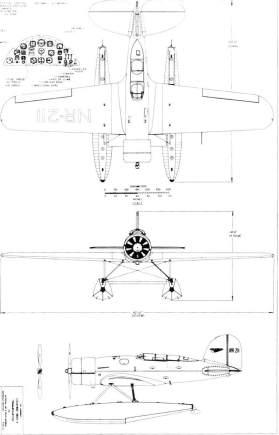

Lockheed F–104A Starfighter

Wingspan:	6.68 m (21 ft. 11 in.)
Length:	16.61 m (54 ft. 9 in.)
Height:	4.11 m (13 ft. 6 in.)
Weight:	Gross, 9,980 kg (22,000 lb.)
Engine:	General Electric J79-GE-3A Turbojet, 11,000-lb static thrust

The Lockheed F-104 Starfighter was nicknamed "the missile with a man in it," since its long, thin fuselage and stubby wings resembled a missile more than a conventional aircraft. The F-104 was the first interceptor in our nation's service to be able to fly at sustained speeds above Mach 2 (twice the speed of sound).

The Starfighter's design was radical for its time, as it was a small, straight-wing aircraft while most contemporary designs were much larger and featured swept-back wings. The wingspan is only 21 feet, 11 inches, and the wings themselves have a 10° negative dihedral. The razor-sharp leading edge requires a specially fitted cover when on the ground to protect the ground crew. A narrow fuselage fits tightly around the power plant, and its forward portion curves down slightly to allow maximum pilot visibility.

The F-104 featured the General Electric 14,800-pound-thrust J79 turbojet engine and afterburner, which occupied more than half the length of the fuselage. The fuel tanks and cockpit took up much of the remainder, so that insufficient space remained for the necessary electronics systems. A series of self-contained electronics packages were

developed which could be "plugged in" to suit the individual mission. Basic armament consisted of an M-61 Vulcan 20-mm gun in the fuselage and a Sidewinder GAR-8 missile on each wingtip. The M-61 was a Gatling type with multiple rotating barrels and an extremely high rate of fire.

Design of the F-104 began in November 1952. The U.S. Air Force had a requirement for a superior day fighter, and Lockheed began work on its Model 83. Two prototypes, powered by the Wright J65 engine, were ordered by the Air Force in March 1953. On February 7, 1954, Lockheed test pilot Tony Le Vier made the first flight in the XC-104. Fifteen YF-104A aircraft, powered by the GE J79 engine, were ordered for testing.

The first F-104A deliveries took place on January 26, 1958. They were delivered to the 83d Fighter-Interceptor Squadron at Hamilton Air Force Base, California. Soon afterward, pilots from this squadron set new world speed and altitude records. Maj. Howard C. Johnson established a world airplane altitude record of 91,249 feet on May 7, 1958. On May 16, 1958, Capt. Walter W. Irvin established a world speed record of 1,404.19 mph. The F-104 also established seven climb-to-

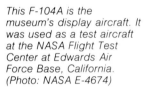

This F-104A is the museum's display aircraft. It was used as a test aircraft at the NASA Flight Test Center at Edwards Air Force Base, California. (Photo: NASA E-4674)

The CF-1-4/F-104G versions of the Starfighter were built for use in NATO and SEATO nations. These F-104s are shown in the markings of Germany, Canada, and Japan, respectively.
(Photo: SI 75-13905)

height records. Four of these replaced old records; the 15,000 meter, 20,000 meter, and 25,000 meter climbs set completely new records.

The major variants were the F-104B, a two-seat version of the F-104A, used as an operational trainer; the F-104C, modified for use by the Tactical Air Command with provision for inflight refueling; and the F-104D, a two-seat version of the F-104C.

The majority of Starfighters were used in foreign service. Most of the F-104Gs, F-104Js, and CF-104s were built under license in NATO and SEATO countries. The basic Starfighter was modified to be a multimission fighter with considerably strengthened structure and different operational equipment.

On October 12, 1959, the Starfighter project was awarded the Collier Trophy.

Starfighters served in the Air Force until the early 1960s. A few saw service in Vietnam, and they were also used in Air National Guard units until 1975. Their European counterparts stayed in service even longer.

The museum's specimen is a Lockheed F-104A, military serial number 55-2961, the seventh F-104A produced (formerly a YF-104A). It was procured by the NASA Flight Research Center (then NACA High Speed Flight Station) at Edwards Air Force Base, California, on August 23, 1956. It was first flown by NASA on August 27, 1956, and logged 1,439 flights over a period of nineteen years.

The airplane, NASA number 818, was used in a number of research programs at Edwards. It was used in the evaluation program of the Starfighter at first and was later used to help confirm wind tunnel data in actual flight, as a flying testbed, and as a chase plane. It was a part of the research program that led to the X-15 airplane program; a particularly important phase was the testing of reaction type controls.

Nineteen pilots flew the 818. Among them were three Apollo astronauts, including Neil Armstrong; seven X-15 pilots, including Joe Walker; and six lifting body pilots. It made its last operational flight on August 26, 1975, and was flown to Andrews Air Force Base, near Washington, D.C., for transfer to the National Air and Space Museum later that year.
Michael E. Dobson

This photograph shows the sleek fuselage of the F-104. When the picture was taken, the engine air scoops were covered for security reasons.
(Photo: SI 75-13906)

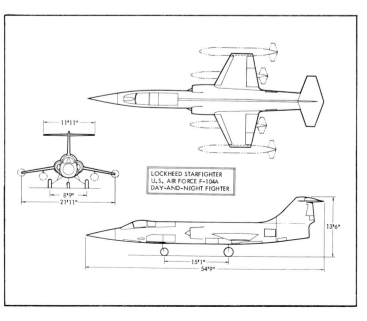

LOCKHEED STARFIGHTER
U.S. AIR FORCE F-104A
DAY-AND-NIGHT FIGHTER

Lockheed U-2C

Wingspan:	24.4 m (80 ft.)
Length:	15.2 m (50 ft.)
Height:	4.6 m (15 ft.)
Weight:	Gross, 10,225 kg (22,542 lb.)
	Empty, 5,929 kg (13,071 lb.)
Engine:	Pratt and Whitney J75-P-13B,
	7,711 kg (17,000 lb.) thrust

Still shrouded in secrecy over 35 years after its creation, the Lockheed U-2 was originally designed as a strategic reconnaissance aircraft, playing a crucial role during the tense years of the Cold War. Built by the famous "Skunk Works" by Lockheed under the direction of Clarence L. "Kelly" Johnson, the U-2 was truly one of the most successful intelligence-gathering aircraft ever produced.

In 1953, on behalf of the Central Intelligence Agency, the U.S. Air Force issued a request for a single-seat, long-range, high-altitude reconnaissance aircraft to monitor the military activities of the Soviet Union and its satellite countries in Eastern Europe. By this time, breakthroughs in film and camera technologies made possible the creation of an aircraft that could take high resolution photographs of strategic sites from extreme altitudes where it would be invulnerable to interception.

In November 1954, Lockheed presented an unsolicited proposal that was accepted by the CIA with President Dwight Eisenhower's approval. Operating under a very strict schedule, the Skunk Works produced the new U-2 just eight months later. Lockheed test pilot Tony LeVier flew the single-seat U-2 on its maiden flight on August 6, 1955. With its narrow chord and sailplane-like wing, the lightly loaded U-2 refused to land until LeVier's fifth attempt brought it back to Earth. The U-2 was subjected to an accelerated test program which

revealed a number of problems that were quickly overcome, particularly that of engine flameouts at high altitude. This was solved by the development of new low-volatility fuel for the single Pratt and Whitney J57 turbojet.

CIA pilot training began in the spring of 1956 and by the summer the first U-2As were operational. On July 4, 1956, a U-2A completed the first overflight of the Soviet Union. Sophisticated electronic and camera equipment was housed in the nose and in a large fuselage bay. Large fuel tanks enabled the aircraft to fly for six hours over almost 4,600 kilometers (3,000 miles) at altitudes in excess of 60,000 feet. Operational U-2As flew routinely from bases in Pakistan and Turkey to Norway, overflying vast stretches of the Soviet Union. These flights gathered much important data and particularly revealed that the so-called "missile gap" in the Soviet's favor was a myth, thus altering the delicate strategic balance. For four years the CIA operated these flights with U-2As and improved U-2Bs until May 1, 1960, when Francis Gary Powers was shot down by a Soviet SA-2 missile over Sverdlovsk, thus sparking an embarrassing diplomatic incident for the United States and halting these flights.

Flights over the People's Republic of China, however, continued unabated from bases in Taiwan, as did flights over Cuba from U.S. bases. On August 29, 1962, a U-2 confirmed the presence of Soviet intermediate-range ballistic missiles on that island

The extreme dimensions of the wings made the suspension of the U-2 in NASM's Looking at Earth gallery a particularly difficult task.
(Photo: SI 85-12771-22)

nation, which led to the Cuban Missile Crisis. U-2s were also in demand to gather information over Vietnam after July 1964, operating continually until the fall of Saigon in 1975. Since then, U-2s have observed the developing situations in the Middle East and other political hot spots.

The U-2's remarkable high-altitude abilities have also made it a valuable tool for scientific research. NASA has operated two of these aircraft in its High Altitude Missions Branch, where the U-2 has proven useful in stratospheric sampling, particularly in gathering volcanic dust after the 1980 eruption of Mt. St. Helens, and has been involved in assessments of natural disasters and water and land use.

Numerous versions of the U-2 have been produced, each one providing important improvements in performance and mission capability, including two-seat models and models that can be operated from aircraft carriers. The most significant change came with the development of the U-2R, which was a virtual redesign that lengthened both the fuselage and wingspan, allowing for much improved handling and electronics and sensor payload. The U-2R retained the general configuration of earlier versions, with its unique bicycle-type landing gear and the powerful Pratt and Whitney J75-P-13B engine of the U-2C. In 1979, after a break in production of 12 years, the TR-1A version of the U-2R was ordered by the U.S. Air Force to provide reconnaissance capability for high-altitude stand-off surveillance of Eastern Europe. A new generation of cameras and sensors that can peer 300 miles away from the aircraft made this possible. NASA has also acquired the earth resources version of the TR-1A, known as the ER-2, for service with the U-2Cs of the High Altitude Missions Branch.

On August 30, 1982, the National Air and Space Museum acquired its Lockheed U-2C from the U.S. Air Force. This particular aircraft, Article 347, Serial Number 56-6680, was the seventh U-2 built. It was delivered on February 9, 1956, and was first employed operationally on July 4. It originally flew as a U-2A model and was subsequently upgraded as a U-2C when refitted with the J75-P-13B engine, which required a significant enlargement of the airframe engine inlets. At one point it was temporarily fitted with an in-flight refueling probe and designated as a U-2F.

When flown by the CIA, the aircraft remained unpainted except for its three-digit production number and was operated from bases at Lakenheath, England; Wiesbaden and Giebelstade, Germany; Akrotiri, Cyprus; and Edwards Air Force Base, California. The aircraft was apparently lent to the Air Force in 1969 and flown over Vietnam. In 1974 the CIA transferred ownership of #347 to the Air Force, which operated it until 1978. The paint scheme now on the aircraft was used by the Air Force during operations from British bases in the Middle East. The airplane remained with the Air Force until its transfer to the Museum in 1982.

F. Robert van der Linden

The cockpit of the U-2 was conventional in appearance. (Photo: SI 83-8082-33)

Clarence L. "Kelly" Johnson created the U-2 in his famous "Skunk Works" at Lockheed. (Photo: Courtesy of Lockheed)

Slipper fuel tanks on the wings extend the range of the U-2 for longer missions. (Photo: Courtesy of Lockheed)

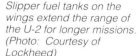

Lockheed XP-80 Shooting Star

Wingspan:	11.3 m (37 ft.)
Length:	10.0 m (32 ft. 10 in.)
Height:	3.1 m (10 ft. 3 in.)
Weight:	Gross, 3,910 kg (8,620 lb.)
	Empty, 2,852 kg (6,287 lb.)
Engine:	Allis-Chalmers H-1 turbojet, 1361 kg (3,000 lb.) static thrust

The National Air and Space Museum's XP-80 is shown at Muroc Flight Test Base, California, during tactical evaluation and engine testing in 1945–46. (Photo: SI 78-7544)

The P-80 Shooting Star program began in 1943 when a team of engineers and designers headed by Lockheed's chief research engineer Clarence "Kelly" Johnson accepted the challenge to build an airplane that could counter the German jet fighter, the Me 262, in aerial combat over Europe. The preliminary design, using a British-designed, 3,000-pound-thrust turbojet, was submitted to the U.S. Army on June 15, 1943, and was designated the XP-80. Kelly Johnson's handpicked team, dubbed the "Skunk Works," built the first XP-80 in just 143 days, and nicknamed the aircraft "Lulu Belle" (serial number 44-83020). The first flight was on January 8, 1944, with Lockheed's chief test pilot, Milo Burcham, at the controls.

While the XP-80 was undergoing flight testing, a new and improved model, the XP-80A, was delivered. This airplane, of which two were built, was slightly heavier and longer than the XP-80 and incorporated the 4,000-pound-thrust General Electric I-40 engine, insuring considerably

improved performance. The first XP-80A, nicknamed the "Gray Ghost" (serial number 44-83021), first flew on June 10, 1944.

On February 12, 1944, Gen. H. H. Arnold, Commanding General, Army Air Forces, gave his approval to build 13 I-40 powered P-80 type aircraft, which would be known as YP-80As (serial numbers 44-83023 to 44-83035). Four of these service test aircraft were deployed to Europe in early 1945 to demonstrate the capabilities of the P-80A to flight crews in England and Italy. One YP-80A crashed in England, while the remaining three continued to fly without further difficulty until the termination of the project on May 7, 1945. None of the YP-80As saw action in combat.

After the war, three P-80A aircraft were assigned to a project to break the transcontinental speed record. Col. William Councill, Capt. Martin Smith, and Capt. John Babel were the pilots assigned. The route began at Long Beach, California, and ended at LaGuardia Field, New York. Colonel

Final version of the F-80 Shooting Star was the F-80C, a rugged and versatile aircraft that performed well in a ground support role during the Korean War. (Photo: Smithsonian Institution)

"Stretching" the F-80C into a two-place aircraft assured the Shooting Star of lasting fame. Lockheed built 5,691 T-33 trainers between 1948 and 1959 and licensed the production of 656 more in Canada and 210 in Japan. (Photo: Smithsonian Institution)

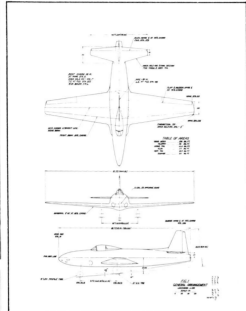

(Diagram: Courtesy of Lockheed Corporation)

Councill's P-80A flew the 2,453.8-mile trip nonstop in 4 hours, 13 minutes, and 26 seconds for an average speed of 580.93 mph. The P-80 went on to break other records, including the world's speed record on June 19, 1947, when Col. "Al" Boyd flew a P-80R nicknamed "Racey" an average speed of 623.8 mph.

The most significant outgrowth of the P-80 program was the evolution of the T-33 trainer. The "T-Bird" was an F-80C, stretched 38½ inches to accommodate a second seat. The prototype first flew on March 22, 1948, and was designated the TF-80C in June 1948, when the Air Force revised the designation given to fighter aircraft from P for pursuit to F for fighter. Designated the T-33 in May 1949, some 5,691 of the aircraft were eventually produced.

The Korean War brought 365 F-80s into operational units of the Far East Air Force. Lt. Russell J. Brown, flying a Shooting Star, destroyed a MiG-15 near the Yalu River on November 8, 1950, thus recording the first victory in an aerial combat between jet fighters. The last close support sortie flown by an F-80 was on April 30, 1953.

After the war, the F-80Cs were completely phased out from active duty forces. Still in use, however, was the drone version, QF-80, which collected fallout samples from radioactive clouds as late as the mid-1960s. Eventually, about 100 F-80Cs went to allied nations under the Military Assistance Program. Even in its declining years, the Shooting Star did not just fade away; in fact, it endured for many years as the F-94 Starfire, an all-weather interceptor.

Custody of the XP-80 *Lulu Belle* was assumed by the Smithsonian on May 1, 1949. The aircraft was disassembled, boxed, and moved from the Museum Storage Depot in Park Ridge, Illinois, to the National Air Museum's Preservation and Restoration Facility at Silver Hill, Maryland, in the early 1950s. *Lulu Belle*, with Allis-Chalmers H-1 engine serial number 000006, remained boxed until late 1976, when the decision was made to restore it. The restoration was completed in May 1978.

Doug Campbell

Macchi C.202 Folgore

Wingspan:	10.58 m (34 ft. 8½ in.)
Length:	8.85 m (29 ft. ½ in.)
Height:	3.02 m (9 ft. 11½ in.)
Weight:	Gross, 2,937 kg (6,636 lb.)
	Empty, 2,357 kg (5,181 lb.)
Engine:	Daimler-Benz DB-601, license-built by Alfa Romeo

One of the most effective fighter planes in the early part of World War II was the Italian Macchi C.202. Outside Italy, however, it failed to achieve as much fame as contemporary fighters of other nations. Known by the pilots who flew it as the Folgore, meaning "lightning," it was the Regia Aeronautica's finest fighter, and raised the level of Italian fighter development to international standards.

Flown initially in August 1940, M.C.202s joined their first unit, the 1° Stormo C.T., in the summer of 1941 for conversion training. By November, that unit was transferred with its new aircraft to Libya to participate in the last stages of the British campaign that led to the raising of the blockade around Tobruk and the retreat of the German and Italian troops in Cyrenaica in late December.

Its late arrival in battle was a contributing factor to the success of the British offensive. This new Macchi made its mark as an outstanding fighter, however. In capable hands, it was a challenge to its North African adversaries, being superior to both the American Curtiss P-40 and the British Hawker Hurricane by a substantial margin. It could outmaneuver any of its opponents and outperform all but the late-model Spitfires and Mustangs. Pilots who flew the Folgore lauded its finger-light handling and its superb agility.

The success of the Folgore was due largely to the use of the in-line, liquid-cooled engine. Although Italy had gained the world speed record in 1934 with its in-line engine-powered Macchi C.72, the Italian aircraft industry ignored this speed potential and stayed with the more easily

maintainable, yet bulky, radial engine. Its fighter force suffered from this policy.

It was not until the opening months of 1940 that the Macchi Company, as a private venture, imported an example of the Daimler-Benz D.B.601 in-line engine from Germany and designed a slender fuselage around it. Utilizing the wings and tail design of the M.C.200, the new airplane became the M.C.202 Folgore.

Results with this new design were impressive, and production began at once. By using major components, as well as special tooling of its predecessor, the M.C.200 Saetta, the changeover in production proceeded rapidly.

Initially, the new Macchi was powered by German-supplied D.B.601 engines, but before long the aircraft production lines had to depend upon the license-built Alfa Romeo version, designated R.A.1000 R.C.41 Monsonie (Monsoon). Production of the new engine was slow and created a bottleneck in the delivery of the new airplane. This necessitated keeping the outdated C.200 Saetta in production alongside the M.C.202. By the end of 1942, however, there were more Folgores than any other fighter in the Regia Aeronautica.

An interesting but hardly noticeable fact is that the left wing of the Folgore is 8⅜ inches longer than the right wing. Only a few aircraft designs have used this asymmetrical method of counteracting the rotational torque of the engine to assist pilot control.

The Macchi C.202 in the National Air and Space Museum is one of only two remaining in the world. The early history of this airplane is obscure, but it

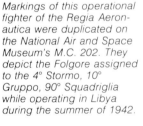

Markings of this operational fighter of the Regia Aeronautica were duplicated on the National Air and Space Museum's M.C. 202. They depict the Folgore assigned to the 4° Stormo, 10° Gruppo, 90° Squadriglia while operating in Libya during the summer of 1942.

This Macchi C.202 in the National Air and Space Museum is the only survivor of its type. (Photo: SI 80–2089)

was one of many enemy World War II aircraft brought to this country for evaluation at the Army's Air Technical Service Command at Wright and Freeman fields. For years after its testing, it remained in storage.

In 1975 National Air and Space Museum technicians completely restored the fighter to exhibit condition. Since there is no record of the original markings, the colors used are of the 4° Stormo, 10° Gruppo, and 90° Squadriglia units operating in Libya in the summer of 1942. The camouflage pattern of light sand and olive green splotches is the type used during that period.

The 4° Stormo, one of the most famous Italian fighter units, distinguished itself particularly during the Axis advance in North Africa and was credited with 500 victories from the time it was formed in 1940. On the nose of their aircraft was inscribed "4° F. Baracca," to memorialize Italy's leading ace, Maj. Francesco Baracca, who had thirty-five World War I victories.

Positive identification of the model series of the museum's aircraft is not known, but it rests somewhere between the late Series VI and IX. For marking purposes, the Series IX was selected along with the arbitrary serial number MM 9476, which falls within the block of numbers for this series. This airplane was originally equipped with 7.7-mm wing-mounted guns in addition to the twin fuselage 12.7-mm guns. Since the correct wing guns could not be located, they are not installed.

Although the M.C.202 was produced in larger numbers than any other Italian monoplane fighter (1,150–1,200), the lack of an effective propaganda effort deprived the Folgore of the reputation it earned in the hands of skilled pilots who flew it. The airplane was used on a small scale by the Germans, and after 1943 it appeared in the small Italian Co-Belligerent Air Force that operated continuously from the Italian Armistice until VE Day. The M.C.202's last days of service ended where it all began, in the North African skies, while in service with the Egyptian Air Force.

Robert C. Mikesh

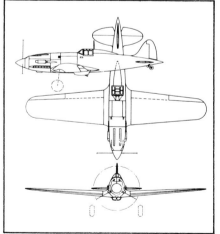

Another aircraft of the 10° Squadriglia crashlanded in mid-1942 at El Alamein after a battle. Flyers of the South African brigade examine the wreckage.

MacCready
"Gossamer Condor"

Wingspan:	29.25 m (96 ft.)
Length:	9.14 m (30 ft.)
Height:	5.49 m (18 ft.)
Weight:	31.75 kg (70 lb.)

Bryan Allen pilots the Gossamer Condor on a test flight prior to the August 23, 1977, Kremer Prize-winning flight.
(Photo: Courtesy Dr. Paul B. MacCready)

On August 23, 1977, the man-powered aircraft *Gossamer Condor* successfully demonstrated sustained, maneuverable manpowered flight and won the £50,000 ($95,000) Kremer Prize.

Pilot Bryan Allen took off from Shafter Airport, Shafter, California, at 7:30 a.m. and landed 7 minutes, 27.5 seconds later. The official circuit, a figure-8 course around pylons one-half mile apart with a 10-foot hurdle at the beginning and the end, covered 1.15 miles. The *Gossamer Condor* traveled a total of 1.35 miles from takeoff to landing. Its flight speed was between 10 and 11 mph, with Allen, a championship bicyclist and hang-glider enthusiast, developing one-third horsepower.

The Kremer Prize was established in 1959 by industrialist Henry Kremer. It was originally set at £10,000 ($14,000), but as the years passed with no winners, the value increased periodically for added incentive until it reached £50,000.

Dr. Paul B. MacCready and Dr. Peter B. S. Lissaman, both of Pasadena, California, designed the *Gossamer Condor,* which is made of thin aluminum tubes covered with mylar plastic and braced with stainless steel wires. The leading edges are made of corrugated cardboard and styrene foam. One advantage of the *Gossamer Condor* over previous manpowered aircraft was the facility with which it could be modified or repaired. After a crash, it could be returned to flying condition within twenty-four hours, enabling the aircraft to be tested extensively and easily modified. Also, MacCready's team did not try to adapt a conventional aircraft design for manpower, as others had mistakenly done; they designed an aircraft solely for its manpowered mission.

The pilot sat in a semireclining position with both hands free for the controls. One hand held a handle that controlled both vertical and lateral movement. For turns, the other hand set a lever located beside the seat that controlled wires to twist the wing.

Dr. MacCready conceived the idea of building a manpowered aircraft in mid-July 1976. After building several models to test structure, Dr. MacCready and his team began building the first complete aircraft in October. The first significant flight, one of 40 seconds, took place on December 26. Throughout the first part of 1977, modifications steadily improved control and efficiency, and all efforts were rewarded with the August 23 prize-winning flight.

In January 1978 the *Gossamer Condor* was donated to the National Air and Space Museum.

Claudia M. Oakes

McDonnell FH-1 Phantom

Wingspan:	12.42 m (40 ft. 9 in.)
Length:	11.82 m (39 ft. 9 in.)
Height:	4.32 m (14 ft. 2 in.)
Weight:	Gross, 4,551 kg (10,035 lb.) Empty, 3,031 kg (6,683 lb.)
Engine:	Two Westinghouse J30-WE-20 axial flow turbojet engines, 708 kg (1,560 lb.) thrust each

The McDonnell FH-1 Phantom was the first U.S. jet aircraft to take off from and land on an aircraft carrier, and subsequently it became the first U.S. jet fighter in operational service with both the Navy and Marine Corps. Its development during World War II was a major technological achievement that played a significant role in transforming U.S. aircraft at sea from piston power to jet propulsion.

In August 1943, the Navy's Bureau of Aeronautics requested the young McDonnell Corporation to begin development of an all-jet, carrier-based fighter aircraft. Westinghouse Electric Corporation was commissioned to design the turbojet engines, and together the teams took on the challenge.

After exhaustive tests on the number and size of the jet engines, it was determined that two 19-inch-diameter turbojets mounted in the wing roots would provide the necessary power and fuel economy. The final configuration emerged with two Westinghouse 19 XB-2B engines, a low-wing, single-tail fuselage with the horizontal stabilizer

*The museum's FH-1, now in the Jet Aviation gallery, is shown as it looked on display at the Paul E. Garber Facility.
(Photo: SI 80-15425)*

clear of the exhaust, and a single cockpit forward of the leading edge of the wing. The nose held four 0.50-caliber guns. The prototype XFD-1 Phantom first flew on January 26, 1945.

Problems anticipated by the engineers designing the jet included the ability of the plane to take off in the relatively short length of the flight deck and the ability of the engine to accelerate quickly enough for a wave-off situation or to deaccelerate quickly enough for a good carrier landing.

It was on July 21, 1946, that the Phantom made the first takeoff from and landing on a carrier—the U.S.S. *Franklin D. Roosevelt.* Impressed with its performance, the Navy ordered production versions, designated the FH-1. Delivery to fleet squadrons began in July 1947, with Fighter Squadron 17A (VF-17A) becoming the first Navy jet squadron to be carrier-qualified and the first operational shipboard jet fighter squadron in the world. This crucial test of the plane occurred during carrier operation trials aboard the U.S.S.

*Flight-deck crewmen prepare the XFD-1 for its first takeoff from the U.S.S. Franklin D. Roosevelt, on July 21, 1946.
(Photo: SI 80-15427)*

*The McDonnell Phantom FH-1 was the first operational shipboard jet fighter in the world.
(Photo: SI A2011)*

*Carrier operation trials for the FH-1 took place aboard the U.S.S. Saipan in May 1948. Here a Phantom is catapulted off the deck.
(Photo: SI 80-15426)*

Saipan in May 1948. Pilots of VF-17A made 176 takeoffs, took wave-offs, and simulated combat maneuvers. The Phantom met all the requirements and proved the soundness of the fundamental concept of carrier-based jet aircraft. With the completion of these trials, a new age in naval aviation had begun.

The first Marine Corps unit to receive the FH-1 Phantom was Marine Fighter Squadron 122 (VMF-122), stationed at the Marine Corps Air Station, Cherry Point, North Carolina. VMF-122 received considerable recognition with its precision aerobatic team of FH-1s known as the Flying Leathernecks.

Sixty Phantoms were built under the Navy

contract and served in the Korean War and as jet trainers. The Phantom's operational career, limited by newer jet fighters, lasted until mid-1950. However, McDonnell successors, the F2H Banshee, the F3H Demon, the F-101 Voodoo, and the F-4 Phantom II, continued the sound design concept and high performance qualities of the FH-1.

The National Air and Space Museum's FH-1, which served with Marine Fighter Squadron 122 (VMF-122), completed its service life in April 1954, with a total of 418 flight hours. It was transferred to the museum by the U.S. Navy in 1959.
Dorothy S. Cochrane

Martin B-26B Marauder "Flak Bait" (nose section)

Wingspan:	21.63 m (71 ft.)
Length:	17.76 m (58 ft. 3 in.)
Height:	6.55 m (21 ft. 6 in.)
Weight:	Gross, 16,783 kg (37,000 lb.)
	Empty, 10,886 kg (24,000 lb.)
Engines:	Pratt and Whitney R-2800-43, 2,000 hp

Flak Bait flew more missions over Europe than any other Allied aircraft in World War II. With 202 operational sorties to its credit, this medium bomber has perhaps the longest and most colorful combat history of any museum aircraft.

The Glenn L. Martin Company of Baltimore, Maryland, developed the B-26 in response to an Army Air Corps specification issued January 25, 1939. Because of the accelerated pace of development, the Marauder was ordered "right off the drawing board" and no prototype was constructed. The first production example flew on November 25, 1940.

A high-wing loading was selected by Martin designers as a means of achieving exceptional performance, with the result that the bomber landed at high speeds and was quickly termed "hot" by its pilots. Early Marauder aircraft flew combat missions in the Pacific Theater of Operations within days of the American entry in World War II.

Engine and propeller malfunctions, inadequate crew preparation, and the demanding flying characteristics of the B-26 led to an initially high rate of accidents in training. Intimidating epithets such as the "Widow Maker" and "One-a-Day-in-Tampa-Bay" served only to add to the bomber's already tarnished reputation, and production was in danger of being halted on several occasions. By war's end, nevertheless, the rugged Marauders had vindicated themselves with the greatest bombing accuracy and lowest loss rate of any American aircraft.

Flak Bait, a B-26B with the serial number 41-31773, was built in April 1943 and flown to England by its crew. Once there, it was attached to the 449th Bombardment Squadron of the 322d Bombardment Group, and given the fuselage identification markings PN-O. The name of the plane was derived from "Flea Bait," the nickname of a dog belonging to the pilot, Lt. James J. Farrell of Greenwich, Connecticut.

The Martin B-26 Flak Bait on its 200th mission leads a group of B-26s over Magdeburg, Germany. (Photo: USAF 57532 A.C.)

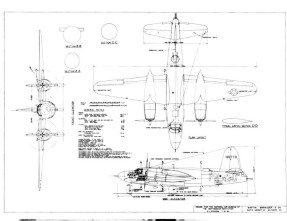

Flak Bait *wears a paper bomb denoting completion of its 200th mission, on April 17, 1945.*
(Photo: SI 78-6656)

Pilot James J. Farrell and crew pose on Flak Bait's wing as mechanics adjust the 2,000-hp Double Wasp engine.
(Photo: SI 76-8506)

Lt. Henry Bozarth and his crew flew Flak Bait *later in the plane's career.*
(Photo: Smithsonian Institution)

The crew of the 200th mission included both the squadron commander and group commander.
(Photo: SI 77-2694)

The plane immediately began living up to its name. Other bombers could pass unscathed, but *Flak Bait* invariably returned full of holes.

"It was hit plenty of times, hit *all* the time," recalls Farrell. "I guess it was hit more than any other plane in the group."

There were also encounters with enemy fighters, such as the mission of September 10, 1943, to Amiens, France. Minutes after turning away from the target, *Flak Bait* was attacked by a Messerschmitt Bf. 109 that came out of the sun. A 20-mm aircraft cannon shell penetrated the Plexiglas nose, narrowly missing the bombardier, and exploded against the back of the instrument panel. Despite having his instruments knocked out, and a metal fragment lodged in his leg, Farrell brought *Flak Bait* back to England.

"It was the best landing I ever saw the boss make," commented Sgt. Don Tyler, tail gunner of Farrell's crew.

The first crew returned to the United States in July 1944, and the plane was assigned to Lt. Graydon K. Eubank of San Antonio, Texas. Soon afterward, *Flak Bait* was reassigned to Lt. Henry "Hank" Bozarth of Shreveport, Louisiana.

"Everybody was afraid of the damn thing," remembers McDonald Darnell, Jr., radio operator in Bozarth's crew, "but she always got back for us. We always had faith in her."

Flak Bait's hour of glory came on April 17, 1945, when it completed its record 200th mission,

leading the entire 322d Bombardment Group to Magdeburg and back.

In its career, *Flak Bait* was based at four airfields—two on the continent after D-Day—and logged 725 hours of combat time. It returned twice on one engine and once with an engine on fire, had its electrical system shot out twice and its hydraulic system shot out once, and it shot down at least three German fighters. It flew against coastal targets and participated in the pre-Normandy invasion aerial offensive; it flew two missions on D-Day; it flew twenty-one missions against V-1 buzz bomb launch sites in the Pas de Calais area of France; and also attacked targets in Holland, Belgium, and France. An interesting historical note is that *Flak Bait* and other European Theater Marauders flew a number of large-scale missions at night—the only American aircraft to do so.

Today, few Martin B-26 Marauders survive. *Flak Bait,* because of its remarkable history, was included in a collection of World War II aircraft from different countries set aside for the National Aeronautical Collection by Gen. Henry H. "Hap" Arnold, and was transferred to the Smithsonian Institution in 1960. The original paint is still bright, but more than a thousand patched flak holes bear witness to the fact that this most famous of Marauders was indeed appropriately named.
Jay P. Spenser

Messerschmitt Bf 109G-6 "Gustav"

Wingspan:	9.92 m (32 ft. 6½ in.)
Length:	9.02 m (29 ft. 7 in.)
Height:	3.40 m (11 ft. 2 in.)
Weight:	Gross, 3,150 kg (6,945 lb.)
	Empty, 2,700 kg (5,953 lb.)
Engine:	Daimler-Benz DB605A-1TA, 1,475 hp

This is the aircraft after which the National Air and Space Museum patterned markings and camouflage for its Bf 109G. The Messerschmitt fighter was from III./JG27, which operated in the Eastern Mediterranean in late 1943.
(Photo: SI 73-1989, courtesy William Green)

The story of air combat over Europe cannot be told without great emphasis being given to the Messerschmitt Bf 109. It gained its fame as the major opponent of the Spitfire during the Battle of Britain and continued intense rivalry with all Allied aircraft until the close of World War II.

Designed by Professor Willy Messerschmitt and manufactured initially by the Bayerische Flugzeugwerke AG, forerunner of the Messerschmitt AG, the single-seat fighter was to gain the distinction of being produced in larger quantities than any other combat airplane except for the Russian IL-2.

The first prototype Bf 109 flew in September 1935, powered, oddly enough, by a Rolls Royce Kestrel 695-hp engine. Follow-on prototypes utilized several other engines until settling on the Daimler-Benz inverted-V, liquid-cooled engine that powered subsequent airframes throughout its wartime production.

The new fighter's first public demonstration took place at the 1936 Olympic Games held in Berlin, but the plane's first real impact on the aviation world came during the international flying meet held in Zurich in the summer of 1937. Five Bf 109s took part and demonstrated outstanding climbing, diving, and maneuverability, along with astonishing speed.

While these impressive demonstrations were taking place, twenty-four Messerschmitt fighters were delivered to Spain for the Condor Legion. By the time England declared war on Germany, the already-proven Messerschmitt was being mass-produced in the Bf 109E series and was ready to enter the fight.

The Spitfire, the Bf 109's first major opponent, was slightly faster and definitely more maneuverable, but its performance at altitude was inferior. There was also little difference in pilot skill between the Luftwaffe and the Royal Air Force, although pilots in the RAF had the advantage of fighting over their own country, while the critical

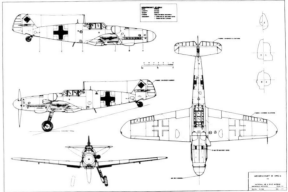

Although the original identity of the museum's Bf 109
had not been recorded, the
aircraft was fully restored
with markings as it would
have appeared in an operational combat unit.
(Photo: SI 74-4294)

On the day of its "roll-out"
at Silver Hill, Maryland, after
restoration, the Bf 109 appears ready for its pilot and
a scramble takeoff.
(Photo: SI 74-4293)

Expert craftsmen restored
the cockpit of the Bf 109 to
near-operational condition.
(Photo: SI 74-4140-1A)

range of the Bf 109s limited German fighting time
to about twenty minutes.

As Allied bomber formations and fighter-
bombers pushed the war into Germany, the
Bf 109s were forced into a combat role for which
they were not designed—that of close ground
support. In this capacity the 109s were heavily
battered by Allied fighters and ground fire. The
Messerschmitt also relentlessly attacked the
massive bomber formations, only to be heavily
pounded by the bombers' defensive crossfire. In
every air encounter over Europe, the 109s could
generally be counted on to appear for a fight.

As new and improved models of Allied fighters
entered the combat scene, the Germans countered
with upgraded models of the Bf 109, primarily with
increased power rating in the Daimler-Benz engine.
When German production stopped, the G series of
the Bf 109 was produced in far greater numbers
than any other model, 21,000 being completed by
the end of 1944. Known as "Gustav," the Bf 109G
was powered by a DB 605 engine. This machine
had two MG 131 machine guns, a single 30-mm
MK 108 cannon firing through the spinner, and
sometimes carried two underwing MG 151/20
weapons. This combination was ideal for bomber
interception but severely reduced the machine's
efficiency in fighter-versus-fighter combat.

It is an aircraft of this type that is in the collection
of the National Air and Space Museum. Nothing is

known of its German operational history, for this
was of little significance at the time of its
unrecorded capture. The fighter was shipped to
the United States with a number of other German
aircraft near the end of the war for evaluation.

It was stripped of all its unit markings and
camouflage; even its serial number was
eradicated. The FE-496 number assigned to it by
the Air Technical Intelligence Command while
operating at Wright and Freeman Field was its only
identity. After a time, the Messerschmitt was
transferred from the Air Force to the National Air
and Space Museum in 1948 along with a group of
other World War II aircraft, which were stored at
O'Hare Field, Illinois. Later, the collection was
moved to the museum's storage facility at Silver
Hill, Maryland, near Washington, D.C.

As plans for the new museum building became
definite, "Gustav" was one of the first aircraft to be
restored for exhibit. By April 1974 the aircraft was
totally restored inside and out, carrying the
selected camouflage and markings of ship number
2 of the 7th Squadron, 3d Group, 27th Wing that
operated in the Eastern Mediterranean in late 1943.
As an escort fighter, it carries the two-tone gray
camouflage pattern design.

This Bf 109G-6 is one of the best preserved
and most completely and accurately restored
Messerschmitt fighters in the world today.
Robert C. Mikesh

Messerschmitt Me 262-1a

Wingspan:	12.48 m (40 ft. 11½ in.)
Length:	12.13 m (39 ft. 9½ in.)
Height:	3.84 m (12 ft. 7 in.)
Weight:	Gross, 6,010 kg (13,250 lb.)
	Empty, 4,419 kg (9,742 lb.)
Engines:	Junkers Jumo 004B, 898 kg (1,980 lb.) static thrust each.

The Messerschmitt Me 262 was the world's first operational turbojet fighter. This aircraft was tested by the U.S. Army Air Force after World War II. The one shown here is in the collection of the National Air and Space Museum. (Photo: SI 79-4622)

The world's first operational jet fighter, the Me-262, flashed into German skies with a shape and a sound that clearly presaged the future. The premier fighter plane of World War II, the *Schwalbe* (Swallow), was powered by two Junkers Jumo 004B turbine engines and had sleekly swept wings and a powerful armament package of four 30-mm cannons.

With a top speed of approximately 540 mph, the 262 was 120 mph faster than the famed North American Mustang at the same altitude and, although not so maneuverable, was able to engage in or break off combat at will.

Conceived in 1938, the Me 262 was designed by a team led by Dr. Waldermar Voigt. It went through a long gestation period, not making its first flight until April 18, 1941, and then only under the power of a Junkers Jumo 210G piston engine of about 700 horsepower. Jet engine development, although more advanced in Germany than elsewhere, was still in a primitive state, and the turbine engines

intended for the sleek fighter were not ready. On July 19, 1942, Flugkapitan Fritz Wendel made the first takeoff under jet power, and from that point on, the Me 262 became a ray of hope in the increasingly dark skies of the German Luftwaffe.

It should be noted here that it was *not* Adolf Hitler's notorious decision that the Me 262 be built solely as a bomber that delayed its introduction into combat, but rather the inevitably slow development of the jet engines that powered it. Hitler's order did have the adverse affect of diverting some 30 percent of production into the Me 262A-2a *Sturmvogel* (*Stormbird*) bomber type.

The vastly superior performance of the Me 262 gave confidence to the fortunate pilots who flew it, but the Allied dominance of the air was so complete that the *Schwalbe* never had a chance to reach its full potential. The airfields from which it flew were under constant attack, and in the last days of the war, the remaining Me 262 units were forced to operate from makeshift bases

The Germans built two main versions of the Me 262. This is the Me 262A-1a Schwalbe (Swallow), a fighter armed with four 30-mm cannon. A fighter-bomber, the Me 262A-2 Sturmvogel (Stormbird) carried a limited variety of bombs.
(Photo: SI 79-4074)

constructed along Germany's famous autobahns.

Although 1,443 Me 262s were completed, it is estimated that only about 300 saw combat. The airplane was reportedly delightful to fly, although considerable care had to be exercised in moving the throttles on the jet engines, to avoid a compressor stall.

The museum's aircraft was captured by a special U.S.A.A.F. team led by Col. (later Maj. Gen.) Harold M. Watson, at Lechfeld, Germany, which at the war's end was a principal experimental and training base of the Luftwaffe. Watson directed Operation Lusty, which involved seizing the most advanced German aircraft and flying them back to France where they could be shipped to the United States for testing.

The museum's aircraft, a Messerschmitt Me 262A-1a, was flown to Cherbourg, where it was placed on an aircraft carrier for shipment to the United States. It was put into flying condition at Newark, New Jersey, and flown, with a single stop at Pittsburgh, to Freeman Field, Indiana, where it received the test number FE-111.

At some time during the testing process, the standard fighter nose of FE-111 was changed for the reconnaissance nose of its sister ship, FE-4012, a Messerschmitt Me 262A-1a/U3. This aircraft was sent to the Hughes Aircraft Company for rebuilding and for comparison with the Lockheed XP-80, while FE-111 was sent to Park Ridge, Illinois, for storage. It was brought to the Silver Hill Facility in 1950, and restoration work began in 1978.

The biggest challenge in the restoration project was to remove the corrosion that had built up over thirty-four years. The second-biggest problem was the restoration of the fighter nose, which involved much tedious but skillful metal work. After 6,077 manhours, the aircraft appeared as it did when it served with the famous Jagdgeschwader JG 7, complete with unit insignia and victory markings, which show forty-two victories over Russian aircraft and seven over the United States.

Although it was not destined to be a significant factor in the outcome of World War II, the Me 262 had many features that were found on later aircraft, including the sweptwing, wing slots, underslung nacelle, and heavy central cannon armament. It was a tribute to the engineering skills of the men who designed it, the people who built it under conditions of almost unimaginable adversity, and the pilots who flew it, and it fully deserves its place in the museum's Jet Aviation gallery.

Walter J. Boyne

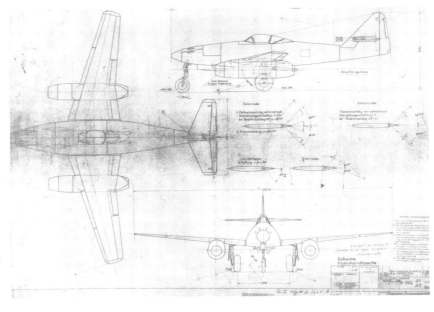

This Messerschmitt Me 262A-1a is being flown by a U.S. Air Force test pilot, Maj. Russ Schleeh. The aircraft had not been painted prior to its acquisition by U.S. forces.
(Photo: SI 79-5981)

Mitsubishi Zero-Fighter Model 52

Wingspan:	11 m (36 ft. 1 in.)
Length:	9.12 m (29 ft. 11 in.)
Height:	3.51 m (11 ft. 6 in.)
Weight:	Gross, 2,733 kg (6,025 lb.)
	Empty, 1,876 kg (4,136 lb.)
Engine:	NKIF Sakae 21, 1,130 hp

One of the major elements in the vast Japanese war machine that contributed to that country's astonishing initial success was the Zero fighter. This plane's performance was so superior in 1940, the year of its debut, that planners within the Japanese Navy felt extremely confident in the ability of the Zero to wrest air control from the enemy over any battle area.

Early in its service life, the Zero did everything expected of it—and more.

Conception of the Zero derived from the Imperial Japanese Navy's need for support for its operations over mainland China. As Japan's bombers penetrated deeper inland, the need for fighter escort increased. The requirements for this fighter included very long range, good maneuverability, and exceptional speed. This seemingly impossible combination was achieved, and when put to the test, it obtained overwhelming success in the air war over China.

To accomplish this, careful attention was paid to weight-saving measures and the use of a new lightweight aluminum alloy developed in Japan. The absence of pilot's protective armor plate and self-sealing tanks to save weight were not oversights or a complete lack of concern for pilot safety. This protection could not be incorporated in the design if the armament and performance requirements were to be met, yet those factors eventually became the Zero's undoing.

Early model Zeros first appeared over Chungking in limited numbers in August 1940, destroying all the defending fighters. So incredible were early reports of the Zero's speed, maneuverability, firepower, and range that American aeronautical experts rejected them as inaccurate and unbelievable.

After the surprise attack on Pearl Harbor, the previously ignored reports of the past year and a half became grim reality. The plane's appearance

*This Zero was one of twelve Japanese fighters captured on Saipan Island in April 1944. The museum's Zero is presumed to have been from this group and has been painted and marked like this fighter of the 261st Naval Air Corps.
(Photo: National Archives 80-G-169187)*

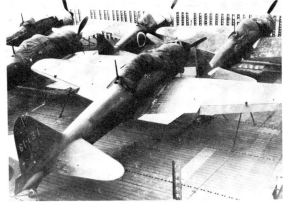

When captured on Saipan, these Zeros were the most airworthy of the Model 52s that fell into Allied hands. Lashed to the deck of the U.S.S. Copahee, they were delivered in haste to the United States for study.
(Photo: SI A49688R)

The aircraft was code-named Zeke by the Allied identification name system and its popular Japanese name was Rei-sen, meaning Zero-Fighter. Functional Japanese identification for this model, however, was A6M5.
(Photo: SI A38634C)

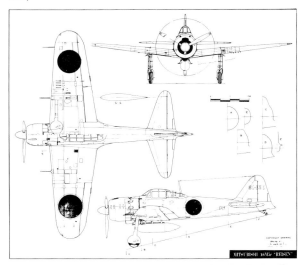

(Diagram by K. Hashimoto, courtesy Koku Fan magazine)

When the Air Technical Intelligence Command concluded its evaluation of the Zero that is now in the National Air and Space Museum, it had been stripped of all Japanese camouflage and unit markings. Here, the Zero makes one of its final landings at Wright Field, Ohio.
(Photo: National Archives 18-WP-172481)

throughout the Pacific in seemingly countless numbers in the opening days of the war created a myth about the Zero. For almost two more years the Zero. or Zeke as the Allies code-named it. remained an ominous threat and frequent victor throughout the Pacific. As American training and experience improved. the Grumman F4F Wildcat. the Zero's main adversary. became a more formidable opponent. It was not until the Grumman F6F Hellcat and the North American P-51 went into action. however. that the Zero lost its relative superiority.

Japan's aviation industry continued to develop advanced fighters to counter these new opponents. Complexities in their production and prolonged pressures of war allowed only a comparatively few of these newer types to be produced. Consequently. the more simply built Zero remained in production throughout the war. Some 10.000 Zeros were produced. more than any other Japanese warplane. From the day that the Zero was introduced into the conflict in China in mid-1940 until the last desperate attempts to counter the ever-building tide of Allied air attacks against Japan. the Zero took part in almost every major action in which the Japanese Navy was committed.

The A6M5 Zero Model 52 on display in the National Air and Space Museum is presumed to have been captured with a group of fighters on Saipan Island in April 1944. Twelve late-model Zeros were taken from the island and sent to the United States for evaluation. The earliest records pertaining to the museum's Zero show that in 1944 it was involved in such an evaluation program at Wright and Eglin fields. The plane was stripped of all its markings and colors for complete inspection. and thereby lost its individual unit identity. All that remained was its serial number 4043. etched and painted on the inside of its major components.

The markings selected for this airplane are those of the 261st Naval Air Corps. patterned after an aircraft of this unit captured at Saipan. The 261st MAC was more commonly known as the Tiger Corps. It was activated on June 1. 1943. and was soon assigned to the newly organized 1st Air Fleet. The Tiger Corps moved to the Marianas on February 16. 1944. where it participated in some of the fiercest fighting of the war.
Robert C. Mikesh

North American F-86A Sabre

Wingspan:	11.3 m (37.1 ft.)
Length:	11.5 m (37.6 ft.)
Height:	4.5 m (14.8 ft.)
Weight:	Empty, 4,750 kg (10,495 lb.)
	Gross, 7,410 kg (16,357 lb.)
Engine:	General Electric J 47-GE-13, 2,360 kg (5,200 lb.) static thrust

The F-86 Sabre joined the ranks of the great fighters high above the Yalu River area of Korea. There, despite the fact that the enemy MiG-15s could not be pursued across the Chinese border, the American Sabre pilots established a victory ratio of more than ten to one.

In the fall of 1944 the Army Air Forces ordered three prototypes of a modified North American FJ-1 Fury, a jet fighter being developed for the Navy. It was designated the XP-86. The design progressed

through the mock-up stage, but by the summer of 1945 it was apparent that the fighter's top speed would be well below the 600 mph called for in the specification. Fortunately, a great deal of captured German aerodynamic data became available to the North American designers with the surrender of Germany in May 1945. These data indicated that a sweptwing delayed the compressibility effects encountered at high subsonic speeds. Sweptwing aircraft could be controlled at a considerably

*F-86As of the 4th Fighter Interceptor Wing are lined up on the steel parking ramp in Korea.
(Photo: SI 74-9690)*

This is a view of the cockpit of the museum's F-86A. (Photo: SI 75-13177-12)

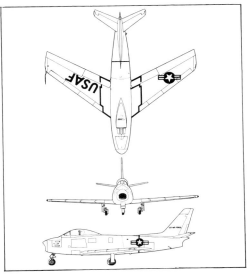

Lt. Col. William F. Barnes, USAF, with the F-86D in which he set a new world's speed record of 715.697 mph on July 16, 1953. Note the nose protrusion housing the radar antenna and the rocket pod, which is extended below the cockpit. (Photo: SI 75-11878)

higher Mach number (percentage of the speed of sound) than a straightwing aircraft of the same general configuration. The sweptwing, however, introduced low-speed stability problems. The designers, after scale model wind tunnel tests, selected a wing that was swept back at an angle of 35 degrees, and added automatic leading edge slats to solve the stability problem.

The first XP-86 flew on October 1, 1947, powered by an Allison J35-C-3, 3,750-pound-thrust engine. In April 1948, the XP-86 exceeded Mach 1 (the speed of sound) in a shallow dive. On December 28, 1947, the Air Force ordered 221 P-86As to be powered by the 4,850-pound-thrust General Electric J47-GE-1 engine. In June 1948, a month after the first P-86A flight, its designation was changed to F-86A.

On September 15, 1948, an F-86A set a world speed record of 670.981 mph. In addition to its high performance, the F-86A had excellent handling characteristics and was well liked by its pilots. The Sabre was armed with six .50-caliber M-3 machine guns mounted in the nose. The Mark 18 manual-ranging computing gunsight was replaced in later models with the A-1CM, which used radar ranging.

In December 1950, the 4th Fighter Interceptor Wing, one of the first of the Air Force's Sabre units, arrived in Seoul to fight the Russian-built

sweptwing MiG-15s, which had appeared in Korea in November. On December 17, in the first known combat between sweptwing fighters, Lt. Col. Bruce H. Hinton shot down a MiG-15. By the end of the Korean War, the Sabres had destroyed almost 800 MiG-15s with the loss of fewer than eighty F-86s.

The F-86 progressed through several improved versions—the F-86E, F, H, D, and K models. The changes, in most cases, included improved armament, more powerful engines, and control-system modifications. The F-86D, however, was an all-weather interceptor with a radar nose, and was armed with rockets instead of machine guns. The F-86K was a D with 20-mm machine guns replacing the rockets. In addition to those produced in California and Ohio, F-86s were built under license by Canada, Japan, and Italy. Of the 8,443 Sabres produced, 554 were F-86As.

The National Air and Space Museum's F-86A was assigned to the 4th Fighter Interceptor Group at Langley Air Force Base, Virginia, in July 1949. It was shipped to Japan in December 1950 with other F-86s of the 4th Group, and flown in Korea. Most of its combat missions against Mig-15s were flown from Kimpo Air Base near Seoul. It is displayed in the markings of the 4th Fighter Wing, the first F-86 unit in Korea. These markings were in use prior to June 1952.

Donald S. Lopez

North American P-51C "Excalibur III"

Wingspan:	11.28 m (37 ft. 5/16 in.)
Length:	9.83 m (32 ft. 3 in.)
Height:	3.89 m (12 ft. 9½ in.)
Weight:	Gross, 5,052 kg (11,800 lb.)
	Empty, 4,445 kg (9,800 lb.)
Engine:	Rolls Royce Merlin, V-1650-9
	1,695 hp

"**N**early every flight that was made by *Excalibur III* broke some kind of record," according to this Mustang's last pilot/owner, Capt. Charles F. Blair, Jr. It was Blair who made it possible for this record-setting airplane to become part of the National Aeronautical Collection in 1953.

The World War II operational life of this Mustang was uneventful, and following the war it was sold as surplus property to A. Paul Mantz. A movie stunt and race pilot, Mantz planned to enter the postwar resumption of the cross-country Bendix Air Race from the West Coast to the site of the National Air Races in Cleveland, Ohio. To eliminate the need for an intermediate stop, he modified the plane, converting the wing into a large fuel tank by sealing the interior. The added fuel capacity of this "wetwing" more than doubled the range of the airplane.

This modification had the desired results, for this P-51C came in first in the 1946 and 1947 Bendix Air Races with Mantz at the controls. In 1948 it

came in second and in 1949 it finished third, flown by hired pilots Linton Carney and Herman "Fish" Salmon respectively. In 1947 Mantz set a coast-to-coast speed record in each direction with this Mustang, then called *Blaze of Noon*.

Following its last Bendix Race, a challenge of a different nature was in store for this airplane. Charles F. Blair became interested in setting a solo, round-the-world speed record and purchased this Mustang from Mantz. Blair was a very experienced pilot, a captain with Pan American World Airways at the time, and had established his reputation by setting records in flying boats during his numerous crossings of the Atlantic during World War II.

With the eruption of the Korean War, however, Blair had to change his plans, since flying across international borders in a combat plane during wartime would not have been prudent. New plans were set for the plane that Blair had renamed *Excalibur III*, from the Excalibur Flying Boat that he

This is a moment of triumph for Excalibur III, *as it arrives back at New York International Airport in May 1951. It has just returned from Europe—the hard way—by flying over the North Pole to Fairbanks, Alaska, and on to New York. (Photo: SI 73-5633)*

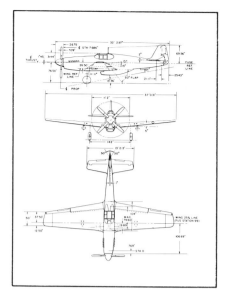

flew for American Export Airlines during World War II. After careful preparations, Blair flew his Mustang from New York to London on January 31, 1951, in 7 hours, 48 minutes, breaking the existing speed record by 1 hour and 7 minutes. This record stands today for reciprocating-engine, propeller-driven airplanes.

In the flight that followed, Blair and *Excalibur III* established their most noted record. Blair had developed a new method of air navigation in polar regions, where the magnetic compass is unreliable, if not useless. By plotting sunlines at predetermined locations and times, a reliable form of navigation was possible, Blair believed. To prove his theory, he left Bardufoss, Norway, with *Excalibur III* on May 29, 1951, heading north over the ice and snow to Fairbanks, Alaska, via the North Pole. There were no intermediate emergency landing points and no communications or radio navigation aids available to him after departing Norway. Exactly as planned, 10 hours and 27 minutes after takeoff on the other side of the world, *Excalibur III* arrived at Fairbanks. Blair financed the project and was solely responsible for every detail of the flight. For this accomplishment, he was awarded the Harmon International Trophy in 1952 by President Harry Truman. Perhaps even more important, this flight of *Excalibur III* changed defense planning for the United States; flights across the northern reaches of the globe by attacking forces were now deemed possible, and steps were taken to prevent them.

This historic flight by *Excalibur III* also carried the first official intercontinental air mail across the North Pole. On the return flight from Fairbanks to New York, another record was set for the first nonstop transcontinental solo crossing of the Alaska-Canadian route from Fairbanks to New York, flown at a leisurely pace in 9½ hours.

For Charlie Blair, there was only one rightful place for this historic airplane and that was the Aeronautical Collection of the Smithsonian Institution. At his suggestion, Pan American purchased the airplane from Blair and donated it to the National Air Museum on November 6, 1953. It was completely restored in 1977.

Robert C. Mikesh

The Merlin engine, noted for its smooth-running operation, was given a complete check by Rolls Royce personnel in England before the polar flight. (Photo: SI 76-5018)

Prior to becoming Excalibur III, this Mustang, in the red and white racing colors of Paul Mantz, leaves the Van Nuys, California, airport for Cleveland, Ohio, to win the Bendix Air Race in 1946. (Photo: Courtesy Don Downie)

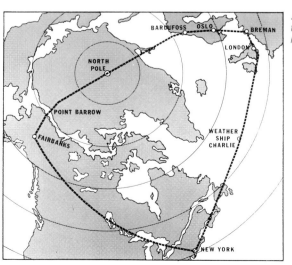

Air routes of historic flights flown by Excalibur III, piloted by Charles F. Blair.

North American P-51D Mustang

Wingspan:	11.28 m (37 ft. 5/16 in.)
Length:	9.83 m (32 ft. 3 in.)
Height:	4.16 m (13 ft. 8 in.)
Weight:	Gross, 5,262 kg (11,600 lb.)
	Empty, 3,232 kg (7,125 lb.)
Engine:	Rolls Royce Merlin, 1,695 hp

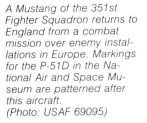

A Mustang of the 351st Fighter Squadron returns to England from a combat mission over enemy installations in Europe. Markings for the P-51D in the National Air and Space Museum are patterned after this aircraft.
(Photo: USAF 69095)

For those who flew it, the North American P-51 Mustang was a fighter pilot's airplane. To others, the name brings to mind one of the best fighter planes of World War II. Unlike other well-known and widely used fighters of that time, the P-51 was the first conceived during the war and built on the basis of combat experience.

The plane got its start because of the Royal Air Force's shortage of airplanes. British purchasing agents came to North American Aviation, Inc., early in 1940 with a request for them to build Curtiss P-40s—a lot of them and fast. The British were not enthusiastic about the P-40, but it was the best American-built fighter available at that time. The company rejected the offer but countered with a proposal to build an entirely new aircraft, superior in every way to the P-40. The British accepted with the proviso that the first airframe be completed in 120 days—a mere four months. At that time such an undertaking usually took a year or more.

The work was carried out at a grueling pace, and in less than the agreed time the new fighter rolled out of the factory doors as North American's Model NA-73X.

The British were impressed with the high speed and spectacular performance of the "Apache," as it was initially called. Within an unusually short time, by summer 1942, the first models were in combat and their popularity among the RAF pilots who flew them was apparent.

While this flow of American-built planes to England continued, two machines were purchased by the U.S. Army for evaluation and were designated XP-51. The British-preferred name of "Mustang" was soon officially adopted for this new U.S. Army Air Forces fighter. The Americans remained cool to the P-51, regarding it as something of a "foreign" design, and busied themselves in perfecting the P-38 and P-47.

In British hands, the Mustangs were the first American-built fighters to carry the war back

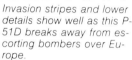

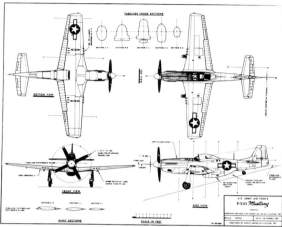

Invasion stripes and lower details show well as this P-51D breaks away from escorting bombers over Europe.
(Photo: USAF 69389A.C.)

across the English Channel after Dunkirk. They were used primarily for reconnaissance and ground support missions, coming in at low altitudes to strafe trains, troops, and enemy installations.

As the Mustangs proved themselves in combat, the USAAF took a greater interest in the plane. American observers in England could see that much of the success of the Spitfire was a result of superior performance of the dependable Rolls Royce Merlin engine with its two-speed blower. As a test, four Mustangs had their Allison engines with the single-speed blower replaced by Merlins. A four-bladed propeller replaced the three-bladed type to better absorb the increased power. From this point on, the Mustang was a spectacular performer.

Conversions on the North American production lines that took place, using the Packard-built Merlins, resulted in the P-51B from the Inglewood, California, plant and the identical P-51C from the Dallas plant. The new models proved to be unquestionable successes. The Nazis learned to fear them at any altitude—as high as their pilots wanted to take them. As for range, the new Mustangs made it possible for the first time for fighters to escort heavy bombers all the way from Britain to Berlin.

Mustangs rapidly filled Army Air Force squadrons in both the European and Pacific theaters of operations. The first land-based fighter strikes against Tokyo, on April 7, 1945, were by Iwo Jima-based Mustangs. High-altitude escort duties remained the prime mission of the P-51, and it possessed a marked edge in speed and maneuverability over all piston-engine enemy fighters.

When the last Mustang was completed, the total had reached 14,819. Unlike so many other combat aircraft that vanished at the end of the war, Mustangs continued serving as the main fighter force in the U.S. Air Force, Reserve, and Air Guard units until replaced by newer jet fighters. Many foreign air forces received Mustangs, and during the Korean War they once again saw combat.

As a representative of this famous fighter, the National Air and Space Museum has in its collection a P-51D-30, Air Force serial 44-74939. It was built late in the war, delivered to the Air Force in July 1945, and first assigned to Andrews Field, near Washington, D.C., and later to Freeman Field, Indiana. After a mere eleven months and 211 flying hours, it was set aside as a museum specimen representative of this type for the Air Force Museum. It was later transferred to the National Air Museum.

For exhibit purposes, this Mustang is painted in the yellow and black checkerboard colors of the 351st Fighter Squadron, 353d Fighter Group, 8th Air Force. This unit converted from P-47s to P-51s on September 30, 1944, while stationed at Raydon, Suffolk, England. It was typical of the many units assigned to escort bombers on missions deep into Germany. After air engagements to protect the bombers, the P-51s would attack enemy aircraft and ground installations on strafing missions on their way home. This fighter group claimed 330½ aircraft shot down and 414 destroyed on the ground. It was awarded the Distinguished Unit Citation for the support of airborne landings in Holland.

Robert C. Mikesh

North American X-15

Wingspan:	6.82 m (22.36 ft.)
Length:	15.47 m (50.75 ft.)
Height:	3.96 m (13 ft.)
Weight:	Launch configuration 17,237 kg (38,000 lb.)
	Landing configuration 5,670 kg (12,500 lb.)
Engine:	Thiokol (Reaction Motors) XLR-99-RM-2, 57,000-lb. thrust at sea level

The North American X-15 rocket-powered research aircraft bridged the gap between manned flight within the atmosphere and manned flight beyond the atmosphere into space. After completing its initial test flights in 1959, the X-15 became the first winged aircraft to attain velocities of Mach 4, 5, and 6 (four, five, and six times the speed of sound). Because of its high-speed capability, the X-15 had to be designed to withstand aerodynamic temperatures on the order of 1,200 degrees F.; as a result, the aircraft was fabricated using a special high-strength nickel alloy named Inconel X.

Air-launched from a modified Boeing B-52 Stratofortress aircraft, the X-15 required conventional aerodynamic control surfaces to operate within the atmosphere and special "thruster" reaction control rockets located in the nose and wings of the aircraft to enable the pilot to maintain control when flying on the fringes of space. Indeed, the X-15 design was so much like that of a space vehicle that during the formative days of Project Mercury, America's first attempt to put a man in orbit, North American and National Air and Space Administration (NASA) engineers gave serious consideration to utilizing a "growth" version

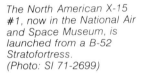

The North American X-15 #1, now in the National Air and Space Museum, is launched from a B-52 Stratofortress. (Photo: SI 71-2699)

of the X-15 for the manned orbiting mission. This plan was dropped in favor of using a blunt-body reentry vehicle. Because of the potential dangers to the pilot should the X-15's pressurized cockpit lose its atmosphere while the aircraft operated in a near-space environment, X-15 pilots wore specially developed full-pressure protection "spacesuits" while flying the experimental plane.

Three X-15 research aircraft were built and flown, completing a total of 199 research flights. The National Air and Space Museum has the historic X-15 #1, Air Force serial 56-6670. The X-15 #2 (56-6671) was rebuilt following a landing accident as the advanced X-15A-2, having increased propellant capacity and, hence, a higher potential performance. The X-15A-2 was the fastest X-15 flown, and it is now on exhibit at the Air Force Museum, Wright-Patterson Air Force Base, Ohio. The X-15 #3 (56-6672) featured an advanced cockpit display panel and a special adaptive control system. The aircraft made many noteworthy flights until it crashed during atmospheric reentry, following pilot disorientation and a control-system failure. The pilot, Capt. Michael Adams, was killed.

The X-15 flew faster and higher than any other airplane. A peak altitude of 354,200 feet (67 +

In 1967, the X-15A-2 was used to test a new ablative coating. (Photo: NASA)

miles) was reached by the X-15, and the X-15A-2 attained a speed of Mach 6.72 (4,534 mph) while testing a new ablative thermal protection material and a proposed design for a hypersonic ramjet. Various proposals were set forth for modifying the aircraft to accomplish new and even more radical tasks. At one point, NASA scientists planned to test a hydrogen-fueled supersonic combustion ramjet engine mounted on the X-15's lower vertical fin. A mock-up of this proposed installation was flight-tested on the X-15A-2. Other ideas included modifying the X-15 with a slender delta wing and using the aircraft as a booster for small satellite launch vehicles. None of these ideas, however, came to fruition.

The X-15 spearheaded research in a variety of areas: hypersonic aerodynamics, winged reentry from space, life-support systems for spacecraft, aerodynamic heating and heat transfer research, and earth sciences experiments. A total of 700 technical documents were produced, equivalent to the output of a typical 4,000-man federal research center for more than two years.

Development of the X-15 began in 1954, in a joint research program sponsored by the National Advisory Committee for Aeronautics (forerunner of NASA), the U.S. Air Force, the U.S. Navy, and private industry. North American was selected as prime contractor on the project following a competition in which Douglas, Republic, and Bell also participated. By the time of its first airborne test, flight research was too complex to rely on simple air-to-ground communications near a test field. The Air Force and the National Advisory Committee for Aeronautics developed a special 485-mile-long test corridor stretching from Wendover Air Force Base, Utah, to Edwards Air Force Base, California. It was planned that the X-15 would be air-launched from a Boeing B-52 near Wendover, then fly down this corridor, the High Range, to Edwards, monitored by tracking stations at Ely and Beatty, Nevada, and at Edwards. The range lay along a series of flat dry lakes, where the X-15 could make an emergency landing, if necessary. Nothing this extensive had previously existed in flight research, and it foreshadowed the worldwide tracking network developed by American manned spacecraft ventures. The X-15 would complete its research mission and then, followed by special Lockheed F-104 chase aircraft, would land on the hard clay of Rogers (formerly Muroc) Dry Lake. Because the X-15 featured a cruciform tail surface arrangement, it was

necessary for the designers to make the lower half of the ventral fin jettisonable prior to landing so that the conventional two-wheel, nose-landing gear and two tail-mounted landing skids could support the aircraft.

Truly a milestone aircraft, the X-15 #1 is on exhibit in the Milestones of Flight gallery.
Richard P. Hallion

Three record-breaking X-15 pilots pose beside the X-15 #1. From left to right are Joseph Walker, NASA; Maj. Robert White, USAF; and A. Scott Crossfield, North American Aviation. (Photo: Rockwell International)

The X-15A-2 is carried to launch altitude by a B-52. (Photo: NASA)

The X-15 #1 lands at Rogers Dry Lake, California, followed by a Lockheed F-104 chase aircraft. (Photo: USAF Systems Command)

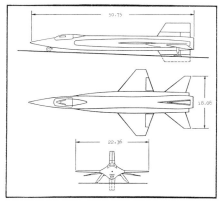

Northrop Alpha

Wingspan:	13.35 m (41 ft. 10 in.)
Length:	8.65 m (28 ft. 4½ in.)
Height:	3.25 m (9 ft.)
Weight:	Gross, 2,043 kg (4,500 lb.)
	Empty, 1,208 kg (2,660 lb.)
Engine:	Pratt and Whitney Wasp, 420 hp

The Northrop Alpha represents a notable point of transition in modern airline design, for it combined features of the past and of the future in a very utilitarian package. The passengers were enclosed in a comfortable cabin, while the pilot remained exposed—and sensitive—to the elements. The modern aspects of the Alpha—an all-metal structure, semimonocoque fuselage, and cantilever wing—were partially offset by the use of a single engine and fixed gear.

John K. Northrop, who had previously designed the Lockheed Vega, conceived of the Alpha as a means of proving his ideas for quantity production of an all-metal airplane with the machine tools existing in the early 1930s. Always pioneering new ideas and new techniques, Northrop became one of the most influential men in the aviation industry.

The Alpha was designed to be a high-performance plane that could carry mail and passengers out of small fields. The plane was attractive to airlines because of its comparatively high top speed (177 mph for later models) and high reliability. The latter was due in large part to the use of the dependable air-cooled Pratt and Whitney Wasp engine of 420 horsepower.

With the advent of the larger twin-engine Boeing and Douglas transports, the Northrop Alphas were relegated to carrying freight, serving well in this capacity. The Alpha could fly from coast to coast in twenty-three hours, carrying such commodities as freshly cut gardenias, silk worms, medical serums, and auto parts. Stops were made at Winslow (Arizona), Albuquerque, Amarillo, Wichita, Kansas City, St. Louis, Terre Haute, Indianapolis, Columbus, Pittsburgh, Philadelphia, and New York.

Although the Alpha served well, its real importance was its demonstration of Northrop's multicellular wing and stress skin construction. These concepts were of fundamental importance to the Douglas DC-2 and DC-3.

The museum's Alpha, NC11Y, was the third to be built. It was rolled out in November 1930 and

The National Air and Space Museum's Alpha, first owned by the U.S. Department of Commerce, served as the personal plane of Assistant Secretary Col. C. M. Young. Note the original style of the landing gear. (Photo: SI 75-12157)

Several Alphas were used by Transcontinental and Western Air, Inc., as a fast mail and passenger plane. Later, the Alpha was used primarily for cargo. (Photo: SI 75-12124)

became the personal plane of Col. C. M. Young, assistant secretary of commerce for aeronautics. Later, it was owned by the Ford Motor Company and National Air Transport before being sold to Transcontinental and Western Air, Inc.

NC11Y was retired sometime after 1934 and was sold to Frederick B. Lee, who outfitted it with floats for a projected round-the-world flight. The project was not completed, and the veteran Alpha passed through the hands of a succession of owners until purchased by Foster Hannaford, Jr., of Winnetka, Illinois, in May 1946. Hannaford hoped to restore the Alpha to flying condition, but was unable to do so before he died in 1971. The airplane was willed to the Experimental Aircraft Association (EAA) in Hales Corners, Wisconsin.

The National Air and Space Museum learned of the Alpha's existence and negotiated with the EAA and with Trans World Airlines for its restoration. TWA undertook the project, and a group of volunteers under the direction of Dan McGrogan brought the aircraft back to its present almost "as new" condition.

Walter J. Boyne

After its retirement from TWA, the museum's Alpha NC11Y became NR11Y when owned by F. B. Lee, and was outfitted with floats for a projected round-the-world flight. (Photo: SI 75-12206)

(Diagram: Courtesy Aerospace Industries Association of America, Inc.)

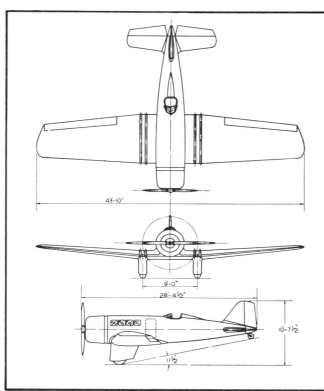

Northrop Gamma 2B "Polar Star"

Wingspan:	14.6 m (48 ft.)
Length:	9.0 m (29 ft. 9 in.)
Height:	2.7 m (9 ft.)
Weight:	Empty 1,589 kg (3,500 lb.)
	Gross 3,178 kg (7,000 lb.)
Engine:	Pratt & Whitney Hornet, 710 hp

On November 23, 1935, explorer Lincoln Ellsworth, with Canadian pilot Herbert Hollick-Kenyon, took off in the Northrop Gamma *Polar Star* from Dundee Island in the Weddell Sea and headed across Antarctica to Little America. This was not the first time that Ellsworth had attempted a transantarctic flight in the *Polar Star*.

Antarctica was the last continent to be discovered and the only one that was mapped entirely from the air. Aerial explorers from the United States, Great Britain, Australia, Norway, Canada, and France can be credited with this feat, and Lincoln Ellsworth was one of the most tenacious of these explorers.

Ellsworth, a World War I pilot, was the son of a Chicago millionaire coal mine owner. He went on his first polar expedition in 1925 with the Norwegian explorer Roald Amundsen. In May 1929, Ellsworth, Amundsen, and Italian dirigible pilot Umberto Nobile made the first transpolar flight in history, from Spitzbergen, Norway, to Alaska, in the airship *Norge*. It was Ellsworth's use of the airplane for exploration, rather than his skills as a pilot, that earned him his place in aviation history.

Ellsworth first took the *Polar Star* to the Antarctic in 1934. Sir Hubert Wilkins, the famous Australian polar explorer, went along as advisor, and the

The Northrop Gamma Polar Star was the first aircraft to make a transantarctic flight. (Photo: SI A4587A)

Polar Star's pilot was Bernt Balchen. The expedition reached the Bay of Whales by ship on January 6, 1934, and Ellsworth intended to make a round-trip flight with Balchen between the Bay of Whales and the Weddell Sea.

However, the 15-foot-thick ice on which the *Polar Star* was standing broke apart and one of the skis slipped through a crack. The aircraft was almost lost, but after long hours of work it was recovered and put back on the ship to be returned to the United States for repairs.

Ellsworth and the expedition went back to Antarctica in September. October and November were considered the best months for flying there, and this time Ellsworth planned to fly from Deception Island to the head of the Weddell Sea. However, before any flight could be made, the *Polar Star* had to be shipped to Magellanes, Chile, for repairs to a broken connecting rod, and by the time the aircraft returned to Deception Island, snow conditions made it impossible to use the runway.

The expedition then tried Snow Hill Island on Antarctica's east coast. On January 3, 1935, Ellsworth and Balchen made a successful flight to Graham Land, but clouds and snow forced them to return to Snow Hill Island after several hours.

That November, Ellsworth and Hollick-Kenyon

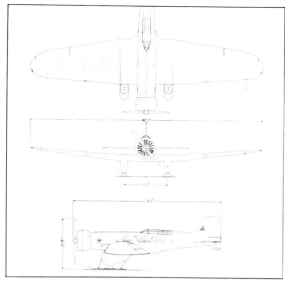

finally succeeded in flying the *Polar Star* across Antarctica. After their takeoff on the 23rd, they flew at an altitude of 13,400 feet; on crossing the 12,000-foot peaks of the Eternity Range, they became the first men to visit western Antarctica. Ellsworth named a portion of that area James W. Ellsworth Land in honor of his father.

The *Polar Star* made four landings during its flight across the Antarctic. After a blizzard that occurred during the night at the third camp, the inside of the plane was packed solid with drifted snow. The two explorers spent a whole day scooping out the dry, powdery snow with a teacup.

On December 5, fuel exhaustion forced them down about 25 miles short of their goal of Little America. They walked for six days to reach there, and then settled down in the camp abandoned by Richard E. Byrd several years earlier.

The British Research Society ship *Discovery II* sighted them on January 15, 1936. Hollick-Kenyon later returned to recover the *Polar Star*. The total distance flown by the *Polar Star* before its forced landing was about 2,400 miles. The U.S. Congress voted Ellsworth a special gold medal for his Antarctic exploration and "for claiming on behalf of the United States approximately 350,000 square miles of land in the Antarctic representing the last unclaimed territory in the world."

The *Polar Star* was one of two Northrop Gammas that were the first aircraft produced in 1933 by the newly established Northrop Corporation of Inglewood, California. The Gamma is a low-wing, all-metal cantilever monoplane with a 710-hp 9-cylinder Pratt & Whitney Hornet engine. The one built for Ellsworth had two seats in tandem with dual controls. The other of these first two Gammas was built for Frank Hawks, who at the time was a pilot for Texaco. Hawks's Gamma was a single-seat model. On June 2, 1933, Hawks set a west-east nonstop record in his Gamma, flying from Los Angeles to Floyd Bennett Field, New York, in 13 hours, 26 minutes, 15 seconds.

In April 1936, Lincoln Ellsworth donated the *Polar Star* to the Smithsonian.
Claudia M. Oakes

Ellsworth and Hollick-Kenyon load supplies into the Polar Star. *The canvas warming hood on the nose of the plane was used for 45 minutes before each start.*
(Photo: SI A37898)

The Polar Star *tandem cockpits had dual controls.*
(Photo: SI 82–5775–12)

Frank Hawks's record-setting Northrop Gamma.
(Photo: SI A1743)

Northrop N-1M Flying Wing

Wingspan:	11.6 m (38 ft.)
Length:	5.2 m (17 ft.)
Height:	1.5 m (5 ft.)
Weight:	1,814 kg (4,000 lb.)
Engines:	2 Franklin 6AC264F2
	6-cylinder, air-cooled, 120 hp

The N-1M (Northrop Model 1 Mockup) Flying Wing was a natural outgrowth of John K. "Jack" Northrop's lifelong concern for an aerodynamically clean design in which all unnecessary drag caused by protruding engine nacelles, fuselage, and vertical and horizontal tail surfaces would be eliminated. Developed in 1939 and 1940, the N-1M was the first pure all-wing airplane to be produced in the United States. Its design was the forerunner of the larger all-wing XB-35 and YB-49 bomber/reconnaissance prototypes that Northrop hoped would win Air Force production contracts and eventually change the shape of modern aircraft.

After serving apprenticeships with the Lockheed brothers and Donald Douglas in the early 1920s and designing the highly successful and innovative Lockheed Vega in 1927, Northrop in the late 1920s turned his attention to all-wing aircraft. In 1928, he left the employ of Lockheed and organized the Avion Corporation; a year later he produced his first flying wing, which incorporated such innovative features as all-metal, multicellular wing and stressed-skin construction. Although the 1929 flying wing was not a true all-wing design because it made use of external control surfaces and outrigger tail booms, it paved the way for the later N-1M, which proved the basic soundness of Northrop's idea for an all-wing aircraft. At the time, however, Northrop did not have the money to continue developing the all-wing idea.

In 1939, Northrop formed his own aircraft company, Northrop Aircraft, Inc., and as a result was in a position to finance research and development of the N-1M. For assistance in designing the aircraft, Northrop enlisted the noted aerodynamicist Dr. Theodore von Kàrmàn, who was at the time Director of the Guggenheim Aeronautical Laboratory at the California Institute of Technology, and von Kàrmàn's assistant, Dr. William R. Sears. Walter J. Cerny, Northrop's assistant design chief, became the overall supervisor for the project. To determine the flight characteristics of an all-wing design, Northrop and Cerny conducted extensive wind tunnel tests on flying wing models. Ultimately, the design of the N-1M benefited from the new low-drag, increased-stability NACA airfoils as well as improved flaps, spoilers, and other aerodynamic devices.

After a period of a year, the N-1M, nicknamed the "Jeep," emerged in July 1940 as a boomerang-shaped flying scale mockup built of wood and tubular steel with a wingspan of 38 feet, a length of 17 feet, and a height of 5 feet. Pitch and roll control was accomplished by means of elevons on the trailing edge of the wing, which served the function of both elevator and aileron. In the place of the conventional rudder was a split flap device on the wing tips; these were originally drooped downward for what was thought to be better directional stability but later straightened.

The Northrop N-1M Flying Wing flies over Muroc Dry Lake, California, during the early stages of flight testing. Downward-drooping wingtips, originally thought to improve the aircraft's directional stability, were later straightened. (Photo: SI 84-10049)

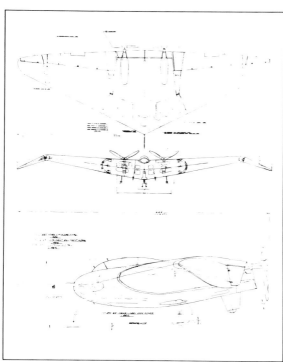

The design team of the Northrop N-1M at work in 1942. From left to right: Walter J. Cerny, Assistant Chief of Design, and supervisor of the N-1M project; John K. Northrop, President and Chief Engineer of Northrop Aircraft, Inc.; and Dr. William Sears, Northrop's Chief of Aerodynamics. Sears, along with Theodore von Kàrmàn, was recruited from the Guggenheim Aeronautical Laboratory at the California Institute of Technology.
(Photo: SI 74-03482)

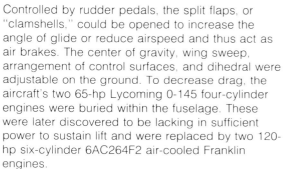

In early 1943, on what was probably its last flight, test pilot John Myers and the N-1M are towed over the California desert by a C-47 transport. When sufficient altitude was reached, the aircraft was released so that Myers could do spin tests.
(Photo: SI 84-10050)

Controlled by rudder pedals, the split flaps, or "clamshells," could be opened to increase the angle of glide or reduce airspeed and thus act as air brakes. The center of gravity, wing sweep, arrangement of control surfaces, and dihedral were adjustable on the ground. To decrease drag, the aircraft's two 65-hp Lycoming 0-145 four-cylinder engines were buried within the fuselage. These were later discovered to be lacking in sufficient power to sustain lift and were replaced by two 120-hp six-cylinder 6AC264F2 air-cooled Franklin engines.

The N-1M made its first test flight on July 3, 1940, at Baker Dry Lake, California, with Vance Breese at the controls. Breese's inaugural flight in the N-1M was inauspicious. During a high-speed taxi run, the aircraft hit a rough spot in the dry lake bed, bounced into the air and accidentally became airborne for a few hundred yards. In the initial stages of flight testing, Breese reported that the aircraft could fly no higher than 5 feet off the ground and that flight could only be sustained by maintaining a precise angle of attack. Von Kàrmàn was called in and he solved the problem by making adjustments to the trailing edges of the elevons.

When Vance Breese left the N-1M program to test-fly the North American B-25, Moye Stephens, the Northrop company secretary, took over testing of the aircraft. By November 1941, after having made some 28 flights, Stephens reported that when attempting to move the N-1M about its vertical axis, the aircraft had a tendency to oscillate in what is called a Dutch roll. That is, the aircraft's wings alternately rose and fell tracing a circular path in a plane that lies between the horizontal and the vertical. Although Stephens was fearful that the oscillations might not be controllable, he found that adjustments to the

aircraft's configuration cleared up the problem. In May 1942, Stephens was replaced by John Myers, who served as test pilot on the project for approximately six months.

Although the exact period of flight testing for the N-1M is difficult to determine because both Northrop and Army Air Forces records have been lost, we do know that after its initial test flight at Baker Dry Lake, the aircraft was flown at Muroc and Rosamond Dry Lake, and at Hawthorne, California, and that late in the testing program (probably after January 1943) it was towed by a C-47 from Muroc to Hawthorne on its last flight with Myers as the pilot.

From its inception, the N-1M was plagued by poor performance because it was both overweight and chronically underpowered. Despite these problems, Northrop convinced General H. H. "Hap" Arnold that the N-1M was successful enough to serve as the forerunner of more advanced flying wing concepts, and the aircraft did form the basis for Northrop's subsequent development of the N-M9 and of the larger and longer-ranged XB-35 and YB-49 flying wings.

In 1945, Northrop turned the N-1M over to the Army Air Forces in the hope that it would someday be placed on exhibit. On July 12, 1946, the aircraft was delivered to Freeman Field, Indiana. A little over a month later, the N-1M was given to the National Air Museum and placed in storage at Park Ridge, Illinois. On May 1, 1949, the aircraft was placed in the Museum's collection, and a few years later moved in packing crates to the Museum's Preservation, Restoration and Storage Facility in Suitland, Maryland. In 1979, the restoration of the N-1M began, and by early 1983, some four decades after it had made its final flight, the aircraft had been returned to its original condition. Dominick A. Pisano

Pentecost Hoppicopter

A personalized and inexpensive device to carry man in free flight has long been an objective of aeronautical inventors. In the late 1930s a Seattle aeronautical engineer named Horace T. Pentecost became convinced that he could design a set of personal wings for inexpensive air transportation. Pentecost was well aware of the shortcomings of man-made flapping wings, so he produced an entirely different solution to the problem. His concept was to have rotating wings like those of the helicopter, which was then coming of age.

Developed during World War II, this air machine was designed for army paratroops and intended to supplant the clumsy and uncontrollable parachute. This 88-pound device attached to the wearer's back was called the "Hoppicopter," because the trooper literally hopped off and landed on his own two feet. It consisted of little more than a 15- to 20-hp engine, a pair of 12-foot coaxial, counter-rotating blades, and a control stick mounted on a tubular frame that curved to fit over the pilot's shoulders and attached to the body by harnesses

The first Pentecost Hoppicopter is exhibited in the Vertical Flight Hall of the National Air and Space Museum.
(Photo: SI 75-13726-7A)

of the type used in parachutes. It was estimated
that this device would carry a man up to 80 mph
and reach a maximum altitude of 12,000 feet.

This concept was impressive, but the
Hoppicopter's dependency upon human legs as
landing gear proved to be its main failing. Should
the wearer stumble or lose balance upon landing,
the whirling blades became a mass of flying
splinters as they churned up the ground.

Follow-on models contained a lightweight tripod
landing gear and pilot seat, and, later, an enclosed
cabin was conceived. As refinements in the
Hoppicopter continued, the original concept
outgrew itself, and further development gave way
to other existing lightweight helicopter designs.

Before the first back-mounted model was
donated to the Smithsonian Institution in 1951, it
flew about twenty hops, with safety cables
attached to the pilot.
Robert C. Mikesh

*The Pentecost Hoppicopter
hangs in the Vertical Flight
gallery. It can be seen in
this photo at left in the rear
of the gallery. In the right
foreground is the Kellett
XO–60 autogiro.
(Photo: SI 77–6381)*

Pfalz D.XII

Wingspan:	9 m (29 ft. 6 in.)
Length:	6.35 m (21 ft.)
Height:	2.7 m (8 ft. 10 in.)
Weight:	Gross, 897.2 kg (1,978 lb.)
	Empty, 712.5 kg (1,571 lb.)
Engine:	Mercedes D.IIIa, 180 hp

The Pfalz D.XII first appeared on the Western Front in 1918 shortly after the June fighter trials at Adlershof, Germany, where a number of aircraft were accepted for production by Idflieg (Inspektion der Fliegertruppen). It was built as a replacement for the dated Albatros and Pfalz D.III scouts and the outclassed Fokker triplane. Of all-wood construction, the Pfalz D.XII was a single-seat, two-bay biplane fighter with a semi-monocoque plywood fuselage. It carried two forward-firing Maxim machines synchronized to fire through the propeller arc. The aircraft's 180-horsepower Mercedes D.IIIa, six-cylinder, water-cooled, in-line engine gave the Pfalz D.XII a top speed of 106 miles per hour and a ceiling of 18,500 feet.

From the time of its introduction until the Armistice on November 11, 1918, the Pfalz D.XII was a match for the Fokker D.VII in a climb or in level flight and could in fact outdive the D.VII. However, it could not turn well and was heavy on the controls. Furthermore, it tended to float when landing, and many accidents occurred when the undercarriage collapsed because of weakness in the spreader bar and overlength struts.

Despite these problems, the Pfalz D.XII performed well enough to relieve the German air service of its shortage of competitive fighters, and

it probably saved lives that might have been lost had the Germans continued to operate the Albatros D. Vas and others. By the time of the Armistice, nearly 800 aircraft had been delivered to front-line service. After the war a substantial number were turned over to the Allies. Of those captured aircraft, four survive. One is on display at the Musée de l'Air in Paris, France, while another is in the Australian War Memorial Collection. The two remaining examples are "ex–movie stars," one of which resides at the Doug Champlin Fighter Museum in Mesa, Arizona, and the other, at NASM.

The wartime history of NASM's Pfalz is obscure. Recently a document from the American Expeditionary Forces of the U.S. Air Service entitled "Reports of Inspection of (Captured) German Airplanes" was discovered, which refers to "two Pfalz D-12 (D.XII) which are among a batch of three (D2558/18, D2630/18 and D2740/18) . . . part of a batch inspected at Coblenz on January 1, 1919." According to a 1949 letter from the donor, Louis C. Kennell, "The two Pfalz aircraft were brought to this country as part of Allied war reparations." Kennell goes on to say, "In 1928 they were purchased from the military as war surplus and brought to Hollywood, California, for use in the original *Dawn Patrol* film." Apparently they were then purchased

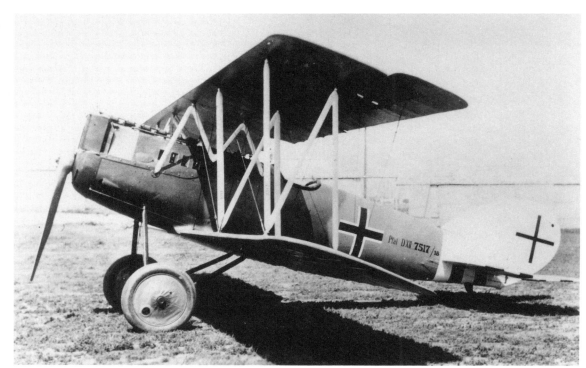

A standard late-war-production Pfalz D.XII. The tail markings indicate that this aircraft belonged to Jasta 23, which operated primarily against the U.S. Army Air Service near Verdun, France. (Photo: SI 87-11838)

Recently discovered documentation indicates that this Pfalz D.XII, captured near Koblenz, Germany, may be the aircraft that is now part of the National Aeronautical Collection. This aircraft and another Pfalz D.XII were sent to the United States in 1919 for testing and evaluation. (Photo: NASM)

NASM's Pfalz D.XII in the preposterous markings it carried in the epic 1930 Hollywood film Dawn Patrol. *This aircraft and another captured Pfalz D.XII were used as movie props throughout the 1930s. Both aircraft survived and are now treasured museum artifacts. (Photo: NASM)*

by Howard Hughes for the epic 1930 film, *Hell's Angels*. Afterward, they were repainted and appeared in First National's *Dawn Patrol*. Most of the existing film coverage of the Pfalz comes from this movie, and there are several stills from the film of the NASM aircraft.

After their use in *Dawn Patrol*, the two aircraft were sent to a Hollywood back lot for storage. One Pfalz was purchased in 1936 by the late Col. G. B. Jarrett. Frank Tallman owned it next, and after his death it was auctioned off as part of the Wings and Wheels Collection in Orlando, Florida. Bought by Doug Champlin, it now rests in his museum.

Our aircraft remained on the lot until 1938, when it was purchased by Paramount Pictures property manager Louis C. Kennell, who restored the aircraft for the motion picture *Men with Wings*. It is not clear if the airplane appeared in the film, however. In 1949, Paul Garber acquired the Pfalz D.XII for the National Air Museum. It remained in storage until 1963, when it was sent to the Experimental Aircraft Association Museum Foundation to be restored in the authentic markings of a "generic" Pfalz D.XII.

In 1989 NASM decided to use the Pfalz D.XII in the new World War I exhibition. Considering the condition of the Pfalz D.XII and the illustrious movie history of this particular aircraft, it was decided to refurbish the Pfalz as it appeared in the Hollywood classic *Dawn Patrol*. The aircraft was inspected, the minor corrosion treated, and a coat of paint applied to the synthetic fabric covering. When authentic fabric becomes available and NASM's five remaining World War I aircraft are restored, the Pfalz will be returned to its original configuration.

Karl S. Schneide

In 1949, Paramount Pictures property manager, Louis C. "Buck" Kennell, flew his Pfalz D.XII from California to Washington, D.C., in order to donate it to the Smithsonian Institution's new National Air Museum. (Photo: SI 41691-B)

Piasecki PV-2

Rotor Diameter: 7.62 m (25 ft.)
Fuselage: 6.42 m (21.5 ft.)
Weight: Gross, 454 kg (1,000 lb.)
Engine: Franklin, 90 hp

The Piasecki PV-2 helicopter was first flown on April 11, 1943, by Frank N. Piasecki, who had only fourteen hours of flying time in a Piper Cub. It was the second helicopter to be successfully flown in the country.

The helicopter was the brainchild of Piasecki and his codesigners, Elliott Daland and Donald Meyers, who together formed the P-V Engineering Forum of Philadelphia. At a time when many helicopter projects were in the experimental stage, Piasecki developed a simply controlled helicopter that was successful on its first flight. The P-V Engineering Forum put together $3,000 and acquired a vacant garage to test their theories using, among other things, a clothesline to hold the helicopter down and an outboard motor to provide gears to the tail rotor.

Piasecki not only designed and built the PV-2 but also taught himself to fly it in the process. He was the first person to receive a helicopter pilot's license without already holding an aircraft pilot's license.

The PV-2 was a single-seat helicopter with a gross weight of 1,000 pounds, and was powered by a 90-hp four-cylinder, Franklin air-cooled engine. Cruising speed was 85 mph with a top speed of 90–100 mph. It had an endurance of two hours and a range of 150 miles.

The three-blade main rotor had a diameter of 25 feet and a tip speed of about 350 mph. The spars of the 12-foot rotor blades were made of tubular steel, while the leading and trailing edges were wood, all fabric covered. For storage, the main rotor blades could be folded back over the fuselage. Its five-foot diameter, two-blade tail rotor was mounted in the right rear of the tail boom.

Several innovative design features were incorporated in the main and tail rotor systems. The blades were dynamically balanced and had flapping restrainers that allowed for quicker response to control movements by the pilot. Directional control was attained by means of a tail rotor, whose blades were attached by wires in tension (but free to twist) and were controlled by

Piasecki at the controls of his helicopter. He was his own test pilot while learning to fly the helicopter at the same time.
(Photo: SI 79-12288)

In the cockpit of the PV-2 is Frank N. Piasecki, founder of P-V Engineering Forum, with Elliott Daland, chief engineer for the project, standing alongside. Note the bulb horn on the side. (Photo: SI 79-12285)

Tipping his hat as he hovers for the photographer, Piasecki shows how easily the PV-2 handles. His goal was to produce a simple and practical helicopter with advanced methods of control and design. (Photo: SI 79-12286)

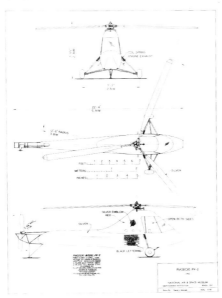

The first public demonstration of the Piasecki PV-2 took place in October 1943 at Washington National Airport. The PV-2 was the second helicopter to be successfully flown in the United States. (Photo: SI 79-12287)

rudder pedals. The combination of main and tail rotor blades utilized the torque reaction method developed by von Baumhauer: the antitorque rotor was geared to maintain a constant speed relationship with the main rotor.

The cyclic pitch control stick was suspended from the roof of the helicopter cabin and the collective pitch of the main rotor could be set so that the craft could be flown with only the throttle. To take off, the collective pitch control was placed in the forward position and the throttle opened. As the rotor speed increased, the helicopter would rise into the air. Then the cyclic pitch control stick was pushed forward for horizontal flight and eased back as the throttle was adjusted to maintain cruising speed.

During the early stages of design, the Navy Bureau of Aeronautics had reviewed the drawings of the PV-2 and was impressed by what it found. After observing the first public demonstration of the maroon and silver PV-2 on October 20, 1943, at Washington National Airport, the Navy awarded a contract to Piasecki and the Forum for the development and construction of a tandem rotor helicopter. The PV-3 (Navy designation XHRP-1), or "Flying Banana," was successfully flown in March 1945 and was subsequently produced as the HRP-1.

P-V Engineering Forum became the Piasecki Helicopter Corporation in 1946 and continued to develop and produce tandem transport helicopters. The PV-2 was never put into production and remained a one-of-a-kind helicopter.

The Piasecki PV-2 was given to the National Air and Space Museum by the Piasecki Aircraft Corporation on July 6, 1965, and spent many years on display at the Marine Corps Museum in Quantico, Virginia. It is now on exhibit in the Vertical Flight gallery.

Dorothy S. Cochrane

Piper J-3 Cub

Wingspan:	10.7 m (35 ft. 2½ in.)
Length:	6.83 m (22 ft. 4½ in.)
Height:	1.9 m (6 ft. 8 in.)
Weight:	Gross, 554 kg (1,220 lb.)
	Empty, 309 kg (680 lb.)
Engine:	Continental A-65, 65 hp

The Piper J-3 Cub is perhaps the most famous light airplane of all. The National Air and Space Museum's Cub was flown to Washington, D.C., from Houston, and is shown here before its 1941 markings were restored.
(Photo: SI 80-3909)

First built in 1938, the Piper J-3 earned its fame as a trainer. So successful was it that the name "Cub" soon came to be a generic term for all light airplanes, and Piper Aircraft became the best known general aviation manufacturer.

The story of the J-3 began in the late 1920s with C. Gilbert and Gordon Taylor, partners in the very small Taylor Brothers Aircraft Company of Rochester, New York. Onetime barnstormers, the brothers had designed and were attempting to market a two-seat monoplane called the Chummy, when Gordon Taylor was killed in a crash.

Gilbert Taylor, who believed there would be a growing market for light planes, moved in 1929 to Bradford, Pennsylvania, where community leaders were anxious to promote new local industries. The Bradford Board of Commerce provided $50,0000 to capitalize the new Taylor company, which built five Chummys before the Great Depression put a halt to construction.

One of the stockholders was an oilman named William T. Piper. Being interested in aviation and believing that the Chummy was too expensive and inefficient, Piper offered to sponsor the development of a small plane to sell for half the Chummy's $3,985. The resulting aircraft, designated the E-2, was completed in late 1930, and fitted with a two-cylinder Brownbach "Tiger Kitten" engine.

Testing had revealed the Tiger Kitten, which was rated at 20 hp, had too little power for the E-2. At full throttle, the small plane was able only to indulge in "grass cutting," rising a few feet into the air before settling back to earth. The Tiger Kitten engine had suggested the name Cub for the airplane, however, denoting the E-2 as the earliest true ancestor of the J-3.

With no suitable power plant, the Taylor company was forced to declare bankruptcy in 1931. Piper bought up the assets, keeping C. G. Taylor on as chief engineer. Later that year, Continental Motors Corporation came out with the

Built as sport and training aircraft, more than 14,000 Piper J-3 Cubs were completed between 1938 and 1947.
(Photo: SI 80-3908)

The sporting aspect of the Piper J-3 is accentuated in this view of a Cub on floats.
(Photo: SI 80-3910)

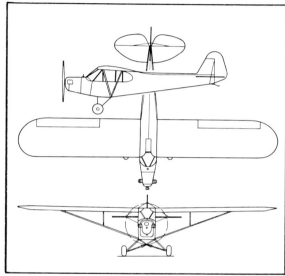

Designated the Piper L-4 Grasshopper and featuring additional window area, the Cub saw Army service in World War II as an observation and liaison aircraft.
(Photo: SI A52,483)

37-hp A-40, and the Taylor E-2 Cub was placed on the market. Twenty-two were sold that year, with sales growing tenfold by 1935.

The following year, the plane was completely redesigned. Redesignated the Taylor J-2, it featured a greatly improved Continental engine. Also in 1936, C. G. Taylor left to establish the Taylorcraft Aviation Company in Alliance, Ohio.

When the plant at Bradford burned down in 1937, Piper moved his manufacturing equipment and more than two hundred employees to an abandoned silk mill in Lock Haven, Pennsylvania. The company resumed production under the name Piper Aircraft Corporation and completed 687 aircraft before the end of the year.

In 1938 Piper introduced the improved J-3 Cub. Powered by 40-hp Continental, Lycoming, or Franklin engines, the J-3 sold for $1,300. Engine horsepower was soon raised to fifty and reached sixty-five by 1940. Piper also standardized a color scheme: just as Henry Ford's Model Ts were all black, so William Piper's Cubs were all bright yellow with black trim.

Immediately before the entry of the United States into World War II, sales of the Cub were spurred by the organization of the Civilian Pilot Training (CPT) Program. In 1940 3,016 Cubs were built and at the wartime peak a new J-3 emerged from the factory every twenty minutes. Seventy-five percent

of all pilots in the CPT Program were trained on Cubs, many going on to more advanced training in the military.

Cubs were also flown during the war as observation, liaison, and ambulance planes. Known variously as the L-4, O-59, and NE-1, these planes rendered valuable service and were nicknamed "Grasshoppers."

By 1947, when production ended, 14,125 Piper Cubs had been built. The J-3 is now finding an ever-increasing popularity among antique airplane buffs, and brand new Cubs are being constructed by homebuilders. Both an excellent trainer and a delightful sport plane, which lends itself to lazy summer afternoons, the Cub might best be summed up by the words "simple," "economical," and above all, "slow."

The National Air and Space Museum's Piper J-3 Cub, serial number 6578, was built in March 1941. Powered by a Continental A-65 engine, it accumulated approximately 6,000 hours of flying time before being completely restored in 1975. It was donated to the National Air and Space Museum in April 1977 by Roland M. Howard, David L. Stirton, W. Howell Cocke, Jr., and Robert J. Randolph, and is now exhibited in the General Aviation gallery.

Jay P. Spenser

Piper PA-12 "City of Washington"

Wingspan:	10.80 m (35 ft. 5½ in.)
Length:	6.85 m (22 ft. 6 in.)
Height:	2.08 m (6 ft. 10 in.)
Weight:	Gross, 793 kg (1,750 lb.)
	Empty, 454 kg (1,000 lb.)
Engine:	Lycoming O-235-C, 104 hp

The end of World War II saw the resumption of private aircraft manufacture. The Piper Aircraft Company, already well known for the J-3 Cub and the J-5 Cruiser, began production of improved models of these aircraft. These were the Piper PA-11 Cub Special and the Piper PA-12 Super Cruiser.

W. C. Jamoneau, who was head of the engineering department at Piper for many years, is given credit for modifying the J-5 into the PA-12. Test flights were made in December 1945, and the first production version of the aircraft appeared in February 1946. A four-place version, known as the PA-14 Family Cruiser and featuring a 115-hp Lycoming engine, was built in 1948.

The original J-5 series were fabric-covered, three-place, high-wing monoplanes powered by 75-hp Lycoming engines initially, and later by 90-hp Lycomings. The PA-12 was also fabric-covered, over a welded metal tubular frame and wooden wing spars, and featured a Lycoming O-325-C engine, fully cowled. Later models of the PA-12 had as optional equipment a slightly more powerful engine. Standard features on the PA-12 included an electric starter, navigation lights, and a cabin heater.

The Piper PA-12 Super Cruiser was used in a number of roles, from private pleasure flying to light cargo carrying. It was also successful in the export market. A number are still flying.

The museum's specimen is the famous *City of Washington,* one of two Super Cruisers to fly around the world in 1947.

Maj. Clifford V. Evans and Maj. George Truman, two Air Force Reserve officers, became interested in the flight as a result of an offhand remark of Evans that a Piper Cub could fly around the world.

Neither Evans nor Truman was wealthy, so they had to convince Piper, Lycoming, and other manufacturers to donate the necessary equipment. Finally, they were able to arrange for two fully equipped, secondhand Piper Super Cruisers to be furnished for the trip. The planes were modified by the addition of a metal rather than wood, fixed-pitch propeller, extra instruments and radio equipment, and extra fuel tanks.

On the morning of August 9, 1947, Evans in the *City of Washington* and Truman in the companion ship, *City of the Angels,* left Teterboro, New Jersey.

The flight took four months and 22,500 miles. Weather was the biggest problem; the only mishap

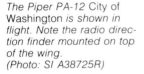

The Piper PA-12 City of Washington *is shown in flight. Note the radio direction finder mounted on top of the wing.*
(Photo: SI A38725R)

George Truman (left) and Clifford Evans are standing by their respective aircraft. (Photo: SI 75-13593)

This is the instrument panel of the City of Washington. It was more elaborate than the panels of most PA-12s. (Photo: SI A38725F)

This route was followed by the City of Washington and the City of the Angels on their around-the-world flight in 1947. (Photo: SI 75-13594)

(Diagram: Courtesy Aerospace Industries Association of America, Inc.)

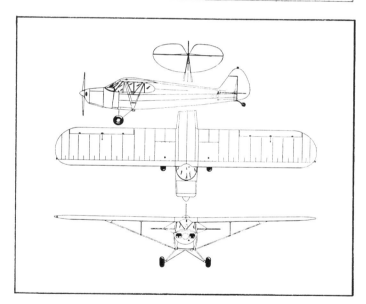

was a damaged tail wheel on one of the landings. In Dhahran, Saudi Arabia, the pilots were detained six days by authorities, even though their papers were in order.

Their successful arrival at Teterboro on December 10, 1947, marked the first around-the-world flight of an airplane of under 100 horsepower.

The *City of Washington* was presented to the National Air Museum by William T. Piper, Sr., on September 17, 1949.
Michael E. Dobson

Pitcairn AC-35

Rotor diameter:	11.06 m (36 ft. 4 in.)
Length:	6.60 m (21 ft. 8 in.)
Height:	2.44 m (8 ft.)
Weight:	Gross, 603 kg (1,330 lb.)
Engine:	Pobjoy Cascade, 90 hp

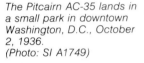

The Pitcairn AC-35 lands in a small park in downtown Washington, D.C., October 2, 1936.
(Photo: SI A1749)

An aircraft in everyone's garage—such was the aim of the Autogiro Company of America's AC-35 roadable autogiro. Work began on this aircraft in 1935 when the Experimental Development Section of the Bureau of Air Commerce awarded a contract for the development of an advanced version of the PA-22, a small cabin autogiro built by the Pitcairn Autogiro Company, of which the Autogiro Company of America was a subsidiary. This new aircraft was one of six experimental aircraft manufactured for the bureau as part of its development program for private-owner aircraft types.

The AC-35 had many features designed to appeal to the public. The rotor blades could be folded back over the fuselage for ground travel and for storage in a 7 × 24-foot space, certainly small enough for the average-size garage. It could be flown by a licensed pilot who did not need rotary-wing-aircraft experience. On the road, the aircraft could reach a modest speed of 25 mph maximum. It seated two in a side-by-side

arrangement and had hand baggage storage space behind the seats.

The 90-hp Pobjoy "Cascade" engine was mounted behind the cabin. A shaft encased in a metal housing extended through the cabin between the two seats to the propeller installation. When the AC-35 made its first flight on March 26, 1936, it was equipped with two contrarotating propellers, but, because they produced excessive noise, they were replaced by a single propeller. The engine was also connected by a shaft to the tailwheel for use on the road. This wheel, on which the aircraft's roadability depended, was the same size as the main wheels.

For road use the rotor blades could be folded back over the fuselage, the propeller disengaged, and the tailwheel put in gear. The front wheels were used for steering.

The fuselage was of welded steel tube construction with wooden fairing strips and metal and fabric covering; the tail section was entirely of

James G. Ray of the Auto-giro Company of America drives the roadable aircraft down Washington's Constitution Avenue.
(Photo: SI 74-2677)

The AC-35's blades are being folded to convert the craft to its roadable configuration.
(Photo: SI A38539H)

wood with fabric covering.

In addition to its use by the public as a pleasure craft, there were endless other possibilities for the AC-35—military and commercial transportation, aerial surveillance and photography, and police and forestry patrol, to mention only a few.

On October 2, 1936, James G. Ray, vice president and chief pilot of the Autogiro Company of America, landed the AC-35 in a small downtown park in Washington, D.C., just north of the Department of Commerce building. There he converted the aircraft to its roadable configuration and drove it to the main entrance of the Commerce Building. It was accepted by John H. Geisse, chief of the Aeronautics Branch, and was taken to the department's hangar at Bolling Field where further test flights were made. It was also demonstrated publicly at air shows and other gatherings during that year.

In 1937 the Bureau of Air Commerce loaned the AC-35 back to the Autogiro Company of America for use in testing and perfecting a new design with which Pitcairn engineers were experimenting. It remained at Pitcairn Field until 1942 when it was returned to the Bureau of Air Commerce. In 1950 it was presented to the Smithsonian Institution for the National Aeronautical Collection.

In 1961 Skyway Engineering Company, Inc., of Carmel, Indiana, signed a contract with the Autogiro Company of America to obtain exclusive design rights, blueprints, test data and analyses, and patent rights in order to once again produce AC-35s. The company planned to replace the original Pobjoy engine with 135-hp Lycoming O-290-D2Bs, raising the cruising speed from 75 to 120 mph and giving the aircraft a rate of climb of 700 feet per minute from a "jump start." This later version was not roadable, however. Its range was 300–400 miles, and for extra convenience floats or skis could be added by the factory at special request. Skyway planned to sell the aircraft for $10,000–$15,000.

One model was built and successfully test flown at Terry Field near Indianapolis in the mid-1960s. Shortly afterward, however, the company was dissolved because of internal problems, and no other AC-35s were built.

Claudia M. Oakes

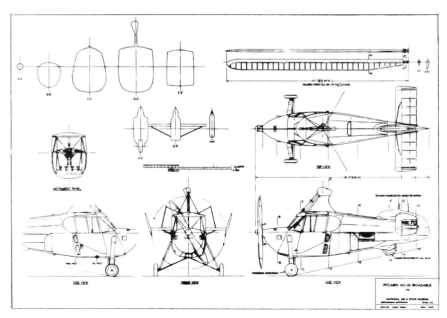

Pitcairn Mailwing

Wingspan:	10.05 cm (33 ft.)
Length:	6.67 m (21 ft. 10½ in.)
Height:	2.83 m (9 ft. 3½ in.)
Weight:	Gross, 1,139 kg (2,512 lb.)
	Empty, 731 kg (1,612 lb.)
Engine:	Wright Whirlwind J-5-C, 200 hp

The "gold" in the golden years of aviation was usually extracted by a winning combination of finances and design genius. Such was the case of Pitcairn Aircraft, Inc., where the money of Harold F. Pitcairn and the talent of Agnew Larsen joined to produce a series of clean, efficient aircraft that were to be of great significance to air transportation.

Perhaps their most important product was the Pitcairn PA-5 Mailwing, a trim, fighterlike, open-cockpit biplane. Considerably smaller than its western counterparts, the Boeing 40A and Douglas M-2, the PA-5 achieved a reputation for efficiency and reliability that resulted in a production run for it and its derivatives of well over one hundred aircraft.

The PA-5's good performance stemmed from three factors—a clean, lightweight airframe; the reliable Wright Whirlwind engine; and the use of a Pitcairn-developed airfoil, which permitted a relatively high top speed of 136 mph and also excellent load-carrying capability.

Larsen and his small team used good, imaginative engineering techniques to create an aircraft that would carry the small loads that could reasonably be expected on the still new airmail routes, thus avoiding the pitfall of many designers

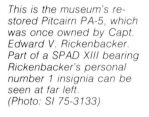

This is the museum's restored Pitcairn PA-5, which was once owned by Capt. Edward V. Rickenbacker. Part of a SPAD XIII bearing Rickenbacker's personal number 1 insignia can be seen at far left.
(Photo: SI 75-3133)

who built airplanes for loads that would not be generated for several years. While the construction was, in the main, conventional, there were several innovative features, including the use of easily fabricated square tubing in the fuselage and an ingenious quick-change engine mounting.

The PA-5 was first used by Texas Air Transport on Contract Air Mail Route 21 on November 27, 1927, only four months after the first Mailwing had been licensed by the Civil Aeronautics Administration. The plane's reputation, however, was really established on the New York-to-Atlanta run, CAM #19, which was flown by Pitcairn Aircraft. Service began on May 1, 1928. The little Pitcairns, flying by night, followed the newly lighted airways between Philadelphia, Baltimore, Washington, Richmond, and Atlanta. The 760-mile route was flown in seven hours, just one-third the time it took by rail.

The forward-looking company took over the Atlanta–Miami route on December 1, 1928, creating the basic structure upon which its successor organization, Eastern Air Transport, would prosper. The new route added 595 miles and permitted fifteen-hour service between New York and Miami by the expanded fleet of sixteen Mailwings.

In its original form, the Pitcairn sometimes had the smooth nose cowling shown here. This is the prototype PA-5, which placed eleventh in the 1927 Ford Reliability Tour and which is on display in the museum. (Photo: SI A46624E)

This PA-5 has the mail bay open, possibly modified to a passenger configuration. Note the very large ailerons, the relatively simple wire bracing, and the generally clean lines. (Photo: SI 75-3134)

Huge landing lights were necessary, as field lighting was nonexistent-to-primitive and every candlepower helped. The elaborate landing gear set-up featured long-stroke oleo struts to ease the shock of rough fields. (Photo: SI 75-3132)

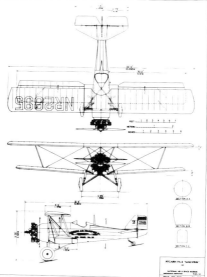

Far from being a gallant pony express operation, the entire Pitcairn route was cleverly planned, having five well-staffed and equipped airports with complete facilities for maintenance and even flight training.

Other airlines bought the PA-5s as well as the later PA-6, PA-7, and PA-8; a partial listing includes Colonial Air Transport, Colonial Western Airways, and Universal Division of American Airways.

The later developments were each slightly more refined, powerful, and streamlined. Detail improvements were added, including more secure mail storage, fire extinguishers, better cockpit heating and ventilation, and larger engines with a mild corresponding improvement in performance.

Civilian versions for sportsman flyers were created, with the mail compartment converted into a commodious two-passenger seat. These aircraft had a glamorous image deriving from their airmail heritage.

Progress ultimately caught up with the Mailwings as improvements in aircraft and increased load requirements made the general type obsolete. They passed from mail service to more general duties, including the dangerous task of crop-dusting, where their great structural strength made them popular with pilots. The stability that had been so advantageous flying the mail did limit their maneuverability in the dusting business, however.

The trim yellow and black Pitcairn on display had an especially exciting history, for it is the prototype Pitcairn PA-5, having the manufacturer's number 1 displayed on its registration plate.

Registered N 2895, the first Pitcairn rode the crest of the national enthusiasm for aviation in the late 1920s. Pitcairn's chief pilot, James G. Ray, placed eleventh in the 1927 Ford Reliability Tour. In the same year, Ray was seventh in the very demanding New York-to-Spokane Air Derby, demonstrating once again the durability and reliability of the plane. He also won first place in the free-for-all races held in Spokane immediately after the Air Derby, to add a flavor of speed to the growing reputation of the Mailwing.

The prototype was sold to Eastern Air Transport, which used it profitably through 1934. It averaged about 500 flying hours per year, an exceptionally high utilization rate for the period. It was then converted to carry passengers, beginning an odyssey through the hands of seven different owners before being repurchased by John Halliburton of Eastern Air Lines, Inc. Halliburton led a group that restored the airplane as a gift for a Capt. Edward V. Rickenbacker, who had guided Eastern for so many years. In 1957 it was donated to the National Air and Space Museum, where it forms an interesting contrast to the more sophisticated planes that followed it.

Walter J. Boyne

Pitts Special

Wingspan:	Upper, 5.28 m (17 ft. 4 in.)
Length:	4.72 m (15 ft. 6 in.)
Weight:	Gross, 476 kg (1,050 lb.)
	Empty, 290 kg (640 lb.)
Engine:	Any engine between 85–180 hp, usually Lycomings 100–180 hp

In 1943 Curtis Pitts of Homestead, Florida, built the first of a line of aircraft that will probably be considered the most famous aerobatic type ever designed—the Pitts Special.

The prototype was wrecked about two weeks after its first flight. Number 2 was *Little Stinker*, built in 1946 and flown at air shows for a year by Phil Quigley, an employee of Pitts. It was then sold to Betty Skelton, who flew it in dozens of air shows and several major competitions before she sold it, some years later. *Little Stinker* went through many hands before getting back to Betty Skelton (now Mrs. Donald Frankman) several years ago.

A few more Pitts Specials were built by Curtis Pitts himself in the 1950s, but the airplane remained a minor type until the early 1960s, when Pitts produced a fine set of construction drawings for sale to interested amateurs for $125 per set. The most commonly seen version of the airplane is the model S-1C, with two ailerons, M-6 airfoils, and any engine from 85 hp up to 180 hp, the most popular being 125–150-hp Lycomings. An estimated 250 Pitts Specials—built in basement workshops and garages—are currently flying.

While most of the Pitts Specials are in the United States, their international reputation is growing fast. These airplanes are now flying in England, Finland, South Africa, Canada, and Jamaica.

The Pitts's role in aerobatic competition dates back to the 1965 U.S. National Aerobatic Championships. Its first win was in 1966, when Bob Herendeen became U.S. champion in his S-1C Pitts. In the same year he competed in the World Championships in Moscow in that plane, arousing considerable interest in Europe.

The S-1S Pitts was flown by two of the three members of the victorious U.S. Aerobatic Team in the 1970 World Championships, and by all three members in 1972. Also in 1972, Individual World Champions Charlie Hillard and Mary Gaffaney flew

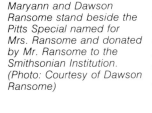

Maryann and Dawson Ransome stand beside the Pitts Special named for Mrs. Ransome and donated by Mr. Ransome to the Smithsonian Institution. (Photo: Courtesy of Dawson Ransome)

The winning team in the 1972 World Aerobatic Championships, from bottom to top: Charlie Hillard, Tom Poberezny, Gene Soucy.
(Photo: Courtesy Judy Booth through EAA, SI 73-5660)

(Diagram: Courtesy Model Airplane News)

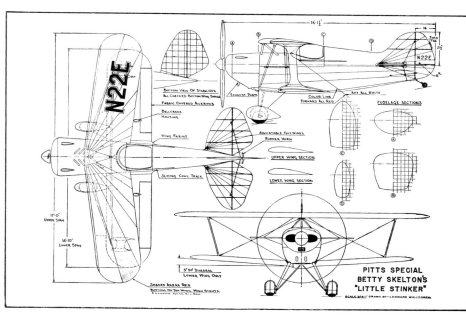

S-1S Pitts Specials. The U.S. National Champion (Men's) has flown an S-1S every year since 1969. and Women's every year since 1967.

In addition, two pilots on the British team flew S-1S Pitts in the 1972 World Championships, and the Canadian team was equipped with S-1S and S-2A Pitts when they entered world competition for the first time in 1974.

The Pitts is perhaps the most popular single design among amateur builders in the United States. Most build the S-1C, although an increasing number are going to the S-1S competition version, which has four ailerons, symmetrical airfoils, and generally, a 180-hp Lycoming engine.

The S-1S has been granted an Approved Type Certificate by the Federal Aviation Administration and is in production at the Pitts factory in Afton, Wyoming. Preceding it in production is the two-seat S-2A, the first truly competitive aerobatic machine commercially produced in the United States.

In 1973, as part of the Smithsonian exhibit to commemorate the U.S. Aerobatic Team winning the World Championships, a Pitts Special of the type used by the team members was on display in the Arts and Industries Building. It was on loan from J. Dawson Ransome, a member of the official delegation to the World Championships. Ransome has since donated the aircraft to the National Air and Space Museum as a lasting national tribute to the team and to exhibition flight.
D. L. Berliner

Rutan Voyager

Wingspan:	33.8 m (110.8 ft.) with winglets
	33 m (108.3 ft.) without winglets
Length:	Fuselage, 7.7 m (25.4 ft.)
	Boom, 8.9 m (29.2 ft.)
Height:	3.1 m (10.3 ft.)
Weight:	Gross, 4,397.4 kg (9,694.5 lb.)
	Empty, 1,020.6 kg (2,250 lb.)
Engine:	Teledyne Continental
	Front, 0-240, 130 hp
	Rear, IOL-200, 110 hp

On December 23, 1986, *Voyager* completed the first nonstop, non-refueled flight around the world. *Voyager*, a unique aircraft constructed almost entirely of lightweight graphite-honeycomb composite materials and laden with fuel, lifted off from Edwards Air Force Base, California, at 8:01:44 a.m., Pacific Standard Time, on December 14, 1986. Nine days later it returned at 8:05:28 a.m., Pacific Standard Time. For their record-breaking flight, the pilots, Dick Rutan and Jeana Yeager; the designer, Burt Rutan; and the crew chief, Bruce Evans, earned the Collier Trophy, aviation's most prestigious award. *Voyager* was the result of six years of design, construction, and development by a talented team of individuals. Designer Burt Rutan had established his reputation with home-built airplanes such as the VariViggen and VariEze and corporate aircraft such as the Beech Starship. Construction began in the summer of 1982 at the Civilian Flight Test Center, Mojave Airport, California. The first flight was made on June 22, 1984.

Voyager was designed for maximum fuel efficiency and, therefore, used lightweight composite materials in 98 percent of its structure. The main material is a .635-centimeter (1/4-inch) sandwich of paper honeycomb and graphite fiber, carefully molded and cured in an oven. The entire airframe was constructed without using metal, and weighs only 425 kilograms (939 pounds). *Voyager*

Roll-out at Mojave Airport, California, 1984.
(Photo: Courtesy of Mark Greenberg, VISIONS)

took more than 22,000 work hours and over 18 months to construct. The long, thin main wing was so flexible that the wing tip deflected upward 0.9 to 1.5 meters (3 to 5 feet) while *Voyager* was in flight. The purpose of the winglets was to raise the fuel vent from the three outboard wing tanks high enough to keep fuel from draining out onto the ground. The cabin area and cockpit were side by side within the fuselage.

Voyager was virtually a flying fuel tank. It had eight storage tanks on each side of the airplane and a fuel tank in the center, for a total of 17 tanks. The pilot shifted fuel from tank to tank during the flight to keep the airplane in balance. The 3,181.3 kilograms (7,011.5 pounds) of fuel aboard at takeoff amounted to 72.3 percent of *Voyager's* gross takeoff weight. At the end of the flight only 48 kilograms (106 pounds) of fuel remained. Two engines, one at each end of the fuselage, powered *Voyager*. The highly efficient 110-horsepower, liquid-cooled main rear engine, a Teledyne Continental IOL-200, ran during the entire flight except for four minutes when a fuel problem caused a temporary shutdown. The 130-horsepower, air-cooled front engine, a Teledyne Continental 0-240, was used for a total of 70 hours and 8 minutes during the initial, heavy-weight phase of the flight, while climbing over weather, and at other critical times. *Voyager* was equipped with

Hartzell constant-speed, variable-pitch aluminum propellers, which proved critical in stretching the aircraft's range enough to bring it home. These propellers were designed, built, and delivered in only 17 days after one of Voyager's original propellers failed.

Voyager's takeoff roll lasted two minutes and six seconds with less than 244 meters (800 feet) of the 4,572-meter (15,000-foot) runway left at liftoff. Both of Voyager's winglets were damaged during takeoff as the wing tips dragged along the runway. Soon after takeoff, an attempt was made to deliberately dislodge the damaged winglets over Edwards Air Force Base so that if structural damage occurred to the aircraft's fuel tanks, Voyager could land as soon as possible. To dislodge the winglets, the crew increased flight speed and maneuvered the airplane to build up side forces sufficiently high to break them free. About eight kilometers (five miles) from the base the right winglet was dislodged and fell into someone's yard. This winglet is now in storage at the Museum's Paul E. Garber Facility in Suitland, Maryland. The other winglet was also successfully dislodged, but was never found.

Following a route determined by weather, wind, and geography, Voyager flew an official distance of 42,212.139 kilometers (24,986.727 miles) at an official speed of 186.11 kilometers per hour (115.65 miles per hour), in an elapsed time of 216 hours, 3 minutes, and 44 seconds. Flying Voyager, Rutan and Yeager established eight absolute and world class records. On the second day of the flight, Voyager was guided by meteorologists through the edges of Typhoon Marge to obtain a "slingshot effect" from tailwinds. These winds increased Voyager's groundspeed to 130 knots (150 miles per hour). Voyager's optimum altitude for fuel economy was 2,438 meters (8,000 feet), but the crew flew as high as 6,248 meters (20,500 feet) over Africa to avoid thunderstorms. Over the Atlantic Ocean near Brazil, a violent storm at night turned Voyager on a 90-degree bank, however the flight through the Caribbean was pleasingly uneventful. A final scare occurred on the last morning when the strain on a small fuel pump and an air pocket in the line starved the rear engine of fuel and it stopped. Voyager lost 1,524 meters (5,000 feet) of altitude while Rutan and Yeager made an emergency restart of the front engine. While the aircraft struggled to climb, the air block was overcome and the rear engine was restarted. The aircraft leveled off at 1,067 meters (3,500 feet) and landed a few hours later at Edwards Air Force Base.

Throughout the flight, the physical and mental capabilities of the pilots were continually tested by mechanical and severe weather problems, as well as by the cramped quarters. The pilot in the cockpit flew the airplane, navigated, maintained ground communication, and transferred fuel to balance the airplane. The other pilot in the cabin area rested, managed the logistics support tasks of the flight, or provided navigation and flight-monitoring assistance. In reality, neither pilot found the time or comfort for much rest, yet both were in remarkably good condition at the end of the flight. Voyager made one

Voyager flies over the clouds along the California coast. A westbound course was chosen to take advantage of the low-altitude, easterly trade winds of the equatorial regions.
(Photo: Courtesy of Mark Greenberg, VISIONS)

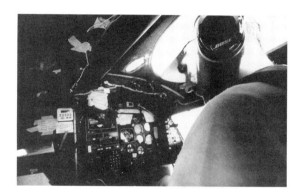

Rutan at the controls in the cramped cockpit. Rutan and Yeager utilized state-of-the-art avionics and maintained constant communication with the Mission Control Center in Mojave, California, for navigational and meteorological data.
(Photo: Courtesy of Mark Greenberg, VISIONS)

December 23, 1986. At the end of the successful and record-breaking nonstop, non-refueled world flight, Yeager and Rutan wave to the crowd at Edwards Air Force Base, California.
(Photo: Courtesy of Mark Greenberg, VISIONS)

last flight on January 6, 1987, when Yeager and Rutan flew it home to Mojave, California.

In the summer of 1987, Voyager was dismantled and trucked across country on a specially modified trailer to NASM's Garber Facility. En route, the airplane made one last stop in Oshkosh, Wisconsin, where it was displayed at the annual Experimental Aircraft Association Convention. Voyager now hangs in the South Lobby of the Museum.
Dorothy Cochrane and Rick Leyes

Ryan NYP
"Spirit of St. Louis"

Wingspan:	14.02 m (46 ft.)
Length:	8.41 m (27 ft. 7 in.)
Height:	2.99 m (9 ft. 10 in.)
Weight:	Gross, 2,329 kg (5,135 lb.)
	Empty, 975 kg (2,150 lb.)
Engine:	Wright Whirlwind J-5-C, 223 hp

"**O**ur messenger of peace and goodwill has broken down another barrier of time and space." So spoke President Calvin Coolidge about Charles A. Lindbergh's extraordinary solo transatlantic flight in 1927. Not until the Apollo 11 moon landing in 1969 was the entire world again as enthusiastic about an aviation event as it was when Lindbergh landed his little Ryan monoplane in Paris.

In 1922, after a year and a half at the University of Wisconsin, Lindbergh left to study aeronautics with the Nebraska Aircraft Corporation. He was a "barnstormer" until 1924, when he enrolled as a flying cadet in the Army Air Service. He won his reserve commission and began serving as a civilian airmail pilot, flying the route between St. Louis and Chicago.

Early in 1927 he obtained the backing of several St. Louis men to compete for the $25,000 prize offered by Raymond Orteig in 1919 for the first nonstop flight between New York City and Paris. In February of that year Lindbergh placed an order with Ryan Airlines in San Diego for an aircraft with specifications necessary to make the flight.

Development began based on a standard Ryan M-2, with Donald A. Hall as principal designer.

The famous Spirit of St. Louis *is ready to take off from San Diego en route to New York and the start of its historic flight.*
(Photo: SI A45132)

Certain modifications to the basic high-wing, strut-braced monoplane design had to be made because of the nature of the flight. The wingspan was increased by 10 feet and the structural members of the fuselage and wing cellule were redesigned to accommodate the greater fuel load. Plywood was fitted along the leading edge of the wings. The fuselage design followed that of a standard M-2 except that it was lengthened 2 feet. The cockpit was moved further to the rear for safety and the engine was moved forward for balance, thus permitting the fuel tank to be installed at the center of gravity. The pilot could see forward only by means of a periscope or by turning the aircraft to look out of a side window. A Wright Whirlwind J-5C engine supplied the power.

Late in April 1927 the work on the aircraft was completed. It was painted silver and carried registration number N-X-211, which, with all other lettering on the plane, was painted in black. Lindbergh made several test flights, and then flew the aircraft from San Diego to New York on May 10–12, making only one stop, at St. Louis. His flight time of 21 hours, 40 minutes set a new transcontinental record.

Charles Lindbergh inspects his Wright Whirlwind J-5 engine.
(Photo: SI A30)

After waiting several days in New York for favorable weather, Lindbergh took off for Paris alone, on the morning of May 20, 1927. Thirty-three hours, 30 minutes, and 3,610 miles later he landed safely at Le Bourget Field, near Paris, where he was greeted by a wildly enthusiastic crowd of 100,000.

Lindbergh and the *Spirit of St. Louis* returned to the United States aboard the U.S.S. *Memphis* on June 11. He received tumultuous welcomes in Washington, D.C., and New York City. From July 20 until October 23 of that year he took the famous plane on a tour of the United States. Then, on December 13, he and the *Spirit of St. Louis* flew nonstop from Washington to Mexico City; through Central America, Colombia, Venezuela, Puerto Rico; and nonstop from Havana to St. Louis. Beginning in Mexico City, flags of the countries he visited were painted on both sides of the cowling.

On April 30, 1928, the *Spirit of St. Louis* made its final flight—from St. Louis to Washington, D.C., where Lindbergh presented the aircraft to the Smithsonian Institution.

Claudia M. Oakes

The Spirit of St. Louis *occupies a place of honor in the Milestones of Flight gallery.*
(Photo: SI 77–3849–1)

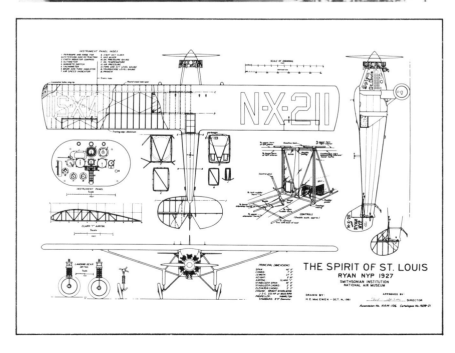

Schweizer 2-22

Wingspan:	13.1 m (43 ft.)
Length:	7.63 m (25 ft 1/2 in.)
Height:	2.74 m (9 ft.)
Weight:	Gross, 376 kg (830 lb.)
	Empty, 240 kg (450 lb.)

The Schweizer 2-22 is being towed aloft. (Photo: SI 75-13910)

Motorless flight is an important part of aviation. Gliding experiments formed the basis of research that led to powered flight—experiments by such aviation pioneers as Sir George Cayley, Otto Lilienthal, Octave Chanute, and the Wright brothers. Gliders were used during World War II as troop and cargo carriers. The German invasion of Crete is an example of the use of troop-carrying gliders. One of the major advantages of the military glider was the cost, since nonessential materials such as wood could be used in their construction. Airplanes like the C-47 were used as glider tugs, and there was even a glider version of the C-47 itself.

It was envisioned that the glider would be used after World War II as a cargo carrier; an airplane on a transcontinental flight could tow several gliders on long cables. At various points during the flight a glider would detach itself and sail safely to the ground with a load or cargo. Postwar aviation technology, however, made this use of the glider unnecessary. The major modern use of gliders is now in sport aviation.

There are two kinds of motorless flight, gliding and soaring. Gliding is the process of flying forward through the air while losing altitude. Soaring, which is the most important kind of motorless flight, is the process of using upward-moving currents in the atmosphere to ascend in altitude while flying. Types of upward-moving currents include thermals, which are masses of heated air, and ridges, which are currents often found on the windward side of hills or cliffs.

Sport soaring in the United States is conducted under the auspices of the Soaring Society of America, which is authorized by the National Aeronautic Association to homologize soaring records. The areas in which soaring pilots try to excel are altitude, duration, and distance. One- and two-seater aircraft are used predominately.

The museum's display sailplane is a Schweizer 2-22, a two-place training and utility aircraft, which

The Schweizer 2-22 (left) and 1-19 are shown together ready for flight. (Photo: SI 75-13909)

Scotty McCray, "Master of Unpowered Flight," was the only person ever granted an unlimited waiver for aerobatics in a sailplane. (Photo: Courtesy Louis S. Casey)

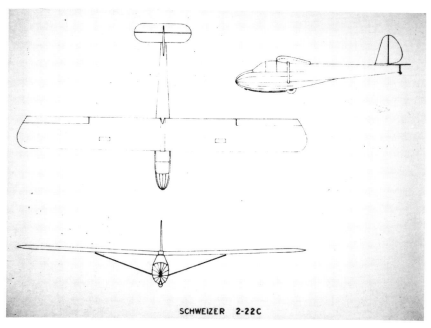

SCHWEIZER 2-22C

was used in aerobatic flight by Byron G. "Scotty" McCray. The Schweizer Aircraft Corporation is located in Elmira, New York, one of the most important centers of soaring in the United States.

The 2-22 was developed in 1945 as a dual instruction training glider. The fuselage is made of fabric-covered welded chromemoly tubing. Wings and vertical tail surfaces are made of sheet metal with some fabric covering. The fin and wings are detachable for trailer transportation.

The 2-22 has a cruising speed of 35 mph and a maximum speed of 89 mph. Its rate of sink in solo flight is 2.8 feet per second. It was designed to be as safe as possible for the student pilot.

The Schweizer 2-22 was in production until 1967, and 258 units were produced. Many are still in use today.

Scotty McCray was the world's foremost aerobatic sailplane pilot. He was the only aviator ever granted an unlimited waiver to perform aerobatics in a sailplane without altitude, maneuver, or inverted flight restrictions by the Federal Aviation Administration. He performed in air shows throughout the United States and in foreign countries.

McCray's performance consisted of aerobatic rolls, loops and other maneuvers in the Schweizer 2-22 from an altitude of 3,000 feet. Many of the maneuvers were previously considered impossible for a sailplane. His flights were so impressive that he was made an unofficial Blue Angel and was named "Master of Unpowered Flight" by the Thunderbirds.

Scotty McCray's performances spanned a period of ten years and numerous air shows. He lost his life in a crash on September 22, 1973, in São Paulo, Brazil, while performing in a Bellanca Decathlon. His Schweizer 2-22 was given to the National Air and Space Museum on March 13, 1975. Michael E. Dobson

Sikorsky UH-34D

Rotor Diameter:	17.7 m (56 ft.)
Length:	14.7 m (46 ft. 9 in.)
Height:	4.8 m (15 ft. 11 in.)
Weight:	Gross, 5,897 kg (13,000 lb.)
Engine:	Wright R-820, 1,525 hp

As the use of helicopters was expanded in the U.S. Navy's antisubmarine warfare program around 1951, a machine of improved capability became necessary. The helicopter that emerged from Sikorsky's Stratford, Connecticut, plant in 1954 was designated the S-58. Replacing the Sikorsky HO4S (H-19) helicopter, which was designed for general purpose duties, the new aircraft was designed specifically for antisubmarine warfare (ASW) missions and was able to carry the increasingly sophisticated sonar equipment used by the Navy.

This new helicopter had more than twice the useful load and engine power, more speed, longer range, and better overall performance than its predecessor, the S-55 (or H-19). In fact, the S-58's performance was so spectacular that it achieved world speed records: 100 kilometers at 141.9 mph; 500 kilometers at 136 mph; and 1,000 kilometers at 132.6 mph.

In meeting the Navy's needs for ASW operations,

the S-58 became known as the "push button" helicopter. The craft could be placed on automatic pilot to maintain 80 knots airspeed 200 feet above the water, then automatically hover at a 50-foot altitude over a preselected spot for lowering sonar equipment. As a result of the Navy's success with the new S-58, the other military services recognized its potential and ordered quantities of the new craft to meet their respective needs.

The Marines used the S-58 (UH-34D) mainly for assault missions, in which the movement of troops from ship to shore was easily and quickly accomplished with the powerful helicopter. In Vietnam, the important role of the helicopter in war was well defined. Aircraft became a primary means of troop transport and casualty evacuation, and UH-34s formed a large portion of the helicopters involved. In 1961 a Marine UH-34D was used in the recovery of astronaut Alan Shepard following his splashdown in Freedom 7. This event marked

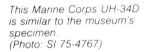

This Marine Corps UH-34D is similar to the museum's specimen.
(Photo: SI 75-4767)

the beginning of helicopter use for space capsule recovery. In all, more than five hundred UH-34s were built for the Marines.

The Army's primary use for the S-58 was as a troop and supply transport; the first Army CH-34 (S-58) flew in March 1955. Various missions were found for it in Vietnam: armed assaults, wire laying, artillery spotting, and many others. In 1957 Sikorsky Aircraft developed an armament system for the CH-34, which gave even greater combat and strike capability to the helicopter. By 1958 the Army's CH-34s were on duty throughout the United States, Europe, and Asia. Of all Sikorsky S-58 models built in the first four years of production, the Army versions had been the most widely used, and had accumulated more than half of the total hours flown by all S-58s.

Many peacetime uses were also found for the S-58. Both the Marines and the Army share responsibility for manning the Executive Flight Detachment for transporting the President and other high-ranking dignitaries. Beginning in the 1950s both services used VH-34s with customized interiors for this responsible mission. Civil uses for the S-58 include commercial passenger service, transportation of heavy equipment, aid in construction projects, fire fighting, and rescue work. A new lease on life has been given to military surplus H-34s by replacing their engines with the more powerful turbo Twin-Pac Pratt and Whitney PT6T-6 engine, thus extending indefinitely the civil use of existing S-58s.

In 1974 a Marine UH-34D was transferred to the National Air and Space Museum to represent medium-size assault helicopters. This particular craft, bureau number 148768, entered Marine service on March 31, 1961, and, during its military life, was assigned to various Marine units at New River, North Carolina; Jacksonville; Santa Ana and El Toro, California; and New Orleans. On November 25, 1970, it was retired and placed in storage at Davis-Monthan Air Force Base, Arizona, having accumulated 3,416 flying hours. Following the transfer of the helicopter to the museum, it was restored by the Sikorsky Aircraft Corporation and Marine personnel of HMX-1 at Quantico Marine Base Virginia. The aircraft has been repainted in 1965 Marine markings, with model number YP-13, to represent a significant aircraft assigned to Marine Medium Helicopter Squadron 163, a combat unit that served in the Da Nang area of Vietnam and became one of the most decorated Marine helicopter squadrons of that war.

Melinda Scarano

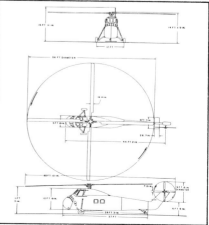

Sikorsky XR-4

Rotor diameter:	11.6 m (38 ft.)
Length:	10.36 m (33 ft. 11½ in.)
Height:	3.78 m (12 ft. 5 in.)
Weight:	Gross, 1,148 kg (2,540 lb.)
	Empty, 913 kg (2,010 lb.)
Engine:	Warner R-500-1 Super Scarab, 175 hp

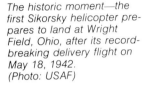

The historic moment—the first Sikorsky helicopter prepares to land at Wright Field, Ohio, after its record-breaking delivery flight on May 18, 1942. (Photo: USAF)

Igor I. Sikorsky's first successful helicopter was the experimental VS-300, which established a world endurance record in 1941 and proved the practicality of this basic design. Because of this success, the U.S. Army awarded a development contract to Sikorsky for a machine that could be produced in sufficient numbers to fill military needs. The XR-4 emerged from Sikorsky's Stratford, Connecticut, plant in December 1941, ready for flight despite its incomplete appearance (being minus its after fuselage covering).

The first flight was made on January 14, 1942. Many subsequent experiments included adding fabric covering to determine what effect this additional surface would have on the control of the aircraft. The XR-4's design was simple, featuring tubular construction, a boxlike cabin with side-by-side seating for a crew of two, and full dual controls.

Many aviation records were established by the XR-4, while it provided dramatic demonstrations of its unique ability to hover motionless. The most significant record was the first extended cross-country flight by helicopter in America. This trip was made for the purpose of delivering the aircraft from the factory at Stratford to the Army's Flight Test Center at Wright Field, Dayton, Ohio—a distance of 761 airline miles. Piloted by C. L.

The hovering capability of the XR-4 was frequently demonstrated by passing objects from the ground up to the helicopter. (Photo: United Aircraft Corp.)

In a simulated rescue, a Coast Guard pilot lands an R-4 on the water within easy reach of a stranded seaman afloat on a raft. (Photo: USCG 411441)

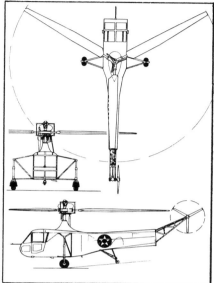

Proud of his helicopter, Igor Sikorsky sits in a rescue sling of an R-4, piloted by Capt. Frank Erikson, USCG, at Brooklyn, New York. (Photo: SI A42717)

Morris, Sikorsky test pilot, the XR-4 made the trip in five days. Sixteen hours and 10 minutes of flying time were logged in sixteen flights.

Stops were made at New Hackensack, near Poughkeepsie, Albany, Utica, Syracuse, Rochester, Buffalo, and Dunkirk, New York; Perry, Willoughby, Cleveland, Mansfield, Springfield, and Dayton, Ohio.

During the entire trip, Morris was accompanied by a support team in a car that had a yellow dot painted on its roof. Turbulent thunderstorms along the route threatened the flight, but the frail-looking craft encountered no difficulties.

On the afternoon of the fifth day, the helicopter landed at Springfield, Ohio, a short flight from its final destination. There it was polished and rechecked for delivery to the Army. Sikorsky flew on this last short hop to Wright Field for the presentation that took place on May 18, 1942.

Army flight tests involved the use of two low-pressure rubberized floats in place of wheels on the XR-4 to examine the versatility of landing on water, dirt, snow, thin ice, and soft marsh ground. In May 1942 further tests were conducted to prove the feasibility of operating the helicopter from a platform on a ship. The tanker S.S. *Bunker Hill*, in Long Island Sound, was used for the tests. The unmodified deck was one that had been used for cargo-carrying purposes and had a clear space only 14 feet greater than the diameter of the main rotor. Col. H. F. Gregory, who was in charge of the Army's Rotary Wing Program, made twenty-four

takeoffs and landings under varying wind conditions. The difficulty of landing on the rolling platform of a ship at sea made it impractical at that time to use helicopters on convoy patrol. Recognizing the air-sea rescue capacity of helicopters, however, the Navy acquired an R-4 for testing by the Coast Guard.

After many minor refinements in the design, the R-4 became the first helicopter in the world to be put into true production. Following the only XR-4 were three YR-4As, twenty-seven YR-4Bs, and 100 R-4Bs, totaling 131 produced during World War II.

First reports of R-4s in action during the war were from Burma. There, R-4s evacuated wounded from points inaccessible by any other means of transportation. One R-4 in Alaska undergoing cold-weather tests was kept in readiness for possible rescue work.

In addition to the use of R-4s by the Army, twenty-three were allocated to the Coast Guard through the Navy, and fifty-two to Britain's Royal Air Force for air-sea rescue operations over the English Channel.

The importance of helicopters increased each day that R-4s were in service, demonstrating their ability to cope with tasks never before accomplished by other types of aircraft.

In 1947 this first record-breaking XR-4 was transferred from the U.S. Army Air Force for exhibit in the National Air Museum.
Robert C. Mikesh

SPAD XIII "Smith IV"

Wingspan:	8.2 m (26 ft. 11 in.)
Length:	6.3 m (20 ft. 8 in.)
Height:	2.4 m (7 ft. 11 in.)
Weight:	Gross, 823 kg (1,815 lb.)
Engine:	Hispano-Suiza 8 Be 8-cylinder vee, 220 hp

The name SPAD, an acronym for Société pour l'Aviation et ses Dérives, evokes a vision of a fast and rugged biplane dogfighting with Fokker D.VIIs high above the muddy trenches of northern France. The SPAD series of aircraft is especially associated with air heroes such as Guynemer, Fonck, Nungesser, Lufbery, Luke, and Rickenbacker, who helped build its reputation as one of the finest fighters of World War I.

SPAD was a respected aircraft manufacturing company in France, originally formed as the Société pour les Appareils Deperdussin in 1910. After the outbreak of World War I, the company was taken over by Louis Blériot and renamed, but the acronym, SPAD, remained the same. Louis Béchereau, Deperdussin's technical director and an innovative designer in his own right, conceived the SPAD fighters. To Béchereau and Marc Birkigt, a Swiss engineer and designer of the Hispano-Suiza engine, must go much of the credit for the success of the SPAD series. The 1918 edition of *Jane's All the World's Aircraft* carries this description of them: "The new Spad biplanes . . . must not be described in detail, but one may say that they are in the very front rank for speed and climbing power, and are recognized as among the finest 'aeroplanes de chasse' or 'destroyers' of the day."

The SPAD XIII was a larger, improved version of the earlier SPAD VII with, among other changes, two fixed, forward-firing Vickers machine guns; a more powerful Hispano-Suiza eight-cylinder engine (220 horsepower for the XIII versus 150 horsepower for the VII); and aerodynamic improvements. The prototype SPAD XIII made its first flight on April 4, 1917, and by the end of the following month, the production aircraft had made its way to the front. By the end of the war, the SPAD XIII had proven itself in combat, particularly over the Western Front in 1918, and it was largely responsible for Allied air superiority over the Central Powers.

The SPAD XIII was manufactured and used in great numbers. In all, 8,472 of the sturdy fighters were constructed. At the end of the war, contracts for an additional 10,000 machines, 6,000 of which were to be built for the United States, had to be cancelled. By the Armistice, almost every French pursuit squadron had them, as did most of the newly formed U.S. Army Air Service squadrons. During the war, SPADs were used by the British, the Italians, the Belgians, and by the Russians.

Surprisingly, in view of the quantities built, only four of these aircraft remain. One of them, *Smith IV*, was assigned to Lt. A. Raymond Brooks, U.S. Army Air Service, who named it after the college attended by his sweetheart and future wife. It later became part of the Smithsonian Institution's collection.

NASM's SPAD XIII was built by the Kellner et Ses Fils piano works in August 1918. It was delivered to

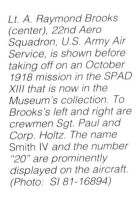

Lt. A. Raymond Brooks (center), 22nd Aero Squadron, U.S. Army Air Service, is shown before taking off on an October 1918 mission in the SPAD XIII that is now in the Museum's collection. To Brooks's left and right are crewmen Sgt. Paul and Corp. Holtz. The name Smith IV *and the number "20" are prominently displayed on the aircraft. (Photo: SI 81-16894)*

Colombey-les-Belles in September 1918 and assigned to the 22nd Aero Squadron, U.S. Army Air Service, where it was given the number "20" and assigned to Ray Brooks. The aircraft was a replacement for another of the same type in which Brooks had earlier crashed. *Smith IV* had one aerial victory, credited to Brooks.

After the war, Maj. Robert L. Walsh, a member of Gen. William Mitchell's staff, proposed the idea of sending two SPAD XIII's to the United States, one of which was *Smith IV*. This aircraft found its way to the Smithsonian Institution on December 17, 1919.

For many years the NASM's SPAD XIII was displayed as an original combat veteran of World War I. Time, however, took its toll and eventually *Smith IV,* its fabric rotted and frayed and its tires missing, was relegated to Building 24 of the Museum's Paul E. Garber Facility. In March 1984 *Smith IV* was retired from display in order to be restored. In 1986 the restoration was completed, and in 1991 the aircraft was placed in the World War I exhibition.

Dominick A. Pisano

This photograph was taken at the Paul E. Garber Facility in Suitland, Maryland, before the restoration of NASM's SPAD XIII. Note the condition of the undersides and trailing edges of the wings. (Photo: SI 83-2241-31)

NASM's SPAD XIII, Smith IV, at the Garber Facility after it had been restored to factory condition in 1986. (Photo: SI 86-12092)

SPAD XVI

Wingspan:	11.06 m (36 ft. 10½ in.)
Length:	7.6 m (25 ft. 4 in.)
Height:	2,525 m (8 ft. 5 in.)
Weight:	Gross, 1,292.75 kg (2,844 lb.)
	Empty, 906.3 kg (1,994 lb.)
Engine:	Lorraine-Dietrich Model 8Bb, 250 hp

All of Europe was embroiled in the "war to end all wars" when the SPAD XVI was introduced to the Allied force in France during 1918. This plane was the "improved" version of the SPAD XI, a two-seat armed reconnaissance biplane. M. Bechereau, the designer of the popular SPAD VII and XIII fighters, also designed both the XI and the XVI, but the latter did not meet with success. The XI was not a poor design; it used the same construction methods as the fighters, but never became popular with the pilots and observers assigned to them. Both the speed and maneuverability had been decreased because of the weight of the additional equipment they carried. They were loaded with flares, cameras, and bombs. A Vickers machine gun was mounted above the fuselage on the starboard side in front of the pilot's cockpit; a Lewis machine gun was mounted on the Scarff ring in the rear cockpit.

The SPAD XVI looked exactly like the XI but had a 230-hp Lorraine-Dietrich 8Fb engine installed in place of the 200-hp Hispano-Suiza, increasing the speed from 110 mph to 116½ mph. By June 1918, these SPADs were being fitted with a 250-hp Lorraine-Dietrich 8Bb engine, further increasing the speed to 122½ mph.

The SPAD XVI differed from the XI in that it was designed to fill two roles: a two-seat fighter and a reconnaissance plane. It was usually armed with twin guns both forward and aft. This SPAD, however, exhibited the same flight problems as the SPAD XI when heavily loaded, so it was not liked any better. Principal among these problems were a too high landing speed and the danger of a tight turn ending in a spin.

Although generally unpopular, the SPAD XVI did earn the distinction of being one of the SPAD versions flown by Brig. Gen. William "Billy"

Gen. William "Billy" Mitchell's SPAD XVI is shown on an airfield during World War I.
(Photo: SI 75-13735)

A SPAD XVI flies over the Compiègne sector in 1918. Note the trenches below. (Photo: SI 75-12263)

General Mitchell poses at the front with one of his planes. Note his personal insignia on the side of the aircraft. (Photo: SI A1134A)

The SPAD XI was the predecessor of the SPAD XVI. (Photo: SI A47964J)

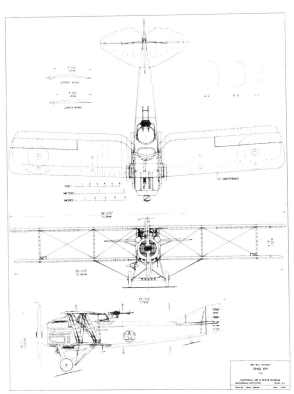

Mitchell, commander of the U.S. Army Air Service during World War I. He used this plane, now part of the National Air and Space Museum's aeronautical collection, when he wanted to take an observer aloft with him. He flew it during the battles at Chateau Thierry and St. Mihiel, and during the operations in the Argonne. After the Armistice, General Mitchell took this plane with him to Coblenz, Germany, where he used it to take the Prince of Wales on an aerial tour of the Rhine River area occupied by American troops. After the war, Mitchell's plane was transferred to the Smithsonian Institution.

Kathleen L. Brooks-Pazmany

Supermarine Spitfire Mk. VII

Wingspan:	17.3 m (40 ft. 2 in.)
Length:	8,975 m (29 ft. 11 in.)
Height:	3,575 m (11 ft. 5 in.)
Weight:	Gross, 3,575 kg (7,875 lb.)
Engine:	Rolls Royce Merlin 64, 1,290 hp at 3,000 rpm

The Spitfire was the end product of many years of design development at the Supermarine works at Woolston, England. There, Reginald J. Mitchell designed racers to enter in the Schneider Trophy Races, with the British government subsidizing the project. Mitchell designed every British winner after World War I, and on September 13, 1931, his S.6B brought the Schneider Cup permanently home to Britain by winning the third consecutive race.

Interest in high-speed competition flying lagged, but Mitchell continued to work on his designs, His seaplane racers gave way to landplane designs, incorporating such new features as an enclosed cockpit, retractable undercarriage, and the new Rolls Royce PV-12 liquid-cooled engine (later named the Merlin). With these elements, he increased the endurance and speed of his planes. The British government was now issuing specifications for fighter aircraft, which reflected its watchful eye on political developments in Germany. When a specification was issued for a

fighter with eight instead of the usual four machine guns installed, Mitchell was ready with the design for the Supermarine Type 300. It surpassed Air Ministry requirements and was accepted. Another specification was written for the construction of the prototype.

On March 5, 1936, Spitfire prototype K5054 took off from Eastleigh Airfield, Southhampton, on its maiden flight. After official trials at Martlesham Heath, a specification covering further development of the Spitfire was drawn up. On June 3, 1936, an order for 310 planes was placed by the Air Ministry. R. J. Mitchell did not live to see his Spitfire reach production; he died of cancer on June 11, 1937, at the age of forty-two. But the groundwork had now been established, and J. Smith, his chief draftsman, took his place as chief designer.

On August 4, 1938, K9789, the third Spitfire off the assembly line, was delivered to the Royal Air Force at Duxford. The first squadron to be

This is the museum's Spitfire, shown as it was delivered to the U.S. Army Air Force in May 1943. (Photo: SI 75-6833)

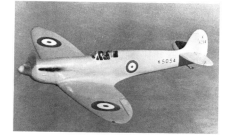

K5054, Supermarine Type 300, the prototype Spitfire. (Photo: SI A2329)

Spitfires are lined up at Duxford in May 1939. (Photo: SI 75-11404)

The second Eagle Squadron flies over the Stars and Stripes as it heads out on patrol. (Photo: SI 75-11403)

reequipped with the new Spitfires was No. 19; No. 66, also at Duxford, began receiving them soon after. When war with Germany was declared, 400 Spitfires were already in service and 2,160 were on order. Nine fighter squadrons were completely equipped with Spitfires; two more were being converted to the fighters.

The Spitfire was an all-metal cantilever monoplane. The shape of the wing, which became its most distinguishing characteristic, was elliptical, reducing drag and increasing speed.

Even while the first deliveries were being made, improvements were being introduced. A metal two-blade controllable pitch propeller replaced the two-blade fixed pitch mahogany airscrew, increasing speed. A tailwheel replaced the tail skid. Bulletproof windshields were installed in Spits already in service and as they came off the production line.

The Spitfire was easy to handle. It became airborne quickly, and once in the air, its maneuverability was outstanding. The combination of its speed and firepower made the Spit a deadly machine. Its eight machine guns concentrated a hail of bullets capable of tearing enemy planes at a point 300 yards in front of the craft.

Since the Spitfire was designed principally as a home defense interceptor fighter, its range was limited. But in 1943 this was increased by adding external (fuel) tanks, which could be jettisoned. This modification enabled the Spitfire to escort bombers to and from targets across the English Channel.

As needs arose, variations on the Spitfire were developed: photo reconnaissance versions to keep track of German movements on the continent and at sea; high-altitude versions to take on the Messerschmitt Bf.109s; low-altitude versions to meet the Focke Wulf Fw.190s. They were also employed in sea-air rescue operations. A Spitfire could quickly reach a downed pilot and drop a dinghy and emergency supplies, often saving the pilot from the cold waters of the channel.

The Spitfire was in service with many different groups and on many different fronts. Belgians, Free French, Poles, Czechs, Americans, and British Commonwealth countries used the fighter. The Eagle Squadron was one of the best known of these foreign units. Composed of American volunteers, the first Eagle Squadron was officially formed on October 19, 1940. They flew Hurricanes until they could be equipped with Spitfires. When the United States entered the war, there were three squadrons of Eagles. On September 29, 1942, these squadrons became the 334th, 335th, and 336th Squadrons of the 4th Fighter Group of the U.S. Eighth Air Force and were reequipped with American fighter craft.

Spitfires took part in operations in the Middle East, North Africa, India, Burma, Australia, and Russia. The neutral governments of Portugal and Turkey were also equipped with Spitfires.

When the war ended, the Spitfire was the only airplane that had been in continuous production throughout the war—20,351 had rolled off the assembly lines.

The museum's specimen is a Mark VII, a high-altitude version, of which only 140 were produced. On March 13, 1943, it was shipped directly from the factory to No. 47 Maintenance Unit at RAF Sealand, Flintshire, near Liverpool. There the plane was dismantled and prepared for shipment to the United States. It was received by the Army Air Force on May 2, 1943, and was used as an evaluation aircraft. It was transferred to the National Air and Space Museum from the Air Force in 1949.

Kathleen L. Brooks-Pazmany

Turner RT-14 Meteor

Wingspan:	7.71 m (25 ft. 3½ in.)
Length:	7.11 m (23 ft. 4 in.)
Height:	3.05 m (10 ft.)
Weight:	Gross, 2,233 kg (4,923 lb.)
	Empty 1,427 kg (3,300 lb.)
Engine:	Pratt and Whitney Twin Wasp, Sr., 1,000 hp

Feeling that his 1934 Thompson Trophy-winning Wedell-Williams was beginning to be outclassed by newer, faster racers, Roscoe Turner in 1936 contracted with the Lawrence W. Brown Aircraft Company of California to build a new racing aircraft. The aircraft, designed by Turner himself and engineered by Professor Howard Barlow of the University of Minnesota, was completed in mid-1936.

When Turner went to California to test fly the aircraft, he decided that it was too heavy for the 22-foot wingspan with its narrow chord. Thus, it was never flown with this small wing but was taken apart and shipped to Chicago, where renowned aircraft designer Matty Laird completely revamped it, using Turner's own design for a new wing. Turner had the span increased by 3 feet, and wing flaps added to reduce landing speed.

The Turner racer began its career with the 1937 National Air Races. That year it was sponsored by Ring Free Oil and was called *Ring Free Meteor*. For a while Turner held the lead in the Thompson

Race, but on the final lap—blinded by the sun—Turner had to recircle a missed pylon. Two aircraft passed him, and Turner finished third with a speed of 253.802 mph.

Turner and his racer returned to the Nationals in 1938, this time sponsored by the Pump Engineering Service Corporation of Cleveland, with the aircraft bearing the name *Pesco Special*. Only minor changes had been made, including the addition of wheel pants, and Turner was more than ready for the race before his second Thompson win. Nineteen thirty-eight was the first year that the same aircraft could not enter both the Bendix and the Thompson races, so Turner and the *Pesco* would have only one shot at a prize. The Thompson Race presented another difficulty to Turner that year. It would be rough going for an aircraft as large as the *Pesco*, since the thirty-lap course was only 10 miles around, not long enough for the larger aircraft to do their best. This situation would also hold true in 1939.

During most of the race Turner flew second

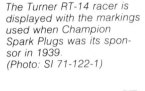

The Turner RT-14 racer is displayed with the markings used when Champion Spark Plugs was its sponsor in 1939.
(Photo: SI 71-122-1)

behind Earl Ortman in his Marcoux-Bromberg. Flying a wide race to be sure of making all the pylons, Turner pushed past Ortman on the sixth lap as Ortman's engine began trailing smoke. Turner went on to take the race at a speed of 283.416 mph—his fastest lap being 293 mph—and thus he became the first two-time winner of the Thompson Race.

Back again in 1939 to attempt a third Thompson win, Turner was sponsored by Champion Spark Plugs. The aircraft, still bearing race number 27, had the Champion insignia on the side and was named *Miss Champion*.

Slow getting off, and sitting in the number four spot, Turner was again plagued as he cut a pylon on the second lap. After going back to recircle the missed one, he trailed the entire field of seven aircraft. But the superior horsepower of Turner's Twin Wasp, Sr., began to make itself felt, and pushing past all other aircraft, Turner went on to an unprecedented third win in the Thompson Trophy Race with a speed of 282.5 mph.

With that race Turner announced his retirement. He returned to Indianapolis to operate the Turner Aeronautical Corporation until his death in 1970. His racer hung in a prominent place from the rafters of his main hangar until restored and placed in the Turner Museum, which was erected near his hangar in Indianapolis.

It was Roscoe Turner's desire that the racer someday be part of the National Aeronautical Collection at the Smithsonian, and with the closing of his museum in late 1972, the plane was gratefully received by the National Air and Space Museum.

Claudia M. Oakes

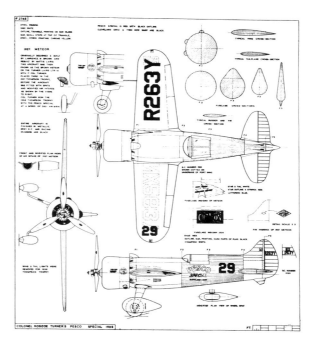

(Diagram: Courtesy Aero Modeller)

Voisin VIII

Wingspan:	18 m (59 ft.)
Length:	11.2 m (37 ft. 9 in.)
Height:	3.2 m (11 ft. 6 in.)
Weight:	Gross, 1,870 kg (4,120 lb.)
	Empty, 1,315 kg (2,900 lb.)
Engine:	Peugeot 8-cylinder vee, 200hp

As two of the first aircraft manufacturers in Europe, Gabriel and Charles Voisin were among France's greatest aviation pioneers, both in setting standards for aircraft design and in tailoring aircraft specifically for military tasks. From 1904 when the Voisin brothers' aircraft factory opened for business until 1908, the fledgling company produced aircraft that were both sturdy and easy to fly. Then in the six years preceding the outbreak of World War I, the Voisins, apparently anticipating the role that their aircraft would one day play in wartime, refined their designs to accommodate weapons. In 1910 they were able to mount a 37-millimeter, quick-firing gun on the nacelle of one of their machines.

By 1914, Voisin aircraft were among the few airplanes that were available for combat duty. During the first half of World War I, the French used Voisins to perform aerial observation missions and by 1916 they were being designed to carry out night bombing missions over the Western Front. As newer types of aircraft designed specifically for these tasks were developed, Voisins were transferred to areas outside the main arena of the Western Front.

The Voisin bomber served in theaters of the war as different as the freezing Russian plains and the broiling Mesopotamian desert. For flying over the snow-covered expanse of central Russia, the Imperial Russian Air Service substituted skis for rubber wheels. Equally adaptable to desert conditions, the sturdy Voisin VIII was used by the British Royal Flying Corps in the Middle East for observation, reconnaissance, and bombing.

Operating Voisin bombers provided the fledgling European air services with valuable experience at flying in harsh and diverse conditions around the world. Perhaps more important than the airplane's versatility, however, was its role as one of the world's first strategic bombers. From 1915 to 1917, Voisin VIIIs carried out the bombings of German towns and factories. Difficulties in finding targets, aiming bombs, and eluding German defenses rendered these French night bombers ineffective, but they remained a portent of things to come.

In the early part of 1917, the United States War Department Bureau of Military Aeronautics purchased a Voisin VIII, which had been used in 1916 on the Western Front, as a representative state-of-the-art night bomber that would demonstrate the advances in aeronautics

The addition of streamlined fuel tanks beneath the upper wings, increased armament, and a more powerful engine made the Voisin VIII more formidable than earlier designs, such as the Voisin III pictured here.
(Photo: NASM)

accomplished by the French. By the time that the Voisin was flown at the Aviation Experimental Station at Langley Field in late 1917 and early 1918, it was already obsolete. As a result of rapid changes in aviation technology in France and in other European countries, the Voisin had become comparatively ungainly and slow.

In July of 1918, the War Department offered the airplane to the Smithsonian Institution for "exhibition purposes or historical record." The Smithsonian accepted the gift, and on September 16 and 17, 1918, three aircraft (a Farman and a Caudron had also been sent) were delivered to the National Museum in six boxes and a crate.

When the packages were opened and inspected, however, it quickly became apparent that the Voisin was not complete. It had been shipped without its engine or propeller. Later, the airplane's propeller was found during reassembly, and in October 1918, the Voisin, without its engine, was suspended from the ceiling of the South Hall of the Arts and Industries Building. Sixty-five years passed before an engine was found for it.

In 1928, the Voisin VIII was removed from the exhibition hall, disassembled, and put in storage at the Paul E. Garber Facility in Suitland, Maryland. More than sixty years later, in 1989, the Voisin VIII was restored for Legend, Memory, and the Great War in the Air, an exhibition addressing the development of military aviation during World War I. Joanne Gernstein and Karl Schneide

The Voisin V carried a 47-millimeter Hotchkiss cannon and was principally used for ground strafing, only one of the roles that the versatile Voisin types played during the war.
(Photo: SI 89-5654)

Reassembled after sixty years of storage, NASM's Voisin VIII prior to restoration.
(Photo: SI 89-8850-10)

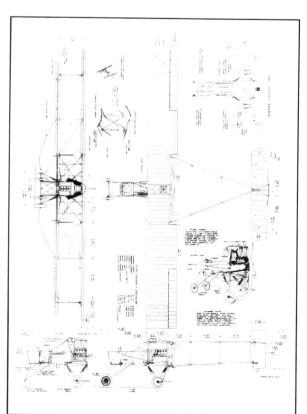

(Diagram: NASM)

Vought F4U-1D Corsair

Wingspan:	12.5 m (41 ft.)
Length:	10.2 m (33 ft. 4 in.)
Height:	4.6 m (15 ft.)
Weight:	Gross, 6,350 kg (14,000 lb.)
	Empty, 4,074 kg (8,982 lb.)
Engine:	Pratt and Whitney R-2800-8W 2,000 take-off hp., 2,250 with Emergency War Power

The F4U Corsair—the distinctive bent wing "U-bird"—has acquired a unique reputation in military aviation for longevity and versatility—a day fighter and a night fighter, a dive bomber and a reconnaissance plane, a land-based and carrier-based fighter.

The F4U Corsair established its distinguished combat record in World War II. Known for its rugged construction, speed, and maneuverability, the Corsair first entered combat service at Guadalcanal in February, 1943. Maj. Gregory "Pappy" Boyington, the leading U.S. Marine ace, flew an F4U-1D as commander of the VMF-214 "Black Sheep" squadron. In the course of the Pacific war the Corsair became an important carrier-based fighter for the U.S. Navy and Royal Navy. During thirty months of combat with the U.S. Navy and Marines, the Corsair destroyed 2,140 Japanese planes in aerial combat.

The U.S. Navy and Marine Corps Corsairs also scored ten aerial victories during the Korean War.

A total of seven Marine and twenty-eight Navy squadrons flew Corsairs in Korea, where the F4U's reputation as an effective night fighter was firmly established.

First proposed in 1938 and then produced in quantity over the next thirteen years (12,571 Corsairs were built), the F4U underwent 981 major engineering changes and nearly 20,000 minor changes. In the post-World War II period, certain models of the Corsair (the high-performance, modified versions of the F2G-1 and 2) participated in numerous air races, capturing the prestigious Thompson Trophy twice.

The genesis of the F4U Corsair can be traced back to Chance Vought Aircraft Company, later the Vought-Sikorsky Division of United Aircraft Corporation, which produced and tested the first Corsair prototype (the XF4U-1). This particular aircraft company had been founded earlier by aviation pioneer Chance Milton Vought (1888–1930). Chance Vought Aircraft remained the

The Vought Corsair Sun Setter *and another member of Marine fighter squadron VMF-113 patrol near Eniwetok, Marshall Islands, on July 9, 1944. The museum's Corsair is painted to depict* Sun Setter. *(Photo: National Archives 80-G-373637)*

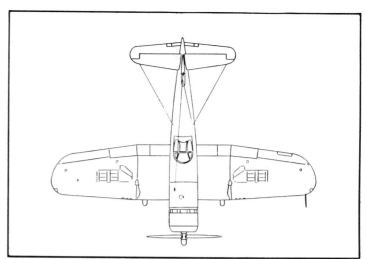

The F4U-1A of Navy Lt. j.g. Ira C. Kepford, fighter squadron VF-17, based at Bougainville, Solomon Islands, February 1944. (Photo: National Archives 80-G-425500)

An F4U-1D of Navy fighter-bomber squadron VBF-83 leaves the U.S.S. Essex, operating near Japan on June 29, 1944. (Photo: National Archives 80-G-333213)

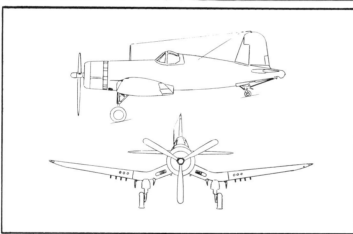

principal manufacturer of the F4U Corsair during World War II. To increase wartime production, however, the U.S. Navy awarded production contracts to the Goodyear Aircraft Corporation and the Brewster Aeronautical Corporation. The F4U Corsair saw service with numerous countries, including Great Britain, New Zealand, and France.

The F4U-1D demonstrated throughout its long career qualities of speed, firepower, and versatility. With its 2,000-hp Pratt and Whitney R-2800-8 engine, the Corsair could range over 1,015 miles (1,633 km) in an air space extending from sea level to an altitude of nearly eight miles. Its impressive climb rate of 2,890 feet (899 meters) per minute and its standard armament of six .50-caliber machine guns made the Corsair a

formidable fighter. It could carry three auxiliary fuel tanks or two 1,000-pound bombs in mounts below the fuselage. Rocket racks on the underside of the outer wing panels could accommodate eight 5-inch rockets. The Corsair ended its operational life in the Navy and Marine air reserve programs.

The National Air and Space Museum acquired its F4U-1D (bureau number 50375) from the Navy in September 1960. It had been delivered to the Navy on April 26, 1944, and continued in active service for two years. The F4U-1D was restored by the museum's restoration craftsmen in 1980.
Garry Cline
Von D. Hardesty

Waco 9

Wingspan:	Upper, 9.54 m (31 ft. 4 in.)
	Lower, 8.99 m (29 ft. 6 in.)
Length:	7.19 m (23 ft. 7 in.)
Height:	2.82 m (9 ft. 3 in.)
Weight:	Gross, 953 kg (2,100 lb.)
	Empty, 600 kg (1,320 lb.)
Engine:	Curtiss OX-5, 90 hp

The name "Waco" has long been synonymous with popular biplanes of the Golden Age of flying (1930s). The first of the pure Waco production design models was the "Nine," which fast became a favorite with pilots, beginning in 1925, when the supply of war surplus types was being exhausted. The bench seat in the front cockpit could snugly accommodate two passengers; the single cockpit for the pilot was in the rear. Aside from its use as an excellent barnstorming plane, it also served in the aerial spray business and in early airline use. Ball Airlines and Embry-Riddle both used Wacos in 1927. (Ball Airlines evolved into Pennsylvania-Central, which later became Capital, now part of United Airlines.)

Barnstormers of the late twenties, in their quest of making a living, often cut corners by using aircraft of questionable airworthiness, flown by pilots with questionable qualifications. This resulted in many accidents and a mounting public demand

The National Air and Space Museum's Waco 9 is shown at the preservation, restoration, and storage facility.
(Photo: SI 72–8833)

that something be done about the menace of the "gypsy pilot." The result was government licensing of pilots and aircraft.

The new Air Commerce Department Regulations of December 31, 1926, required that all aircraft manufacturers secure an Airplane Type Certificate, or ATC, for their product. In order to be issued an ATC, the manufacturer had to submit strength calculations for his design and then demonstrate through static tests on a prototype that it met or exceeded minimum standards. Aircraft production today must still meet these requirements.

Since neither of the designers of the Waco 9 had more than a high school education, it was feared that the airplane was doomed. However, a professor at MIT made stress calculations for the plane, and the U.S. Army even bought one and static-tested it to destruction at McCook Field. The Air Commerce regulations required the structure to be able to withstand a load 6.5 times its own

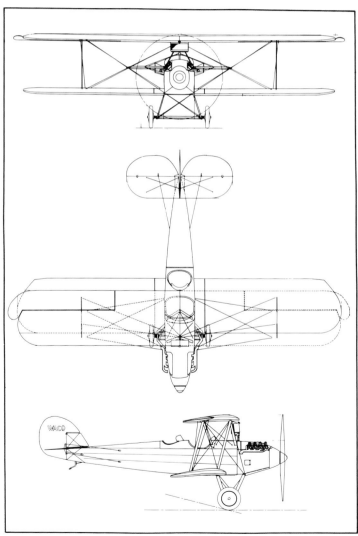

weight. The Waco 9 held up to a load factor of 7.5 and subsequently was issued ATC number 11 in July 1927.

Construction of the "Nine" was typical of the time: welded steel tubing with all-wood wing structure, entirely fabric-covered. The standard finish was silver-painted fabric with blue paint on the exposed metal parts. In all, 120 model 9s were produced from 1925 to 1927.

The museum's Waco 9 was flown by its owner, Marion McClure of Bloomington, Illinois, until 1966, when changing flight-safety requirements caused it to be stored until modifications could be made. The codesigner and Waco Company partner, Clayton J. Bruckner, wishing to contribute something of Waco to the museum, purchased the plane in 1972 for donation to the Smithsonian's National Aeronautical Collection.

D. L. Rush

Wittman "Chief Oshkosh"/ "Buster"

Wingspan:	4.59 m (15 ft. 1 in.)
Length:	5.31 m (17 ft. 5 in.)
Height:	1.22 m (4 ft.)
Weight:	Empty, 227 kg (500 lb.)
Engine:	Continental, 85 hp

The aircraft that enjoyed what was perhaps the longest, and one of the most successful careers in air racing history was Steve Wittman's *Chief Oshkosh,* known in the post-World War II era as *Buster.* From 1931 until its retirement in 1954, this midget racer set records and took numerous trophies in class races and free-for-alls, including two wins in the Goodyear Trophy Races.

The *Chief Oshkosh* was Wittman's first homebuilt racer. It was a Cirrus-powered midwing monoplane with a tripod landing gear; its wheels were too tiny to permit brakes. Wittman used his own design for the 19-foot-span wings. The aircraft was entirely red and had an Indian head with "Chief Oshkosh" painted on the nose.

During the 1931 National Air Races *Chief Oshkosh* developed wing flutter and was entered only in the 400-cubic-inch class race, in which it took third with a speed of 150.27 mph.

Wittman had modified *Chief Oshkosh* by the time of the 1932 Nationals. He had replaced the

American Cirrus with a 349-cubic-inch Cirrus Hermes. The cowl and canopy had been painted silver, with the fuselage still red. That year Wittman beat Ben Howard's *Pete* in one race and also took a second, a fourth, a sixth, and a seventh in other races. Later in 1932 he won the Glenn Curtiss Trophy in Miami with a speed of 166.9 mph.

Nineteen thirty-three proved to be an excellent year for Wittman and the *Chief.* Early in that year he placed third in the Miami races and got two thirds, one fourth, and two fifths at the International Air Races in Chicago. At the 1933 Nationals he took first in the 350-cubic-inch class with a speed of 159.8 mph. That win, along with two seconds and two thirds in the 375-cubic-inch events, was enough for first place overall.

Still bothered by wing-tip flutter, Wittman decided to decrease the size of the wings. By the time the *Chief* was ready for the 1934 Nationals, its span was down to 16 feet and its area to 42 square feet. That year the aircraft picked up two

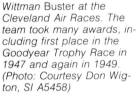

Bill Brennand stands in the Wittman Buster at the Cleveland Air Races. The team took many awards, including first place in the Goodyear Trophy Race in 1947 and again in 1949. (Photo: Courtesy Don Wigton, SI A5458)

Chief Oshkosh —*the plane that later developed into* Buster —*is shown in the mid-1930s.*
(Photo: Courtesy C. G. B. Stuart, SI A5050)

third places, two fourths, and two fifths with a top speed of 186.60 mph.

Competition was stiffer in 1935, and Wittman souped up the *Chief*'s Cirrus to the limit. He managed two thirds and two fifths at the Nationals and one second and two thirds in Miami. His best speed was 202.22 mph.

The Cirrus was replaced in 1936 by a Menasco CS-4 363-cubic-inch engine. The tripod landing gear was replaced by a multiple leaf type with spring steel struts, and the wing span was cut to 13 feet. During the Nationals that year, however,

the *Chief* ran into trouble. Wittman developed engine problems as he was holding down second place in the Shell 375-cubic-inch race. He misjudged on his forced landing and slammed into the top of a parked Northrop A-17. Neither Wittman nor the *Chief* was badly injured, but they were out of the races for 1936.

Wittman and the *Chief* returned in 1937 with more modifications to the aircraft. The multiple leaf landing gear had been replaced by a single leaf type, and the cockpit had been altered to give greater visibility. The aircraft took three firsts, placed second in the Greve Trophy Race, and set a new world's record for its class over a 100-kilometer course at Detroit with a speed of 238.22 mph.

In 1938 Wittman crash-landed the *Chief* at the Oakland, California, races. The aircraft was not raced again until 1947, when it was revamped, fitted with new wings, and renamed *Buster*.

Nineteen forty-seven was also the year of the first of the three Goodyear Trophy Races for midget planes with 190-cubic-inch engine displacement, fixed props and landing gears, and 500-pound empty weights. Bill Brennand, a jockey-sized protégé of Wittman, piloted the red and yellow *Buster* to victory with an average speed of 165.9 mph.

In the 1948 Goodyear Race, Brennand and the *Buster* could manage only fourth place with a speed of 167.063 mph.

Nineteen forty-nine, however, proved to be a different story. With Brennand at the controls, the *Buster* again won the Goodyear Trophy with a speed of 177.3 mph, took second in the Continental Motors Race in Miami (for aircraft with Continental C-85 engines), fourth at San Diego, third at Newhall, California, and fourth at Ontario, California.

Continuing to pilot the *Buster* in the early 1950s, Brennand finished fifth in the 1950 Continental Race at Miami, first at White Plains, New York, first at Chattanooga, and second in the 1950 Rebat Trophy Race at Reading, Pennsylvania.

Bob Porter took over flying the aircraft in 1951. He and the *Buster* took a third and a fourth at Chattanooga, second in the 1951 Rebat Race, and fourth in the 1952 Continental Race at Detroit.

Porter flew the *Buster* to third place in the aircraft's last race at Dansville, New York, on July 4, 1954. The racer was retired after this race and is now part of the Smithsonian's National Aeronautical Collection.

Claudia M. Oakes

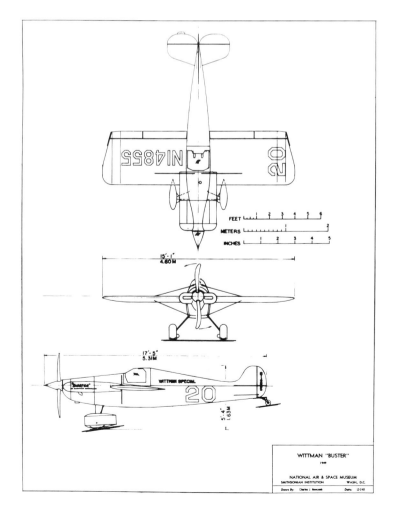

WITTMAN "BUSTER"
1949

NATIONAL AIR & SPACE MUSEUM
SMITHSONIAN INSTITUTION   WASH., D.C.

Wright EX "Vin Fiz"

Wingspan:	9.60 m (31 ft. 6½ in.)
Length:	6.53 m (21 ft. 5 in.)
Height:	2.23 m (7 ft. 4 in.)
Weight:	Gross, 410 kg (903 lb.)
Engine:	Wright, 35 hp

In 1911, after seventy landings, enough replaced parts on his plane to build about four aircraft, and repeated accidents, including an in-flight run-in with an eagle, Calbraith Perry Rodgers, descendant of two naval heroes, became the first man to make a transcontinental United States flight. His aircraft was a spruce and wire Wright EX biplane. Rodgers had learned to fly only a few months earlier at the Wrights' school in Dayton, but he quickly demonstrated his abilities by soloing after only ninety minutes of instruction, and in August of that year he won an award at a Chicago air meet for logging the most time in the air.

William Randolph Hearst was offering a prize of $50,000 to the first man who could make a transcontinental flight in thirty days or less. Three men, including Rodgers, decided to make the attempt. One was forced to abandon the project because his funds ran out, and another was discouraged by a crash about a week after his start.

Rodgers took off from Sheepshead Bay, Long Island, on September 17, 1911. His sponsor was the Armour Company of Chicago, which at that time was marketing a grape-flavored soft drink called "Vin Fiz." The aircraft was decorated with the Vin Fiz trademark, and in addition to the prize money, should he win it, Rodgers was to receive $5 from Armour for every mile flown with his aircraft so lettered.

The aircraft itself was constructed of a framework of spruce trussed with steel wire; the wings were covered with rubberized duck fabric. It was powered by a Wright 35-hp, four-cylinder engine and had a gas tank designed to hold 15 gallons, which would give 3½ hours' air time.

Accompanying Rodgers along the route was a special train carrying mechanics, spare parts, and equipment. Also on board were Rodgers's wife and mother and several representatives from the Armour Company.

Rodgers landed at Middleton, New York, on the

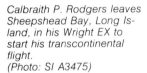

Calbraith P. Rodgers leaves Sheepshead Bay, Long Island, in his Wright EX to start his transcontinental flight.
(Photo: SI A3475)

Rodgers relaxes with a cigar while a mechanic works on the Vin Fiz. *(Photo: SI A42906A)*

The Vin Fiz *trails hay after taking off from a pasture. (Photo: SI A45502B)*

night of the seventeenth, and the next morning on takeoff he experienced his first crash—he flew into a tree and so damaged the aircraft that it took three days to repair it.

The only directional indicator on the aircraft was a piece of string fastened to the front cross brace; the direction in which it waved showed whether the aircraft was climbing, descending, or drifting. Rodgers intended to navigate by following railroad tracks whenever possible. In fact, a stretch of tracks for about 25 miles west of Jersey City had been whitewashed to help guide him. This plan was not infallible, however, because at one point he followed the wrong line at a track switch and ended up in Scranton, Pennsylvania, instead of Elmira, New York.

Rodgers continued undaunted, but the last date on which he could qualify for the Hearst prize found him only as far as Oklahoma. But with the Armour Company's backing, and his own determination to succeed, Rodgers continued west.

On November 5 he reached his original goal, Pasadena, California, 4,321 miles from Sheepshead Bay. His total flying time had been 82 hours, 2 minutes, and his average speed 52 mph. The only original parts of the aircraft remaining were the vertical rudder and two wing struts. Replacement parts had included eighteen wing panels, twenty skids, and two engines.

Rodgers did not feel that his flight would be complete until he actually reached the ocean. So on November 12 he took off from Long Beach, only to be forced down at Covina and Compton. During the Compton landing Rodgers's ankle was broken, and he was grounded until December 10. But on that date, on crutches in his repaired aircraft, Rodgers flew on to the beach and taxied the wheels of the *Vin Fiz* into the Pacific.

In 1934 the Smithsonian obtained the *Vin Fiz* as a gift from the Carnegie Museum in Pittsburgh, Rodgers's hometown.

Claudia M. Oakes

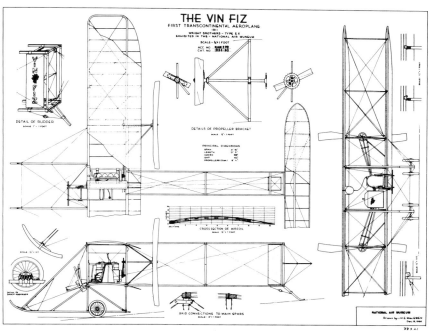

Wright 1903 Flyer

Wingspan:	12.29 m (40 ft. 4 in.)
Length:	7.41 m (21 ft. ⅜ in.)
Height:	2.82 m (9 ft. 3¼ in.)
Weight:	Empty, 274 kg (605 lb.)

On December 17, 1903, Wilbur and Orville Wright realized a dream that had eluded man for centuries—successful controlled, powered, manned, heavier-than-air flight.

The Wright brothers' interest in flight began when they were boys in Dayton, Ohio, after their father brought home a small flying toy powered with rubber bands. They were fascinated by the toy's ability to flutter around the room, and were introduced to the elements of aviation when they tried to repair it and make others like it. Orville became adept at building and flying kites; later, as young men in about 1885, the brothers began reading about the experiments of Otto Lilienthal, the famous German glider pioneer.

In 1899 Wilbur and Orville wrote to the Smithsonian Institution for information about the aerodynamic experiments of Samuel P. Langley, third Secretary of the Smithsonian. About this same time they also wrote to Octave Chanute, an early glider experimenter, for advice. To find the best location for their own experiments, the Wrights checked with the Weather Bureau and decided that Kitty Hawk, North Carolina, with its large sand dunes and steady winds, might be well suited.

From the autumn of 1900 until their historic 1903 flight, the Wrights worked intermittently at Kitty Hawk on their experiments. Their first large glider was a biplane, which they flew unmanned like a kite. Their 1901 glider supported a pilot, and gave the brothers experience in operating their control system. Even with their patented method of lateral control, the 1901 glider did not always perform as expected, so Orville rigged up a wind tunnel to test the reactions of variously shaped surfaces as air was blown through the tunnel. The Wrights' glider, built in 1902, had a vertical tail surface and a better system of operating the wing-warping wires: the pilot's hips fit into a saddle, and he operated the wires by moving his hips insteading of pressing foot pedals. To counteract the tendency of the lower wing to drag, the Wrights combined the rudder action with the warping system so that a single pilot movement operated both.

Back at their shop in Dayton the Wrights built their next machine, which they planned to power

With Orville Wright at the controls, the Flyer rises into the air on December 17, 1903, as Wilbur Wright watches.
(Photo: SI A26767B)

The Wright Flyer sits at Kitty Hawk ready for another flight.
(Photo: SI A26767A)

with an engine and propellers. When they could not find a suitable engine, their mechanic, Charles Taylor, built one for them. It was a four-cylinder, water-cooled engine with a 4-inch bore and 4-inch stroke, developing 12 horsepower. The cylinders were in-line and horizontal. There was no carburetor per se; the gasoline was vaporized after dripping on a distribution plate that extended to the cylinder ports, an elementary form of fuel injection.

The aircraft was shipped to Kitty Hawk and was made ready to fly on December 14, 1903. Wilbur won the coin toss and took his place at the controls. The restraining wire was released and the machine rolled down the launching rail. It rose into the air, but Wilbur elevated the front too high; the plane stalled and settled down awkwardly, causing some damage.

On December 17 the brothers were ready to try again. This time it was Orville's turn. The aircraft ran 40 feet along the rail and rose into the air. It flew 120 feet in 12 seconds. This was the first flight in history in which a machine carrying a man had raised itself by its own power into the air, had flown forward under control without a reduction in speed, and had landed at a point as high as that from which it had started.

Three more flights were made that day: the longest was 852 feet in 59 seconds, with Wilbur as pilot.

Damaged when a gust overturned it later in the day, the aircraft was crated and returned to Dayton. In 1916 it was repaired and reassembled for display at the Massachusetts Institute of Technology, and then it was exhibited at several air shows. In 1928 the Flyer was loaned to the Science Museum in London, where it stayed for twenty years; during World War II it was stored in a London subway for safety.

On the forty-fifth anniversary of the famous flight, December 17, 1948, the Wright 1903 Flyer was returned to the United States and was hung inside the entrance to the Smithsonian's Arts and Industries Building. It now occupies a place of honor as the first aircraft a visitor sees when he enters the new National Air and Space Museum.
Claudia M. Oakes

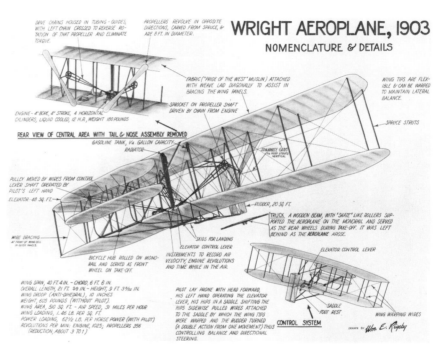

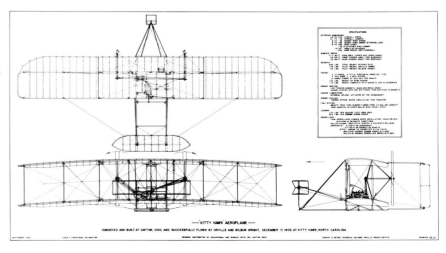

Wright 1909 Military Flyer

Wingspan:	11.12 m (36 ft. 6 in.)
Length:	8.82 m (28 ft. 11 in.)
Height:	2.46 m (8 ft. 1 in.)
Weight:	333 kg (735 lb.)
Engine:	Wright, 25 hp

"**S**ealed proposals in duplicate will be received at this office until 12 o'clock noon on February 1, 1908, on behalf of the Board of Ordnance and Fortification for furnishing the Signal Corps with a heavier-than-air flying machine."

So read Signal Corps Specification Number 486, issued December 23, 1907, to provide the U.S. Army with its first heavier-than-air aircraft—the first military aircraft in the world.

The general requirements continued as follows: that it be designed to be easily assembled and disassembled so that an army wagon could transport it; that it be able to carry two people with a combined weight of 350 pounds, and sufficient fuel for 125 miles; that it be able to reach a speed of at least 40 mph in still air, which would be calculated during a two-lap test flight over a 5-mile course, with and against the wind; that it demonstrate the ability to remain in the air at least one hour without landing, and that it then land without causing any damage that would prevent it

from immediately starting another flight; that it be able to ascend in any sort of country in which the Signal Corps might need it in field service and be able to land without requiring a specially prepared spot; that it be able to land safely in case of accident to the propelling machinery; and that it be simple enough to permit someone to become proficient in its operation within a reasonable amount of time.

The purchase price was set at $25,000 with 10 percent added for each full mile-per-hour of speed over the required 40 mph and 10 percent deducted for each full mile-per-hour under 40 mph.

The Wright brothers constructed for the project a two-place, wire-braced biplane with a Wright 25-hp, four-cylinder engine driving two wooden propellers. It had a wooden framework, with fabric-covered wings and control surfaces. Wooden skids served as landing gear.

This aircraft made its first demonstration flight at the Fort Myer, Virginia, parade grounds on

The Wright 1909 Military Flyer rounds the tower set up at Fort Myer, Virginia, for flight tests, July 2, 1909. (Photo: SI A42699)

Orville Wright and Lt. Thomas O. Selfridge are seated in the 1908 aircraft. (Photo: SI A42869E)

Lieutenant Selfridge was the first military man to lose his life in an aircraft, September 17, 1908. (Photo: SI A18470)

September 3, 1908. Several days of very successful and increasingly ambitious flights followed. On September 17, however, tragedy occurred. At 5:14 p.m. Orville took off with Lt. Thomas O. Selfridge as a passenger. The machine had circled the field four and a half times when a propeller blade shattered. The aircraft, then at 150 feet, safely glided to 75 feet, when it plunged to earth. Orville received several injuries, including a broken hip, but Lieutenant Selfridge was killed and the aircraft was destroyed.

On June 3, 1909, however, the Wrights returned to Fort Myer with a new machine. The engine was the same as in the 1908 aircraft, but the 1909 model had a smaller wing area and modifications to the rudder and the wiring. Lt. Frank P. Lahm and Lt. Benjamin D. Foulois, as future Army pilots, were the Wrights' passengers.

Flights continued into July. During one of these demonstrations a sudden stalling of the engine caused the aircraft to glide into a tree, breaking the skids and ripping a wing. But the damage was repaired in four hours, showing a great advantage for military purposes.

On July 26 President Taft went to Fort Myer to watch the proceedings and was privileged to witness the aircraft ascend under its own power without use of the starting weight. A strong headwind assisted its takeoff with Wilbur running alongside to guide it.

The next day the aircraft satisfied the endurance requirement with a record flight of 1 hour, 12 minutes, and 40 seconds, covering approximately 40 miles in the process.

A course to establish the speed of the aircraft was set up from Fort Myer to Shooter's Hill in Alexandria, Virginia, a distance of 5 miles. After waiting several days for optimum wind conditions, Orville and Foulois made the 10-mile test flight on July 30. The out-lap speed was 37.735 mph and the return lap was 47.431 mph, giving an average speed of 42.533 mph. For the 2 mph over the required forty, the Wrights earned an additional $5,000.

Other training flights continued during the year at College Park, Maryland. Among the Army officers who learned to fly there from the Wrights was Lt. H. H. "Hap" Arnold, the future Army Air Force Chief.

The Smithsonian acquired the aircraft from the War Department in 1911.
Claudia M. Oakes

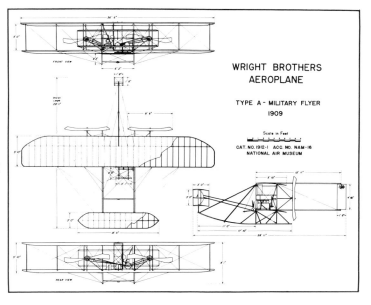

WRIGHT BROTHERS AEROPLANE

TYPE A - MILITARY FLYER
1909

Scale in Feet

CAT. NO. 1912-1   ACC. NO. NAM-16
NATIONAL AIR MUSEUM

Aircraft on Exhibit

By Gallery:

Milestones of Flight *(Gallery 100)*
Bell X-1 *Glamorous Glennis*
Langley Aerodrome No. 5
North American X-15
Ryan NYP *Spirit of St. Louis*
Wright 1903 Flyer

Air Transportation *(Gallery 102)*
Boeing 247D
Douglas DC-3
Douglas M-2
Fairchild FC-2
Ford 5-AT Tri-motor
Grumman G-21 Goose
Northrop Alpha
Pitcairn Mailwing

Vertical Flight *(Gallery 103)*
Bell 206L LongRanger II *Spirit of Texas*
Bensen Gyro-glider and Gyro-copter
Focke-Achgelis Fa 330
Hiller XH-44 Hiller-Copter
Kellett XO-60
Pentecost Hoppicopter
Piasecki PV-2
Sikorsky UH-34D
Sikorsky XR-4

Special Aircraft Exhibits *(Gallery 104)*
Boeing P-26A
Curtiss P-40E Warhawk
Grumman G-22 *Gulfhawk II*

Golden Age *(Gallery 105)*
Beechcraft C17L
Curtiss Robin J-1 Deluxe *Ole Miss*
Hughes H-1
Northrop Gamma 2B *Polar Star*
Wittman *Chief Oshkosh/Buster*

Jet Aviation *(Gallery 106)*
Lockheed XP-80 Shooting Star
McDonnell FH-1 Phantom
Messerschmitt Me 262-1a

Early Flight *(Gallery 107)*
Blériot Type XI
Curtiss D
Ecker Flying Boat
Lilienthal Standard Glider
Wright 1909 Military Flyer

South Lobby *(Gallery 108)*
Rutan Voyager

Flight Testing *(Gallery 109)*
Bell XP-59A Airacomet
Hawker XV-6A Kestrel
Lockheed 5C Vega *Winnie Mae*

Looking at Earth *(Gallery 110)*
Dayton-Wright (de Havilland) DH-4
Lockheed U-2C

Sea-Air Operations *(Gallery 203)*
Boeing F4B-4
Douglas A-4C Skyhawk
Douglas SBD-6 Dauntless
Grumman FM-1 (F4F-4) Wildcat

World War II Aviation *(Gallery 205)*
Macchi C.202 Folgore
Martin B-26B Marauder *Flak Bait*
Messerschmitt Bf 109G-6 "Gustav"
Mitsubishi Zero-Fighter Model 52
North American P-51D Mustang
Supermarine Spitfire Mk.VII

Legend, Memory, and the Great War in the Air *(Gallery 206)*
Albatros D.Va
Fokker D.VII
Pfalz D.XII
SPAD XIII *Smith IV*
Voison VIII

Pioneers of Flight *(Gallery 208)*
Curtiss R3C-2
Douglas World Cruiser *Chicago*
Fokker T-2
Lockheed 5B Vega (Amelia Earhart)
Lockheed 8 Sirius *Tingmissartoq*
MacCready *Gossamer Condor*
Wright EX *Vin Fiz*

East Moving Staircase
Douglas D-558-2 Skyrocket

West Moving Staircase
Lockheed F-104A Starfighter

By Aircraft:

Albatros D.Va *Gallery 206*
Beechcraft C17L *Gallery 105*
Bell 206L LongRanger II *Spirit of Texas Gallery 103*
Bell X-1 *Glamorous Glennis Gallery 100*
Bell XP-59A Airacomet *Gallery 109*
Bensen Gyro-glider and Gyro-copter *Gallery 103*
Blériot Type XI *Gallery 107*
Boeing 247D *Gallery 102*
Boeing F4B-4 *Gallery 203*
Boeing P-26A *Gallery 104*
Curtiss D *Gallery 107*
Curtiss P-40E Warhawk *Gallery 104*
Curtiss R3C-2 *Gallery 208*
Curtiss Robin J-1 Deluxe *Ole Miss Gallery 105*
Dayton-Wright (de Havilland) DH-4 *Gallery 110*
Douglas A-4C Skyhawk *Gallery 203*
Douglas D-558-2 Skyrocket *East Moving Staircase*
Douglas DC-3 *Gallery 102*
Douglas M-2 *Gallery 102*
Douglas SBD-6 Dauntless *Gallery 203*
Douglas World Cruiser *Chicago Gallery 208*
Ecker Flying Boat *Gallery 107*
Fairchild FC-2 *Gallery 102*
Focke-Achgelis Fa 330 *Gallery 103*
Fokker D.VII *Gallery 206*
Fokker T-2 *Gallery 208*
Ford 5-AT Tri-motor *Gallery 102*
Grumman FM-1 (F4F-4) Wildcat *Gallery 203*
Grumman G-21 Goose *Gallery 102*
Grumman G-22 *Gulfhawk II Gallery 104*
Hawker XV-6A Kestrel *Gallery 109*
Hiller XH-44 Hiller-Copter *Gallery 103*
Hughes H-1 *Gallery 105*
Kellett XO-60 *Gallery 103*
Langley Aerodrome No. 5 *Gallery 100*
Lilienthal Standard Glider *Gallery 107*
Lockheed 5B Vega (Amelia Earhart) *Gallery 208*
Lockheed 5C Vega *Winnie Mae Gallery 109*
Lockheed 8 Sirius *Tingmissartoq Gallery 208*
Lockheed F-104A Starfighter *West Moving Staircase*
Lockheed U-2C *Gallery 110*
Lockheed XP-80 Shooting Star *Gallery 106*
Macchi C.202 Folgore *Gallery 205*
MacCready *Gossamer Condor Gallery 208*
McDonnell FH-1 Phantom *Gallery 106*
Martin B-26B Marauder *Flak Bait Gallery 205*
Messerschmitt Bf 109G-6 "Gustav" *Gallery 205*
Messerschmitt Me 262-1a *Gallery 106*
Mitsubishi Zero-Fighter Model 52 *Gallery 205*
North American P-51D Mustang *Gallery 205*
North American X-15 *Gallery 100*
Northrop Alpha *Gallery 102*
Northrop Gamma 2B *Polar Star Gallery 105*
Pentecost Hoppicopter *Gallery 103*
Pfalz D.XII *Gallery 206*
Piasecki PV-2 *Gallery 103*
Pitcairn Mailwing *Gallery 102*
Rutan Voyager *Gallery 108*
Ryan NYP *Spirit of St. Louis Gallery 100*
Sikorsky UH-34D *Gallery 103*
Sikorsky XR-4 *Gallery 103*
SPAD XIII *Smith IV Gallery 206*
Supermarine Spitfire Mk.VII *Gallery 205*
Voisin VIII *Gallery 206*
Wittman *Chief Oshkosh/Buster Gallery 105*
Wright EX *Vin Fiz Gallery 208*
Wright 1903 Flyer *Gallery 100*
Wright 1909 Military Flyer *Gallery 107*

Aircraft on Loan

Boeing 307 Stratoliner	Pima Air Museum, AZ
Boeing 367-80 (prototype 707)	Boeing Aircraft, Seattle, WA
Boeing FB-5	U.S. Marine Corps Museum, VA
Consolidated PBY-5 Catalina	National Museum of Naval Aviation, FL
Curtiss A-1 Hydro	National Museum of Naval Aviation, FL
Curtiss C-46 Commando	The Warplane Museum, NY
Curtiss F9C-2 Sparrowhawk	National Museum of Naval Aviation, FL
Curtiss N-9H	National Museum of Naval Aviation, FL
Curtiss NC-4	National Museum of Naval Aviation, FL
Curtiss SB2C-5 Helldiver	National Museum of Naval Aviation, FL
Curtiss (N.A.F.) TS-1	National Museum of Naval Aviation, FL
De Havilland DH-4 *Old 249*	San Diego Aero-Space Museum, CA
Douglas R4D-5 *Que Sera Sera*	National Museum of Naval Aviation, FL
Fairchild 71 *Stars & Stripes*	Virginia Aviation Museum, VA
Fisher XP-75C Eagle	Air Force Museum, OH
Focke-Wulf Fw 190D-9	Air Force Museum, OH
Gates Learjet 23	Science Museum of Virginia, VA
Goodyear Inflatoplane	Naval Air Test and Evaluation Museum, MD
Goodyear *Pilgrim* (gondola)	National Museum of Naval Aviation, FL
Goodyear ZPG-W (gondola)	Davis-Monthan AFB, AZ
Grumman F9F-6 Cougar	Grumman Aerospace Corp., NY
Grumman US-2B Tracker	Davis-Monthan AFB, AZ
Halberstadt C.L. IV	Verkehrs Museum, Germany
Hiller YROE	Naval Air Test and Evaluation Museum, MD
Huff-Daland Duster	Delta Airlines, GA
Lockheed SP-2H Neptune	Davis-Monthan AFB, AZ
Lockheed XP2V-1 Neptune	National Museum of Naval Aviation, FL
Lockheed CL-475 Helicopter	Army Aviation Museum, AL
Loening OA-1A *San Francisco*	Air Force Museum, OH
MacCready *Gossamer Albatross*	Science Museum, England
MacCready *Solar Challenger*	Science Museum of Virginia, VA
Martin 162A Mariner (3/8 scale)	Baltimore Museum of Industry, MD
Martin PBM-5A Mariner	Pima Air Museum, AZ
Mignet-Crosley *Pou du Ciel*	Experimental Aircraft Association, WI
Mitsubishi A6M7 Zero	San Diego Aero-Space Museum, CA
Monocoupe 70	California Museum of Science and Industry
Monocoupe 110 Special *Lil Butch*	Virginia Aviation Museum
Montgomery Evergreen	San Diego Aero-Space Museum, CA
N.A.F. N3N Yellow Peril	U.S. Naval Academy Museum, MD
Nagler-Rolz NR 54 V2	Hubschrauber Museum, Germany
Nakajima Ki-43 Hayabusa *Oscar*	Experimental Aircraft Association, WI
North American FJ-1 Fury	National Museum of Naval Aviation, FL
North American P-51C *Excalibur III*	California Museum of Science and Industry
Northrop M2-F1 Lifting Body	NASA/Dryden Research Center, CA
Piper L-4B Grasshopper	45th Infantry Division Museum, OK
Ryan X-13 Vertijet	San Diego Aero-Space Museum, CA
Ryan XV-5B Hummingbird	Army Aviation Museum, AL
Sikorsky VH-34C (S-58) Choctaw	Davis-Monthan AFB, AZ
Spad XVI (Mitchell)	Air Force Museum, OH
Stits SA-2 Skybaby	Experimental Aircraft Association, WI
Verville-Sperry M-1 Messenger	Air Force Museum, OH
Vickers Viscount	Sussex County Airport, DE
Vought XF8U-1 Crusader	Museum of Flight, WA
Waco CG-4A Hadrian	Air Force Museum, OH
Westland Lysander	Air Force Museum, OH

Aircraft at the
Paul E. Garber Facility

On Exhibit:

Aeronca C-2
Aichi M6A1 Seiran
Akerman Tailless
Antonov AN-2 *Colt*
Applebay Zuni II
Arado Ar 234-B Blitz
Arlington Sisu 1A
Arrow Sport A2-60
Bachem Ba 349 (BP 20) Natter
Baldwin Red Devil
Bede BD-5
Beechcraft 35 Bonanza
Bell ATV VTOL
Bell Model 30
Bell P-39Q Airacobra
Bell P-63A King Cobra
Bell UH-1M Iroquois
Bell VH-13J (Eisenhower)
Bellanca 14-13 Cruiseair Sr. (crated)
Bellanca C.F.
Benoist-Korn
Bertelson Aerobile (hovercraft)
Boeing B-29 Superfortress *Enola Gay*
  (fuselage)
Boeing KC-97L (cockpit section)
Boeing-Stearman N2S-5 Kaydet
Boeing-Vertol VZ-2A
Bowlus Baby Albatross
Bowlus–du Pont Albatross I *Falcon*
Caudron G-4
Cessna 150L Commuter
Cessna 180 *Spirit of Columbus*
Cessna O-1A (L-19) Bird Dog
Culver TD2C-1
Curtiss F6C-1 *Gulfhawk IA*
Curtiss JN-4D Jenny
Curtiss XP-55 Ascender
Curtiss-Wright CW-1 Junior
Curtiss-Wright X-100
Custer CCW-1 Channel Wing
Dassault Falcon 20
De Havilland D.H.98 Mosquito Mk.35
Douglas B-26B (A-26B) Invader
Douglas DC-3 (cockpit section)
Eipper-Formance Cumulus 10
Erco 415 Ercoupe
Felixstowe (N.A.F.) F-5L (fuselage)
Focke-Wulf Fw 190F-8
Fowler-Gage Tractor
Frankfort TG-1A
Franklin PS-2 *Texaco Eaglet*
Grumman F6F-3 Hellcat
Grumman F8F-2 Bearcat *Conquest I*
Grumman TBF-1 Avenger
Grunau Baby IIb
Hawker Hurricane Mk. IIC
Heinkel He 162A Volksjager
Helio No. 1
Herrick HV2A Convertoplane
Hiller Flying Platform
Hiller HOE-1
Hispano HA-200B Cairo
Kaman K-225
Kugisho Ohka 11 (22)

Laird Super Solution LCDW 500
  (fuselage)
Lockheed P-38J Lightning
Lockheed XC-35 (10E) Electra
Mahoney *Sorceress*
Martin, J. V., K-III Kitten
McDonnell RF-101C Voodoo
  (forward fuselage)
McDonnell XV-1 Convertiplane
Messerschmitt Me 163B Komet
Mitchell U-2 Superwing
Mitsubishi G4M3 *Betty* (forward fuselage)
Morane Saulnier MS 500
  (Fieseler Fi 156 Storch)
NASA Paresev (Rogallo wing)
Nelson BB-1 Dragonfly
Nelson PG-185B Hummingbird
North American F-86A Sabre
North American SNJ-4
Northrop N-1M
Piper PA-12 *City of Washington*
Piper PA-18 Super Cub
Pitcairn AC-35
Pitts Special S-1S (Ransom)
Princeton Air Scooter (hovercraft)
Radioplane DQ-14 (unmanned) (2)
Republic P-47D Thunderbolt
Republic XP-84 (forward fuselage)
Rotorway Scorpion Too
Saab J-29
Schulgleiter SG.38
Schweizer 2-22
Sikorsky JRS-1 (S-43)
Sikorsky XR-5 (VS-317) Dragonfly
Stinson SR-10F Reliant
Turner RT-14 Meteor
Valkyrie
Verville Sport Trainer
Vought F4U-1D Corsair
Vought OS2U Kingfisher
Waco 9
Waco UIC
Windecker Eagle I
Wiseman-Cooke
Yakovlev Yak-18 *Max*
Zimmerman Flying Platform

In Storage:

Abrams Explorer
Aichi B7A1 Ryusei *Grace*
American Aerolights Double Eagle
Arado Ar 196A
Avro Canada VZ-9V Avrocar
Beechcraft 18
Bell Rocket Belt
Bennett Delta Wing Mariah M-9
Bennett Delta Wing Model 162
Bennett Delta Wing Phoenix 6
Bennett Delta Wing Phoenix 6B
Bennett Delta Wing Phoenix Streak 130
Bennett Delta Wing Phoenix Viper
Berliner Helicopter
Blohm & Voss Bv 155B
Boeing B-17D Flying Fortress *Swoose*
Bücker Bü-133 Jungmeister
Bücker Bü-181 Bestmann
Burgess-Curtis
  (Shoemaker-Cannonhouse)
Cascade Kasperwing 180B
Cessna 0-2 Skymaster
Convair 240 *Caroline*
Convair XF2Y-1 Sea Dart
Convair XFY-1 Pogo
Crowley Hydro-Air (hovercraft)
Curtiss E Boat (fuselage)
De Havilland DHC-1A Chipmunk
Dornier Do 335 Pfeil
Double Eagle II (gondola)
Douglas A-1H Skyraider
Douglas XB-42A
Douglas XB-43 *Versatile II*
DSI/NASA Oblique-Wing RPRV
  (unmanned)
Eberhart Target Glider (unmanned)
Fairchild PT-19A Cornell
Farman Sport
Focke-Wulf Ta 152H
Fulton FA-3-101 Airphibian
Gotha Go 229 (Horton IX)
Heinkel He 219A Uhu
Horton Ho II
Horton Ho III (no wings)
Horton Ho III-H (two-seat)
Horton Ho VI
Icarus I
Junkers Ju 388L
Kawanishi N1K1 Kyofu *Rex*
Kawanishi N1K2-J Shiden Kai *George*
Kawasaki Ki-45 Toryu *Nick*
Kellett XR-8
Kreider-Reisner KR-34C
Kugisho MX7Y-K2 Ohka (two-seat trainer)
Kugisho P1Y1-C Ginga *Frances*
Kyushu J7W1 Shinden
Langley Aerodrome A
Lippisch DM-1
Lockheed T-33 Shooting Star
McDonnell XHJD-1 Whirlaway
McDonnell F-4A Phantom II *Sageburner*
Maupin-Lanteri Black Diamond
Messerschmitt Me 410 A-3 Hornisse
Mikoyan-Gurevich MiG-15

Mooney M-18C Mite
Nakajima B6N2 Tenzan *Jill*
Nakajima C6N1-S Saiun *Myrt*
Nakajima Ki-115 Tsurugi
Nakajima Kikka
Nakajima J1N1-S Gekko *Irving*
Nieuport 28C-1
Noorduyn YC-64 Norseman IV
North American F-100D Super Sabre
North American RO-47A
Northrop P-61C Black Widow
Northrop XP-56 Black Bullet
Olmstead Pusher
Piasecki-Vertol XHRP-1 Rescuer
Piper J-2 Cub
Piper J-3 Cub
Pitcairn-Cierva C-8
Pitcairn-Cierva PCA-1A
Pitts Special S-1C *Little Stinker*
Platt-LePage XR-1
Radioplane DQ-2A/TDD-1 (unmanned) (3)
Radioplane OQ-2A/DQ-2A (unmanned)
Radioplane XKD2R-1 (unmanned)
Republic RC-3 Seabee
Republic F-105D Thunderchief
Rutan Quickie
Rutan VariEze
Rutan VariEze (kit)
Standard J-1
Stanley Nomad
Stearman-Hammond Y
Stinson L-5 Sentinel
Stout Skycar
Ultraflight Lazair SS EC
Vought V-173 Flying Pancake
Vultee BT-13A Valiant
Waterman Aeromobile
Waterman Whatsit
Weedhopper JC-1

Aircraft in Storage at Washington Dulles International Airport

Boeing B-17G Flying Fortress
Consolidated B-24D (nose section)
Goodyear K-Car (gondola)
Junkers/CASA Ju-52/3m
Lockheed C-130A Hercules
Lockheed SR-71 Blackbird
Lockheed 1049 Constellation
McDonnell F-4S Phantom II
Martin EB-57B Canberra
North American B-25J (TB-25M) Mitchell
Vought RF-8G Crusader